PORTRAITS
OF THE NEW ARCHITECTURE 2

© 2015 Assouline Publishing
601 West 26th Street, 18th floor
New York, NY 10001 USA
Tel.: 212-989-6769 Fax: 212-647-0005
assouline.com
ISBN: 9781614282679
All rights reserved.
Design by Camille Dubois.

PHOTOGRAPHS BY RICHARD SCHULMAN

INTRODUCTION BY PAUL GOLDBERGER

PORTRAITS
OF THE NEW ARCHITECTURE 2

ASSOULINE

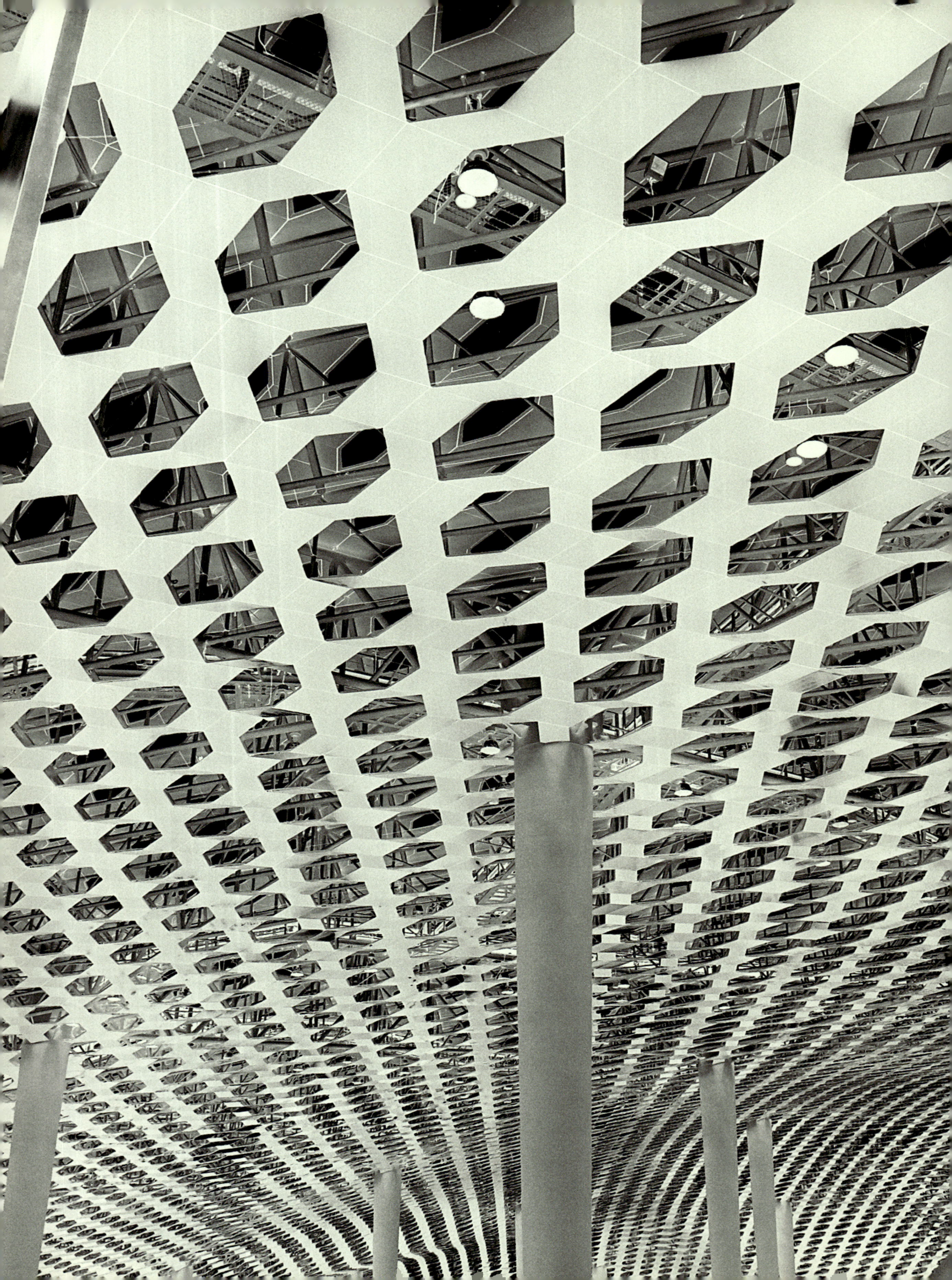

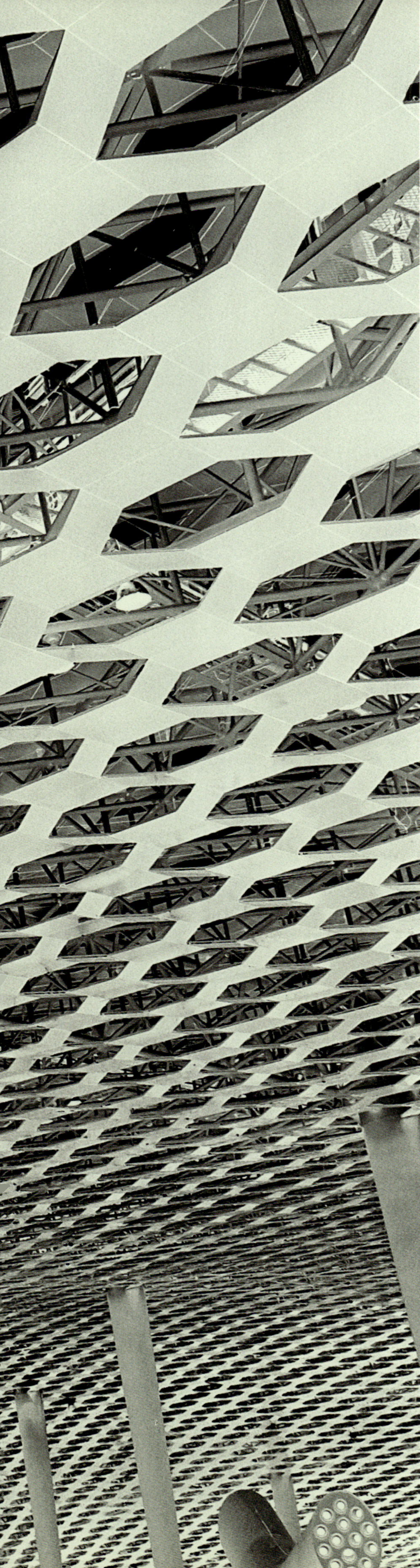

CONTENTS

FOREWORD

BY RICHARD SCHULMAN

Portraits of the New Architecture 2 is the perfect opportunity for me to declare that architecture and its designs are making a greater impact on our lives than ever before.

Ten years ago, in the first *Portraits of the New Architecture* book, my camera celebrated architecture. Most of the personalities from that book—Frank Gehry, Rem Koolhaas, Zaha Hadid, Jean Nouvel, Herzog and de Meuron, Peter Zumthor, and more—are still among the most important voices on the subject. Today, to continue my experience, I am still trying to absorb what the architects in this new volume share with me, and in turn to deliver a more articulated vision than before. This is more than just volume 2: This is a book with the intention to continue engaging the personalities of the architects and their architecture.

After photographing architecture for so many years, I now realize that I need to be more vigilant toward discovering what each building is saying. We make photographs today to show people in the future about our past. Architects design buildings today, and in the future those buildings will reflect how we live in the moment and how we lived in the past. Architecture is rooted in ideas and in our urban and rural needs. Therefore architecture is a culture of young and older personalities fulfilling our needs and designing our future.

I have traveled more than half the world looking for the dialogue, looking for what architecture is about. What I have found most intriguing is that architecture is now a world event. Now more than ever, architects are circling the globe to create new works

Previous pages: Terminal 3 at Shenzhen Bao'an International Airport.

for municipalities and private commissions. There has never been an international dialogue that is so present in our lives as what is going on in sustainable building and design right now.

This book is a combination of the personalities of the architects and the spirit of the architecture. Many photographers run around the world taking pictures of every building they can find. I have the good fortune not only to photograph the buildings, but also to spend time with the architects.

When I am confronted with the challenge of finding a way to create a language about how photography marries architecture, I hear the voices of David Adjaye, Kengo Kuma, Bjarke Ingels, Massimiliano Fuksas, Eduardo Souto de Moura, Jeanne Gang, Fumihiko Maki, and many more. Photography has a vocabulary that, if used properly, helps to build an image. A photographer constructs an image using words like narrative, space, light, and volume. Those words conform to a similar aspect in architecture. It is simply like Legos: So many pieces make a whole.

I fly into Shenzhen, China with an agenda to engage the airport designed by Massimiliano Fuksas. I have seen renderings of the airport. How do I own the moment? How do I photograph the airport that speaks to his design and my vocabulary? In this case, I realize what, specifically, is Fuksas—and what is so unique to his design that I need to illustrate.

For this new book, I do exactly that in thirty cities with thirty architects. I land in São Paulo, Aix-en-Provence, Porto, Rotterdam, Copenhagen, Los Angeles, and Mexico City and still try to define the moment for each building. A photographer's life is a moment in time. A building's moment is sometimes defined by that same moment.

I am engaging with intriguing and famous designers and architects who exhibit their talents in a most unique way. We celebrate fame, but famous people's imagination is the nobler subject to celebrate.

INTRODUCTION

BY PAUL GOLDBERGER

When Richard Schulman published *Portraits of the New Architecture* in 2004, I don't think it was intended to be the beginning of a series. But that book now no longer stands alone: Its success inspired Schulman to keep going, continuing to travel around the world to document not only buildings, as most architectural photographers do, but architects themselves. At the crux of his images is his attempt to explore the elusive connection between architects and their work, a subject that traditional architectural photography almost invariably ignores. For *Portraits of the New Architecture 2* (I suppose that the original book is now, retroactively, *Portraits of the New Architecture 1*), Schulman has found many figures whose careers had barely begun a decade ago—in 2004, David Adjaye, Bjarke Ingels, and Jeanne Gang were far from the household names they have become—and several others who have been around for a while and who could well have been photographed a decade ago, but for whatever reason were not. Thus *Portraits 2* includes Rafael Moneo, Nicholas Grimshaw, Paulo Mendes da Rocha, Álvaro Siza, Fumihiko Maki, Moshe Safdie, and Stanley Tigerman. Several of them are Pritzker Prize winners, all of them have had important careers that are now many decades long, and, most important, all of them have continued to produce architecture that is significant enough that it would be unthinkable to pass over them a second time.

This book may be a mix of new and old names, then, but all the architecture it contains is new. Every architect here, from the youngest to the oldest, is represented by a compelling piece of work that was completed in the last decade, since the publication of *Portraits 1*. The projects included here may not in and of themselves constitute a summary of the architecture of the last decade, but they certainly show us its range and its preoccupations. And *Portraits of the New Architecture 2* demonstrates, even more powerfully than *Portraits 1*, how long, and how gradual, the arc of an architect's career is. What is considered young in architecture would be middle-aged in almost any other career (except sports and much of the entertainment world, where people the age of "young" architects are probably already retired). I don't know that there's any profession other than architecture in which someone in his or her fifties can be called young and is still on the upward trajectory of his or her career. Louis Kahn's first significant building, the Yale Art Gallery, came when he was 51; Frank Gehry's house for himself in Santa

Monica, which first established him as a national figure, was completed when he was 50, and his Guggenheim Museum in Bilbao, Spain, was finished when he was 68. But if it takes most architects a long time to get established, the good news is that they usually keep going. Fumihiko Maki and Paulo Mendes da Rocha are both 86; Rafael Moneo is 77; Moshe Safdie is 76; and Nicholas Grimshaw is 75. All of them are not only still working, they are still producing architecture that demands our attention.

Every now and then there is an exception: Moshe Safdie completed Habitat, at Expo 67 in Montreal, when he was 28; Bjarke Ingels became internationally known when he was in his early thirties (he is only now 40); and David Adjaye achieved fame early as well. I'm not sure that early success is necessarily a lucky thing in architecture, since one of the benefits of the long and gradual career arc is that you have plenty of time for ideas to gestate, plenty of time to learn your craft, and plenty of time to figure out your voice. And early success makes you as vulnerable in architecture as anywhere else to the challenges of acclaim before you are seasoned enough to put it in perspective.

But whenever a career begins to rise, architecture is a long game, not a short one. I've never heard of an architect retiring, or giving up his practice to do something else, the way lawyers and bankers and hedge fund managers do when they've earned enough money and figure it is time to start doing something they like. Architects have always been doing something they like, and they want to keep doing it as long as nature permits. You can see that in Richard Schulman's portraits. Some architects seem formal and some seem relaxed, but none of them seem uncomfortable. Many are photographed at their offices, and others in front or inside of one of their buildings, and they all look as if they are perfectly content to be there, and that they—like Schulman— want the surroundings to be part of the picture.

I will not play the game of trying to suggest that the architects' faces somehow give you some insight into the nature of their architecture—a notion that, however tempting to ponder, is as silly as the old line about people resembling their dogs. But these portrait photographs, like those in *Portraits 1*, do tell you a fair amount about these people as personalities. As with any gifted photographer, Richard Schulman knows how to capture people and make them reveal something about themselves, whether it is David Adjaye and Michael Maltzan standing rather grandly before their own shadows; Stanley Tigerman looking quizzical; Moshe Safdie affably content; or Leo Marmol and Ron Radziner trying to appear as straight as the lines in their buildings. Fumihiko Maki seems to be dreaming of another world, and Bjarke Ingels shows off his contentment at being in this one.

A book of photographs of individual architects, or of partners, inevitably raises the question of just how much architecture is, or is not, a pursuit of creative people acting on their own. It would seem, at first glance, to be reinforcing the phenomenon known by the unfortunate word "starchitect"—the idea that architecture is primarily a matter of form-making and shape-making by people who have become famous for the special forms and shapes that they devise. To some extent, of course, that has been true for much of the last generation—and it is not entirely a bad thing, since whatever else the notion of the star architect has done, it has put architecture far more into the public eye and into the center of the civic and cultural discourse. The fact that our culture cares about putting up buildings that people will notice and derive pleasure from is no small thing.

But the world of those who conceive of striking shapes is only a small portion of the architectural universe—and in any case, to view any building, whether its form is memorable or not, as the product only of a single creative mind is to misunderstand architecture. No architect of any stripe gets very far on his or her own. Bringing a building from a creative idea into constructed reality requires support of all kinds, from a team of architects alongside the person whose name is on the door to the contractors and engineers who enable design to be realized. It takes a village to build even a piece of a village. And I have not even mentioned clients, without whom there is no architecture. The best clients do much more than pay for buildings—their dialogue with architects is a critical part of the design process. Any architect who does not believe his work is honed and refined by interaction with clients either does not understand what he is doing or is in denial of the way architecture is made.

View from the Aqua Tower, Chicago.

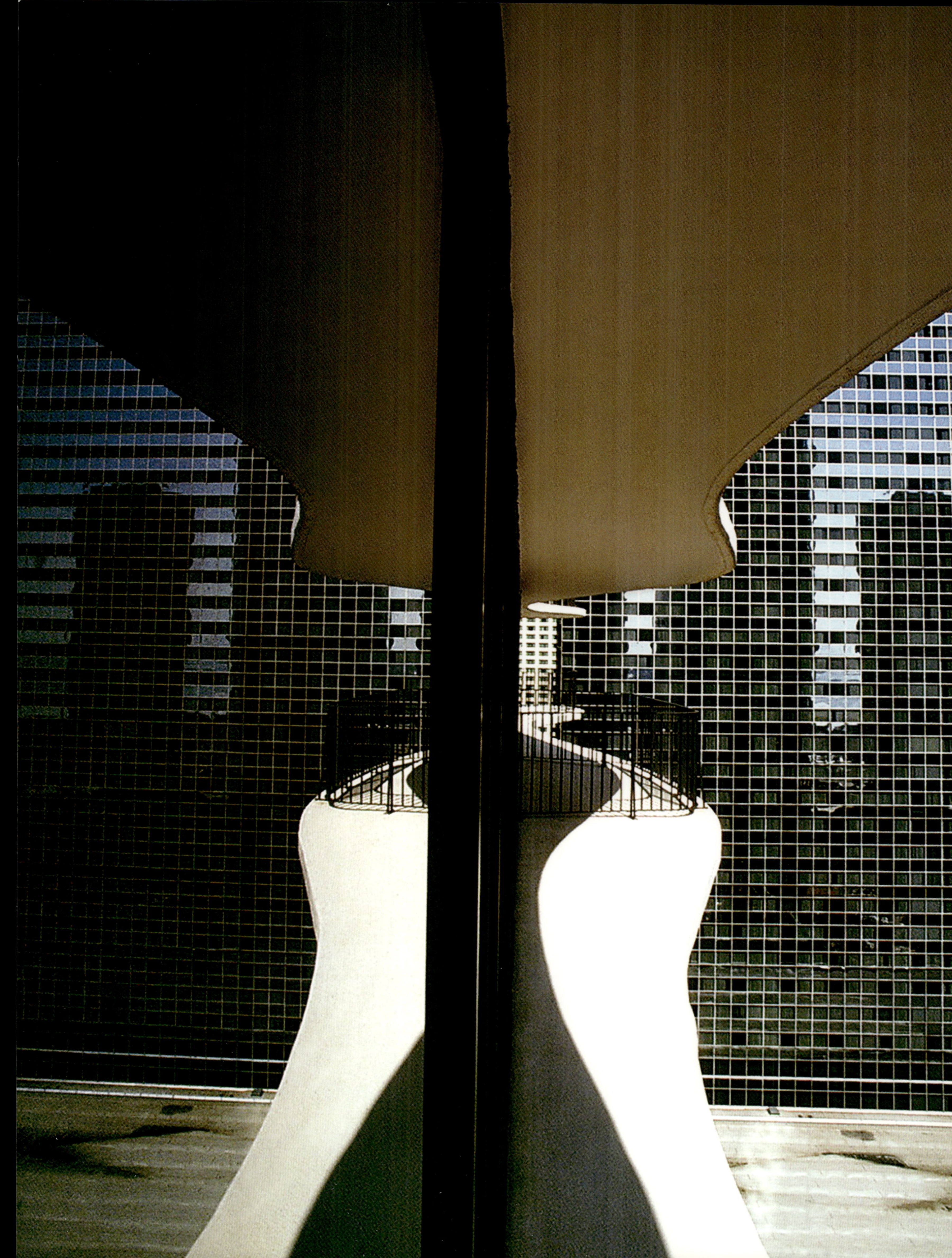

If anything significant has happened in architecture in the decade since Richard Schulman published *Portraits 1*, it is that all of these notions are better understood today than they were before, when the idea of the celebrity architect had a certain novelty. A decade ago, an architect's fame could sometimes seem directly proportionate to the extent to which he or she produced arresting, eye-catching shapes. Today we are more nuanced, less comfortable thinking in such terms—not, I hope, less entranced with lyrical architectural form when we see it, but more willing to see the breadth and depth of what architecture is, more likely to think in terms of process, and more comfortable acknowledging the social as well as the formal dimension in architecture. Buildings exist to serve us as well as to entertain us. Cities are complex entities, not collections of foreground objects. Society's priority should be building to house people who need roofs over their heads, not building to amuse those who are already well taken care of.

Of course we knew all of that a decade ago, but I think it is fair to say that the architectural world was less inclined to focus on these reasonable truths then than it is now. Still, welcome though the acknowledgment of architecture's broader social presence might be, it is easy to slip from this into a realm of thinking in which ambitious and visually strong architecture is viewed as some kind of mistake, as a distraction, or—even worse— as a detriment to the social goals of building. Awarding the Pritzker Prize, architecture's highest honor, to the Japanese architect Shigeru Ban in 2014 in recognition of his work in creating inexpensive, temporary housing and other structures following natural disaster was not, as some critics have tried to suggest, a rejection of aesthetics in favor of social responsibility. Ban's work was notable not because of his indifference to design, but because of his attempt to bring aesthetics into the realm of emergency building. Form did not cease to matter to the Pritzker jury; it was trying to observe that aesthetically meaningful architectural form could be found in more places, and in different kinds of circumstances, than we have been accustomed to expect. But the prize still sought to honor an architect's striving for aesthetic value, as it always has. Design is never solely a matter of aesthetics—but it is never not a matter of aesthetics, either.

I'm not sure, in the end, that the architects represented in *Portraits 2* build all that differently from their colleagues, whom Richard Schulman photographed a decade ago. They rely more heavily on digital technology, and that often creates a greater fluidity of form, as the work of Jeanne Gang, Massimiliano Fuksas, Jürgen Mayer, Ben van Berkel, and Hani Rashid and Lise Anne Couture—among others—demonstrates. But it can often yield work of exceptional elegance, too, as Peter Bohlin's Apple store on Fifth Avenue in New York reminds us.

Without question, many of these architects are producing forms that are as memorable, and sometimes as flamboyant, as anything made a decade ago. Do buildings like MVRDV's Spijkenisse library, Rafael Moneo's Columbia University laboratory, Michael Maltzan's house in Beverly Hills, Roger Duffy's University Center at the New School, Ben van Berkel's auto museum for Daimler-Benz, and David Adjaye's Sugar Hill housing—to cite but six of the more compelling projects in this book—tell us anything about the architecture of our time? Perhaps it is worth noting that none of them are art museums, but what of it? All but one of these projects serve a public function of one kind or another, although of these, only Adjaye's building, which contains publicly assisted housing, could be said to represent the current uptick in awareness of architecture's social responsibility.

In the end, I think that the architecture in this book offers no neat, pat conclusion about the architecture of this moment. What it does tell us is that architects remain as committed to the challenge of making new forms as they have ever been. They welcome the presence of new digital tools to help them—but they were doing that a decade ago too, if less ubiquitously, and we are beginning to see more and more new forms that show the effect of the tools by which they were made. The architectural medium is at least part of the message, as it always has been.

But the real conclusion I draw from Richard Schulman's work isn't about the specific buildings shown on these pages. It's in the fact that this architecture is shown alongside the architect who led the creative process that brought it into being. That doesn't have to make more of architectural celebrity than it's worth. It can also be a reminder of something far more important: that every building, whatever its place or its purpose, is both a social and an aesthetic statement, and who is making that statement continues to matter.

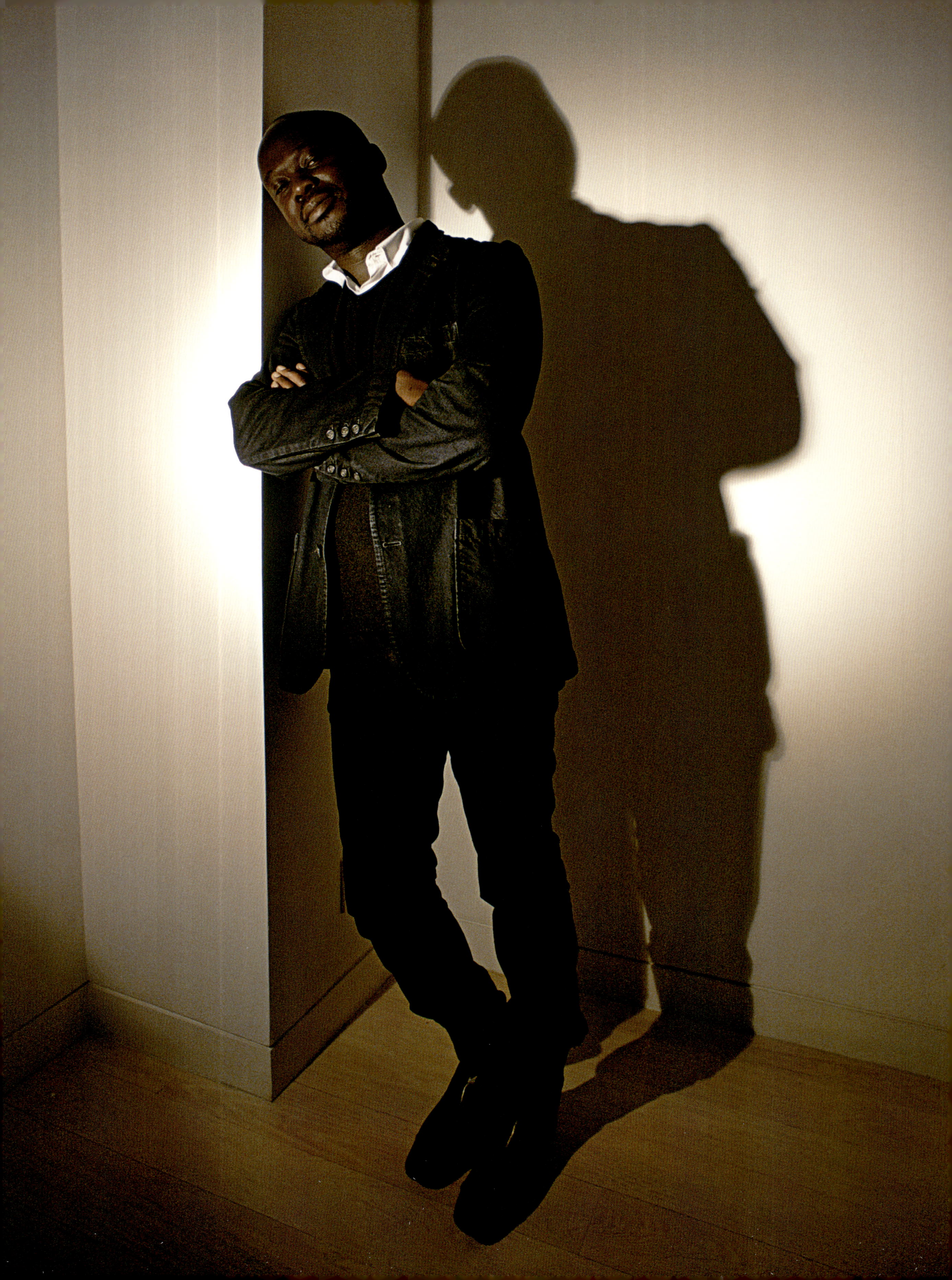

DAVID ADJAYE

For David Adjaye, connecting with the history and culture of the African American communities where many of his most acclaimed projects are located is more than just part of the job—it's his responsibility as a man with African roots. Born in Tanzania in 1966 and raised in Egypt, Lebanon, Yemen, and the United Kingdom, Adjaye, who was educated at the Royal College of Art in London, has spent the golden years of career in the United States, where he has received a number of high-profile commissions.

The most prestigious of these is for the National Museum of African American History and Culture on the National Mall in Washington, D.C.: a box of steel and glass covered in a layer of aluminum panels—inspired by ornamental metal castings made by slaves in the antebellum period—which is scheduled to open in 2015. But the project that has most affected the community where it is located is Sugar Hill (2014), a low-income housing project in the Harlem neighborhood famous for once being the home of Duke Ellington, W. E. B. Du Bois, and Willie Mays, among other celebrities. Located on 155th Street and St. Nicholas Avenue, the structure is covered in a pattern that, in certain light, reveals images of roses. It contains 124 apartments, twenty percent of which have been reserved for the homeless. Although the young Adjaye has received plenty of critical praise, he says that it is projects like the Sugar Hill housing project that remind him of why he became an architect—to service the communities that most need help.

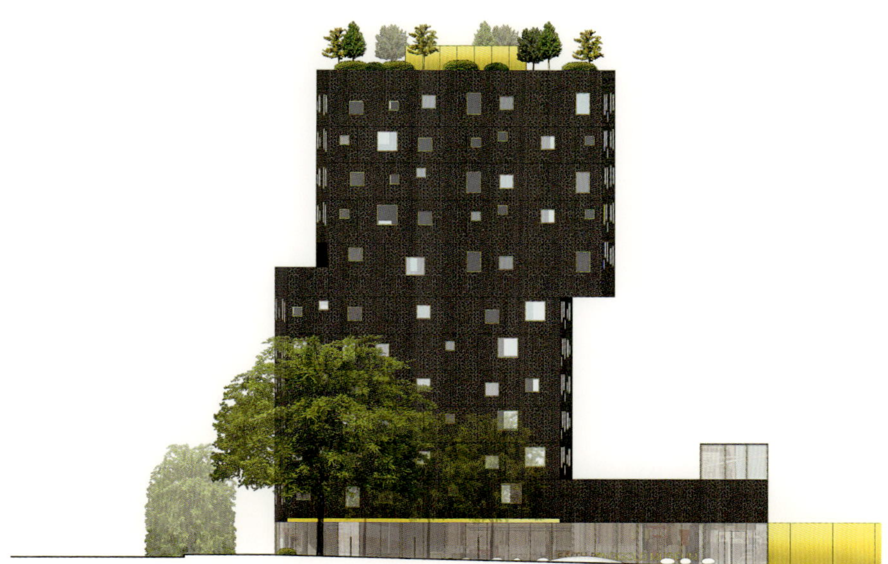

Rendering of the Sugar Hill housing development. *Opposite:* David Adjaye.

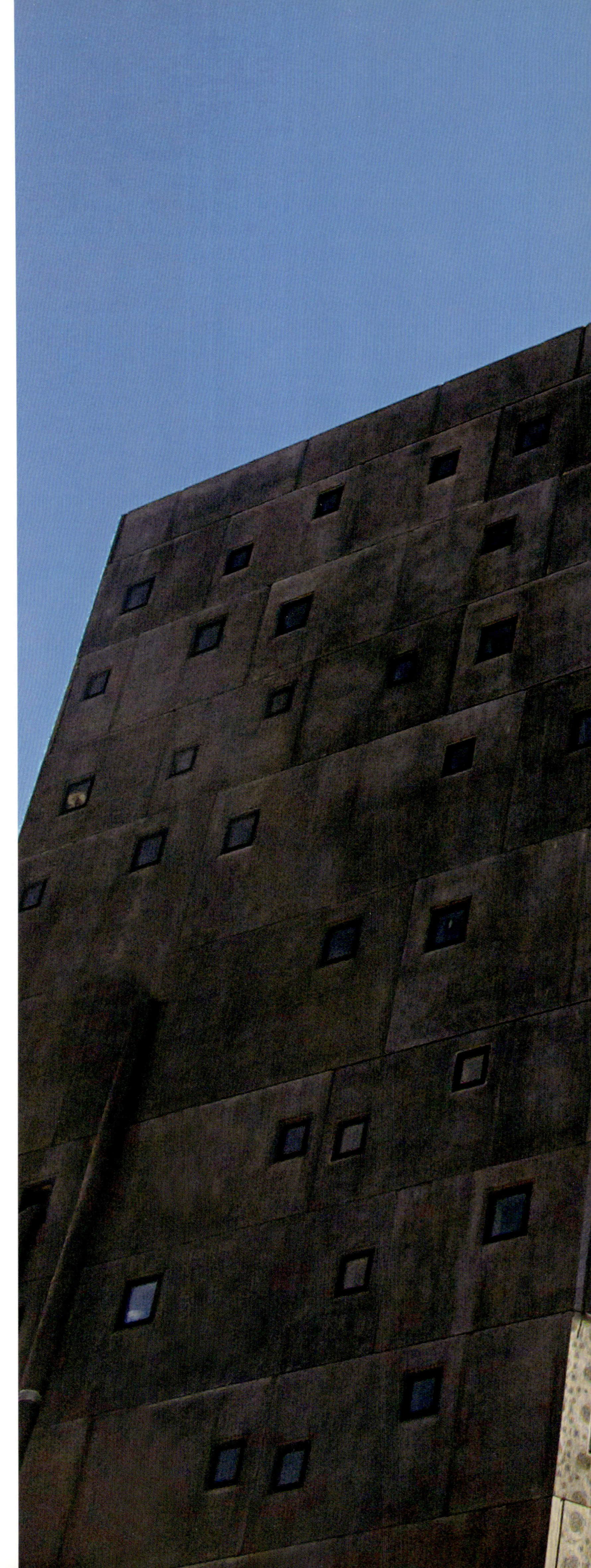

Adjaye Associates. Sugar Hill housing development,
New York City, 2014.

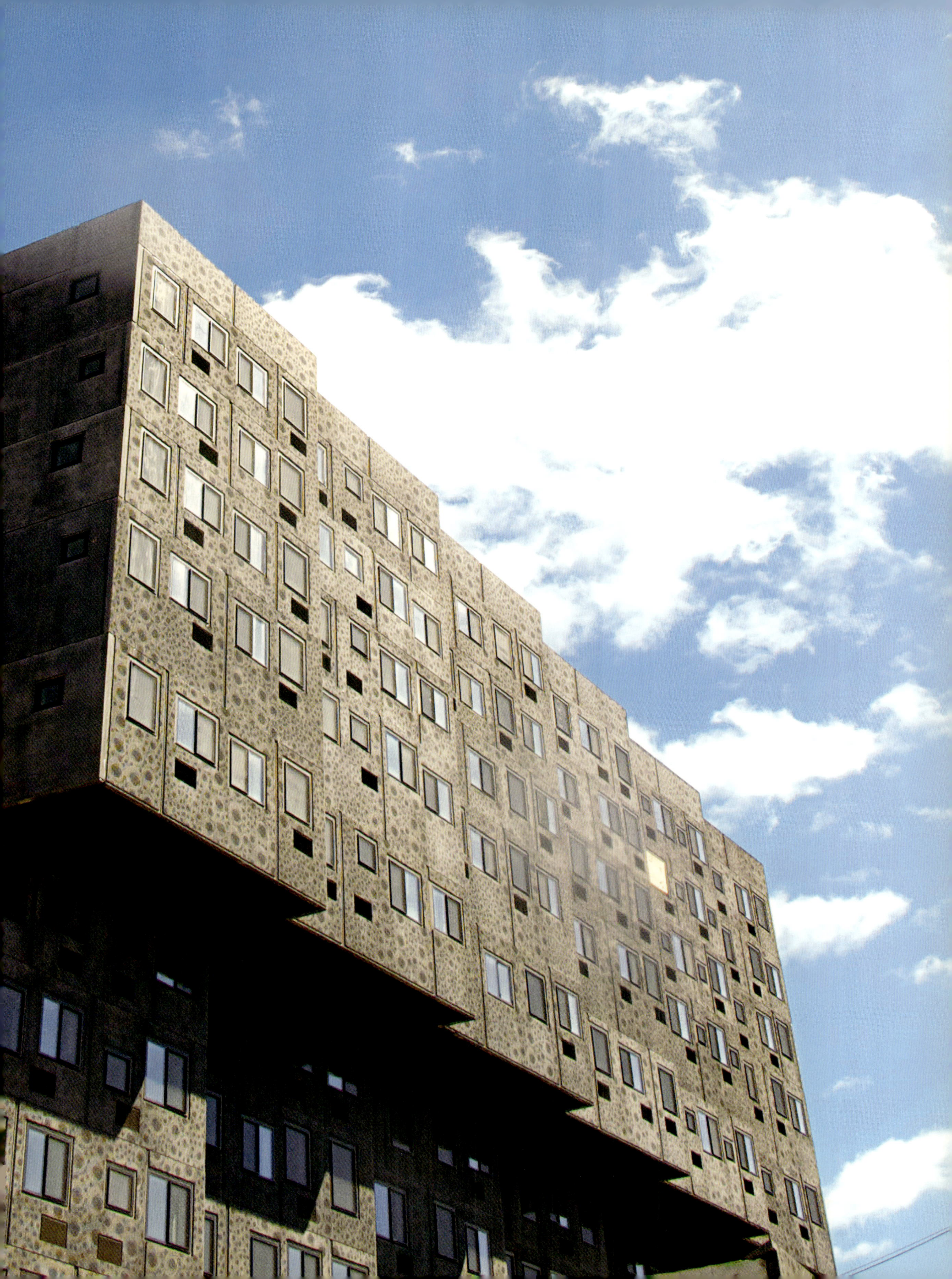

ASYMPTOTE ARCHITECTURE

Coming upon one of Asymptote's buildings feels something like arriving into a future where our landscape has been populated by structures whose technologies exceed our present time. Named after a term in analytic geometry to describe the distance between a curve and a line as it tends to infinity, Asymptote is a New York-based practice founded in 1989 by Hani Rashid and Lise Anne Couture. Known for buildings such as the River Culture Pavilion (ARC) in Daegu, South Korea (2012) and the Yas Viceroy Hotel in Abu Dhabi (2010), the firm has also received acclaim for its virtual reality installations, including Flux 3.0 M_Scapes (2002), a digitally augmented environment derived from the skylines of Tokyo, New York, and Hong Kong that first appeared at Documenta XI in Kassel, Germany.

166 Perry Street is Asymptote's first building in New York. Expanding on the link their work has with art and photography, Rashid and Couture designed the project as an aesthetic gift to its surrounding neighborhood. The two types of glass that make up its facade effectively transform the structure into a reflection of all nearby activity, allowing it to blend seamlessly with its West Village environment. Inside, there are myriad details that welcome in a new age and speak to how residents will want to live decades from now: Aeronautically curved Corian counters fit over the refrigerator, and sliding glass doors separate the bedroom or reconnect it to the remainder of the apartment. Asymptote's focus on both innovative details and creating a building that is a work of art has ensured that the firm's presence will extend well into the future.

Hani Rashid and Lise Anne Couture of Asymptote Architecture.

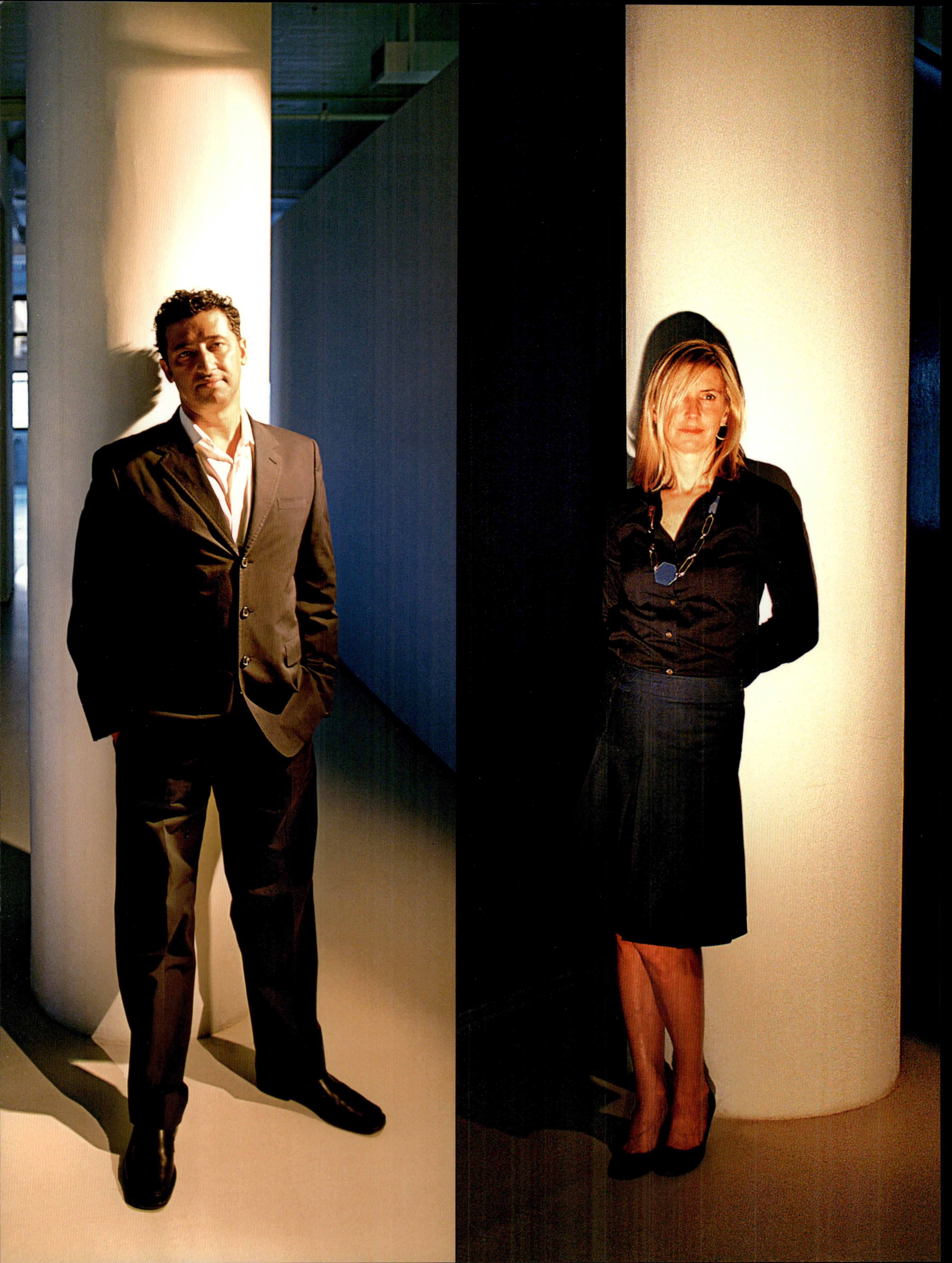

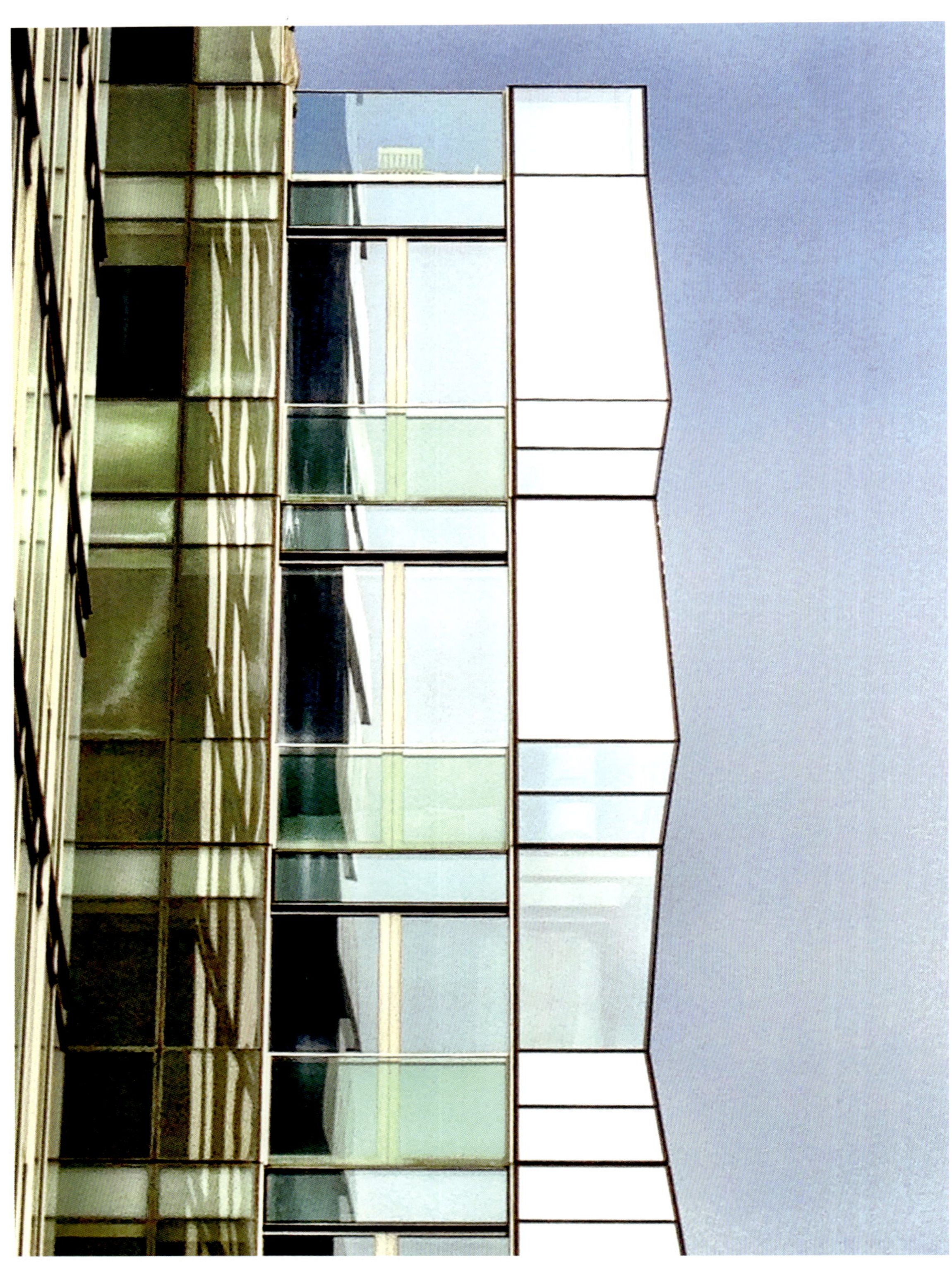

Asymptote Architecture. 166 Perry Street, New York City, 2012.

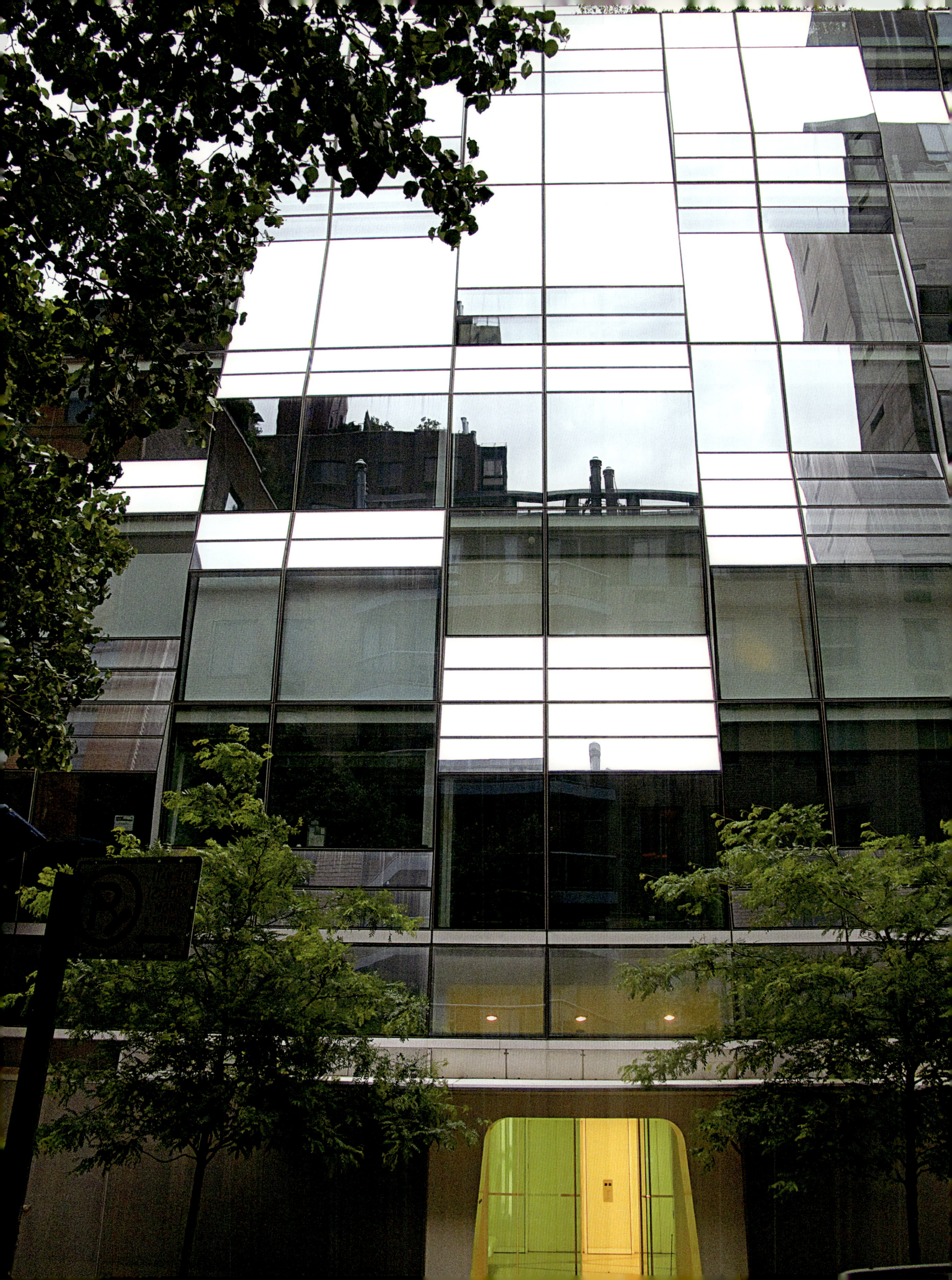

BOHLIN CYWINSKI JACKSON (BCJ)

It's no small feat to create a structure on Fifth Avenue in New York, one of the most iconic retail locations in the world, without disrupting the existing urban balance. But that's exactly what the architects at Bohlin Cywinski Jackson (BCJ) did with their design for the Apple Store (2006). Located at 767 Fifth Avenue, on a corner between 58th and 59th streets and adjacent to both Bergdorf Goodman and FAO Schwarz, the store is buried in the underground retail concourse of the General Motors Building. To entice viewers inside, BCJ designed a thirty-two-foot-high vertical glass cube replete with a glass elevator and a glass staircase, making the structure both visible from the street and transparent. During the day, the cube permeates the underground store with natural light. At night, it beckons consumers with the otherworldly glow of technology emitted from inside.

It's no surprise that BCJ—which was founded in 1965 in Wilkes-Barre, Pennsylvania, and currently has offices in Philadelphia, Seattle and San Francisco—was able to so seamlessly blend a structure into the cramped landscape of midtown Manhattan. The firm has excelled at responding to the subtleties of place for half a century, whether those places are ensconced in the natural world, as was the case with the firm's Grand Teton Discovery and Visitor Center on the banks of the Snake River in Jackson, Wyoming, or in the realm of the academic, as is evinced by the Schlinger Laboratory at the California Institute of Technology, where the firm was tasked with enhancing the quality of life for researchers and students. As a result, BCJ has received more than 540 awards, and continues to make a mark.

Sketch of the Apple Store Fifth Avenue.
Opposite: Peter Bohlin of Bohlin Cywinski Jackson.

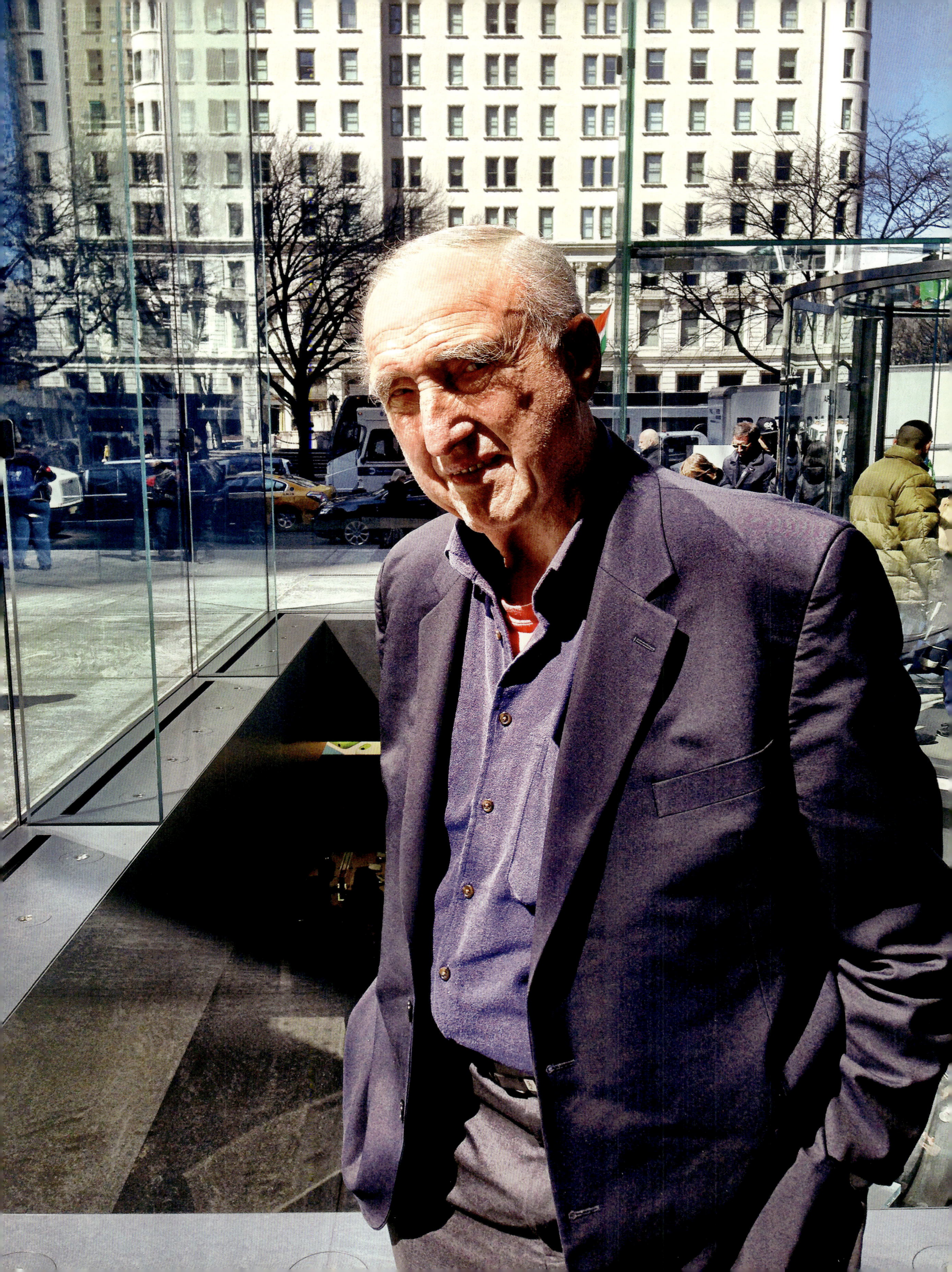

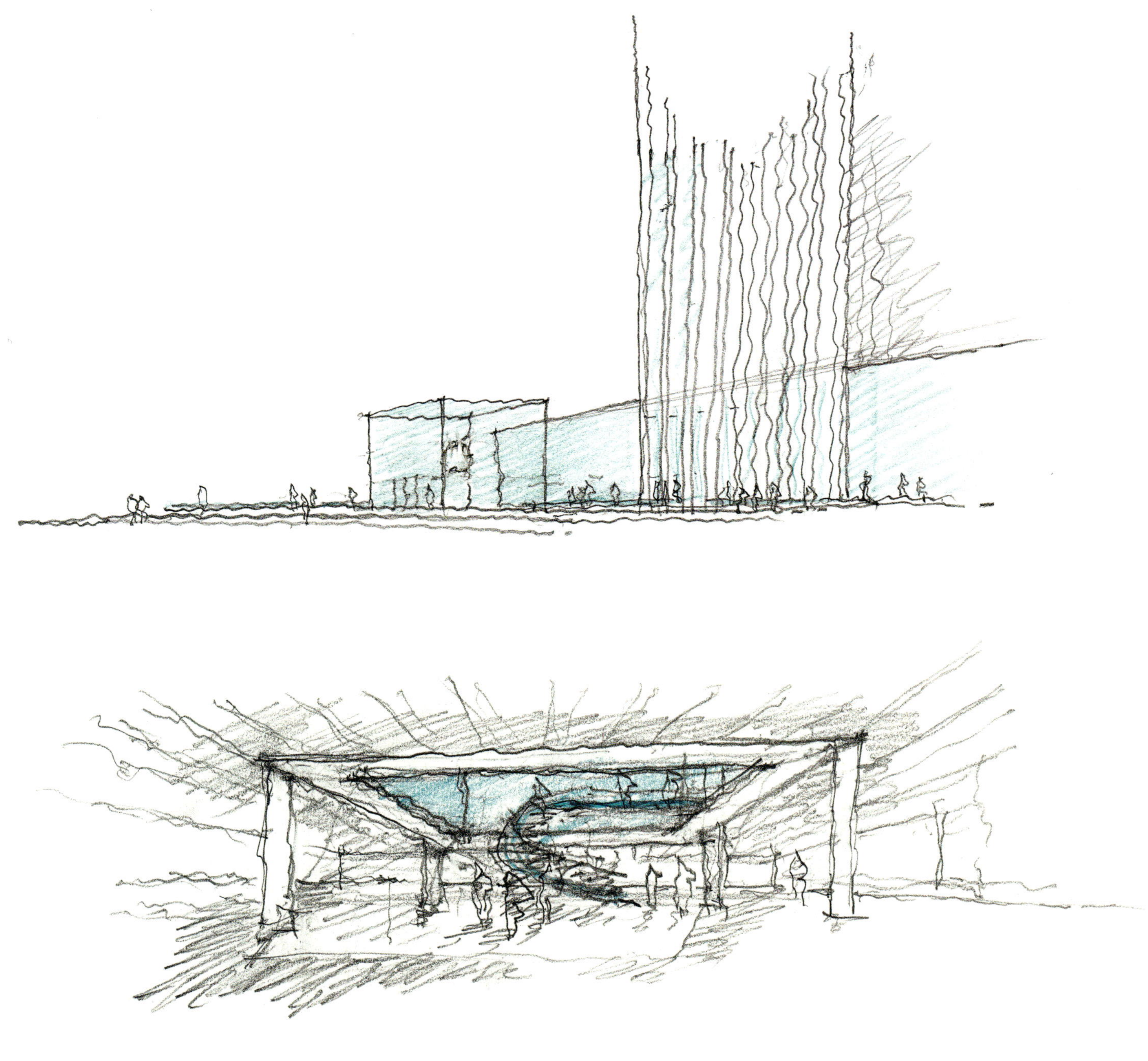

Sketches of the Apple Store Fifth Avenue.
Opposite: Bohlin Cywinski Jackson. Apple Store Fifth Avenue, New York City, 2006.

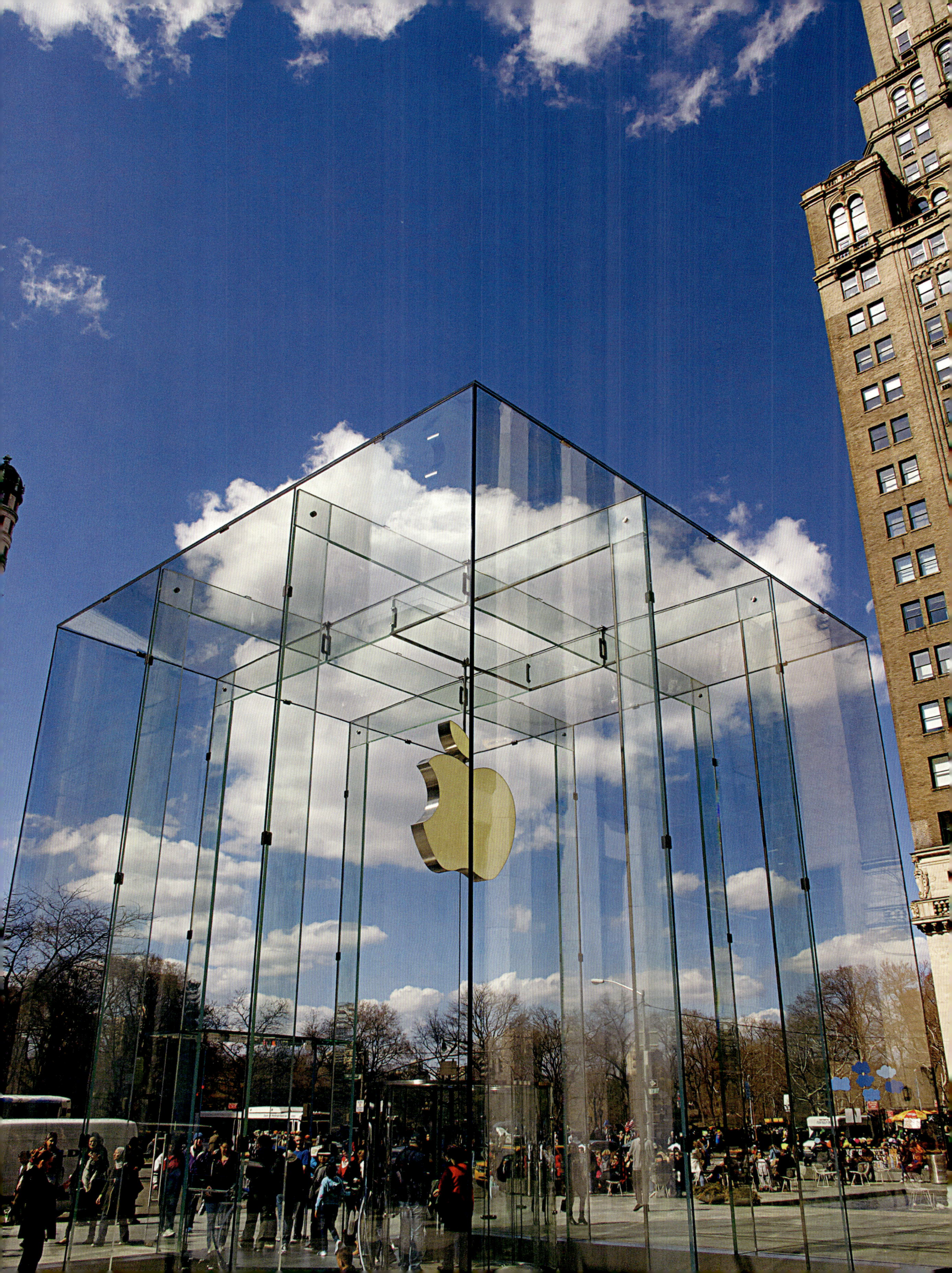

BJARKE INGELS GROUP (BIG)

Founded in 2005 by Bjarke Ingels, a Danish architect born in 1974 and educated at the Royal Academy in Copenhagen, BIG has made its mark with ambitious and highly photogenic projects. These include the Mountain Dwellings (2008), a residential project in Copenhagen consisting of manicured modular units terraced together to form a housing block, and West 57th Street, a pyramid-shaped apartment complex that resembles less a building than an optical puzzle in an M C. Escher painting. The latter, still under construction, is a coup d'état for the young architect—upon its completion, it will place him in the elite category of architects who have made their mark on the Manhattan skyline.

Although the acronym of the firm's name might suggest otherwise, BIG works just as well on a small scale as it does on the monumental. For the Danish National Maritime Museum in Helsingør (2013), rather than building upward, the firm placed the galleries underground, in the 65,000-square-foot footprint left behind by a dry dock originally built in the 1950s. Within the subterranean space, three double-level glass bridges unfold. They contain galleries that tell the history of the Danish shipbuilding industry up to the present day. Part of an initiative by the Danish government to bring tourists to the port, which is most famously known as the town where Shakespeare's *Hamlet* was set, the museum's location allows it to be visible to pedestrians without blocking views of the city's most famous attraction—the sixteenth-century Kronborg Castle. This clever juxtaposition of the historic with the new certainly guarantees a spot for the young Ingels in the history of his birth country's built environment.

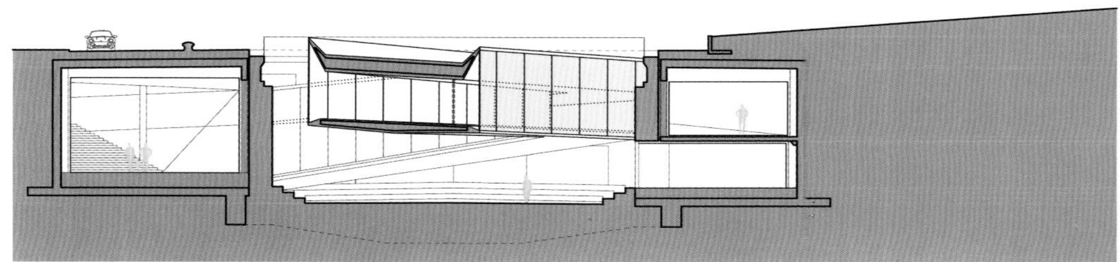

Above and following pages: Renderings of the Danish National Maritime Museum.
Opposite: Bjarke Ingels.
Pages 30–31: Bjarke Ingels Group. Danish National Maritime Museum, Helsingør, Denmark, 2013.

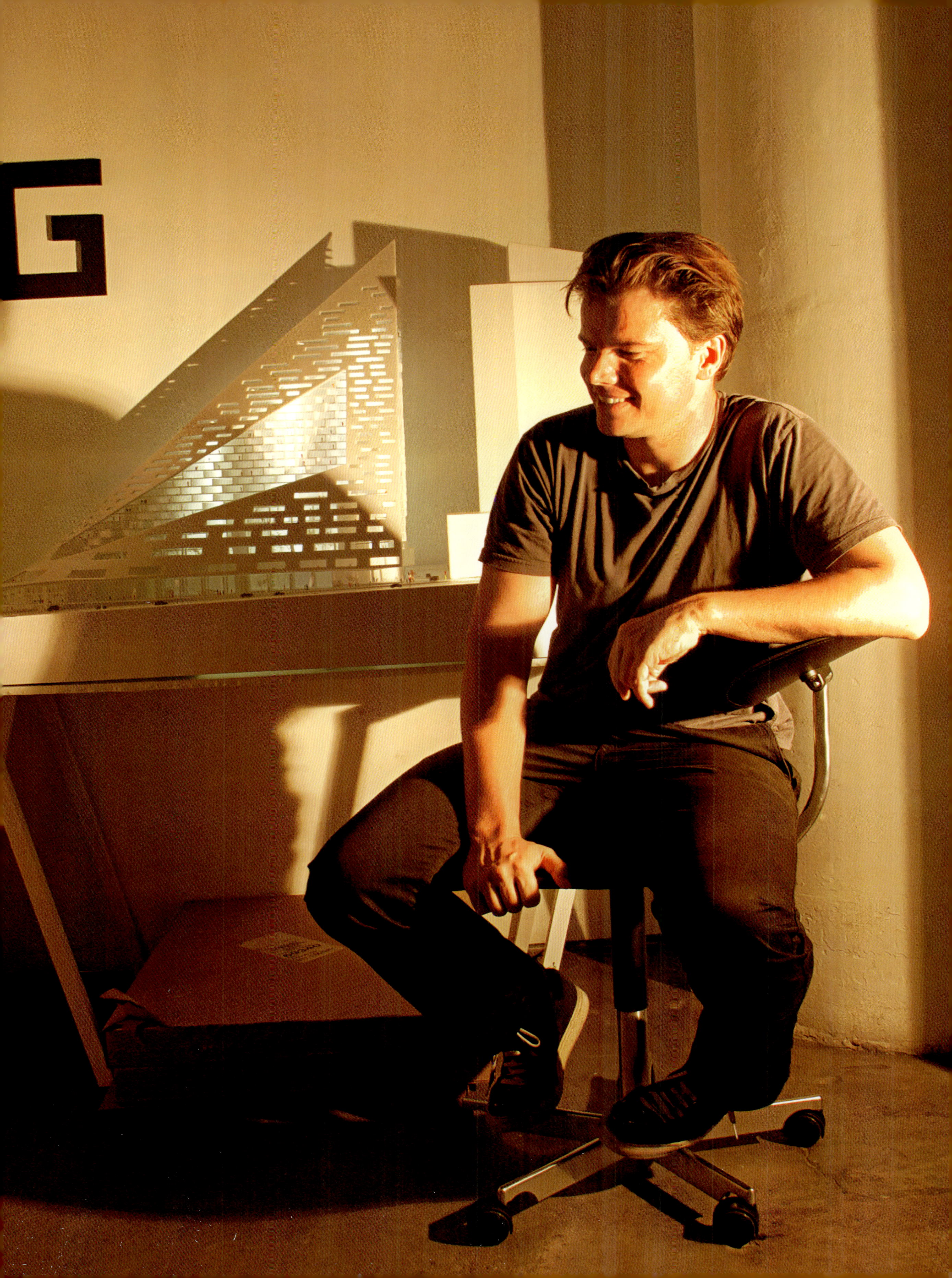

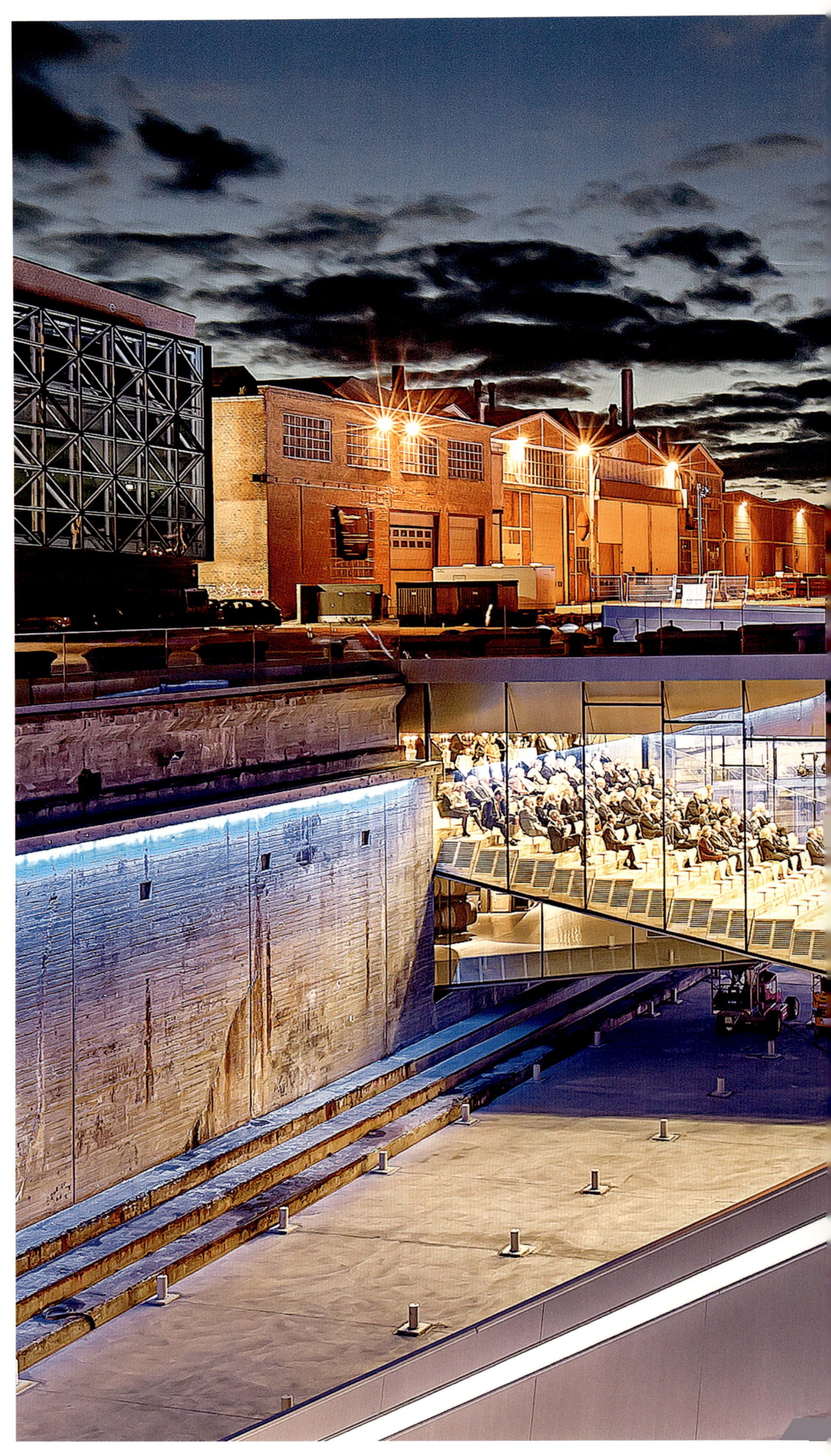

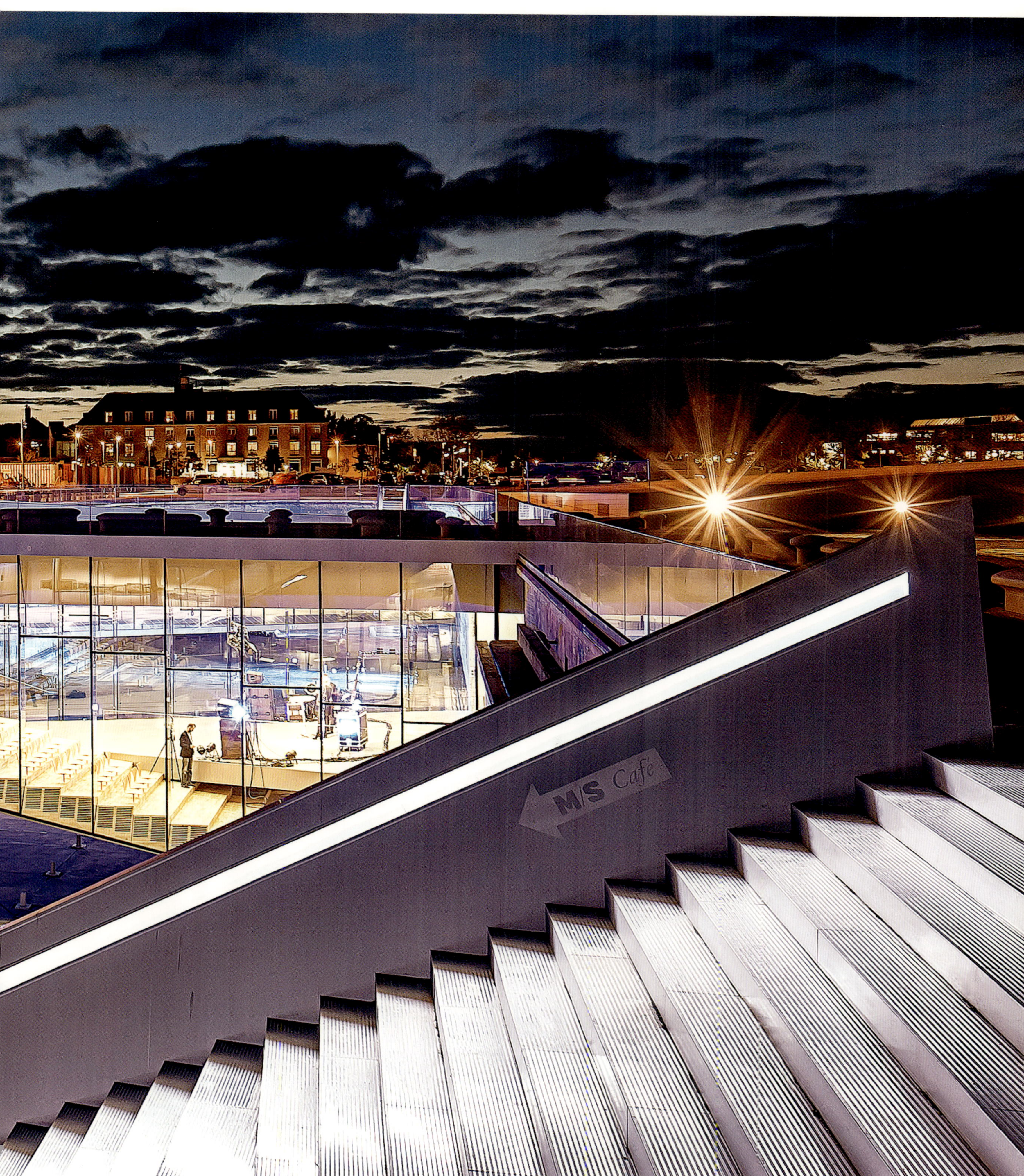
M/S Café

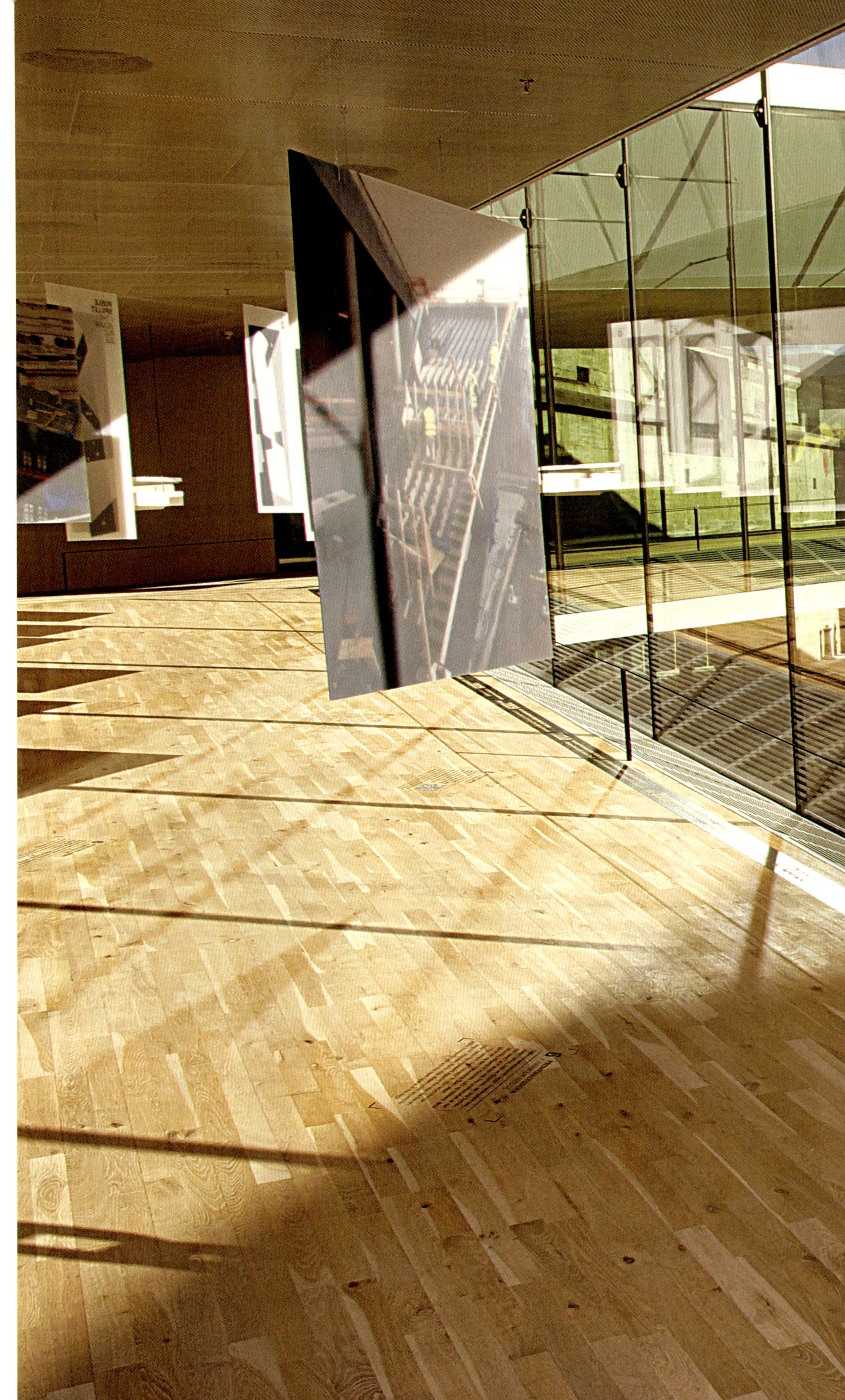

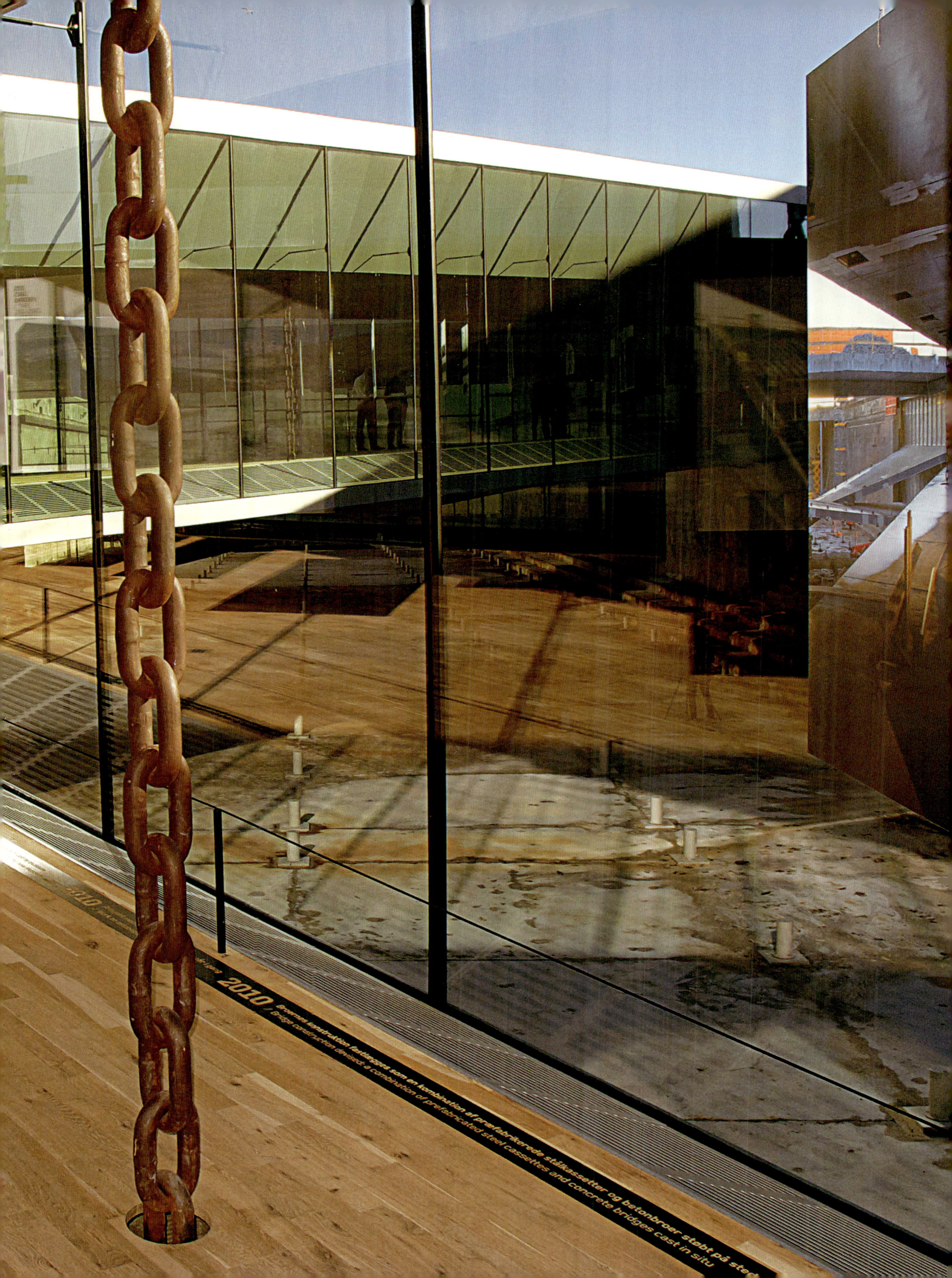

2010
Broens konstruktion fastlægges som en kombination af præfabrikerede stålkassetter og betonbroer støbt på ste[d]
Bridge construction devised: a combination of prefabricated steel cassettes and concrete bridges cast in situ

TATIANA BILBAO

Constructed out of a colony of articulated pentagons that rise from the mountains outside of Monterrey, Mexico, Tatiana Bilbao's Casa Ventura is an elevated structure that looks like a segmented, futuristic tree house from the outside, but flows like a single space within. The building is designed for a couple with six children whose only requirement was to have a house all on one level. Bilbao faced the challenge of creating such an interior on a forested hillside with an uneven foundation. Her solution was a series of cantilevered concrete blocks that respond to the terrain—for example, the living and dining areas are woven around several existing trees. Limited to a palette of concrete, wood, and glass, the house offers clean, often breathtaking views of the forest, and below, the city of Monterrey.

Clean, light-imbued spaces that somehow manage to feel organic are characteristic of Bilbao, a Mexico City-based architect born in 1972 who does not rely heavily on computer programs or sophisticated models to create her impossibly elegant structures. Rather, she designs using simple materials—she states that they are "rock, paper, scissors"—which allows for a purer expression of mathematical forms. Working very closely with her clients, who include the famed Mexican artist Gabriel Orozco, she is conscious that the laborers who work on her buildings in Mexico are not skilled with new technologies. For Orozco's house in Roca Blanca (2009), which was based on an observatory in Delhi, India and revolves around a spherical pool on the roof, she had to monitor the process of construction on a daily basis. It gave her the desire to simplify her language enough so that her structures could be built anywhere.

Resulting works have caught international attention, enough so that Bilbao landed on the short list to add an extension to the Menil Collection, originally designed by Renzo Piano—the commission went to someone else, but Bilbao continues to be in high demand, especially in her native city.

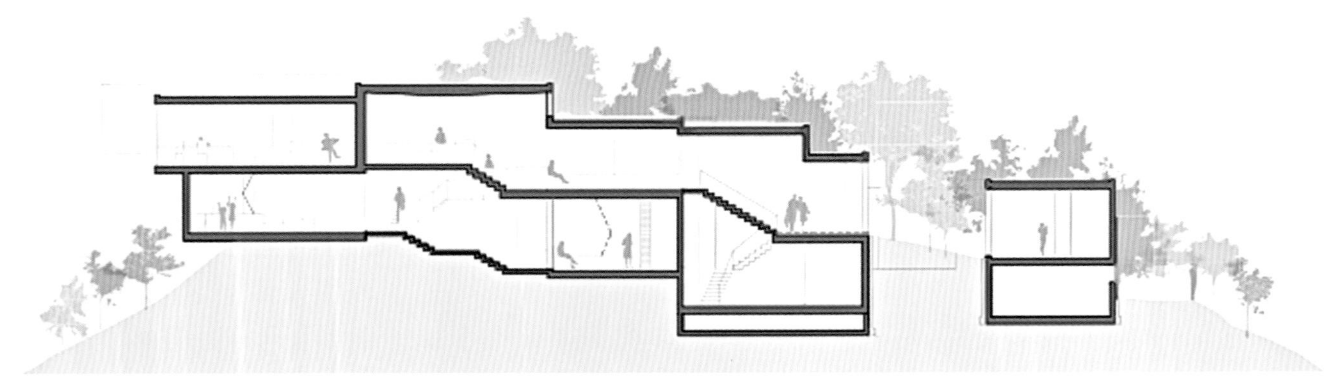

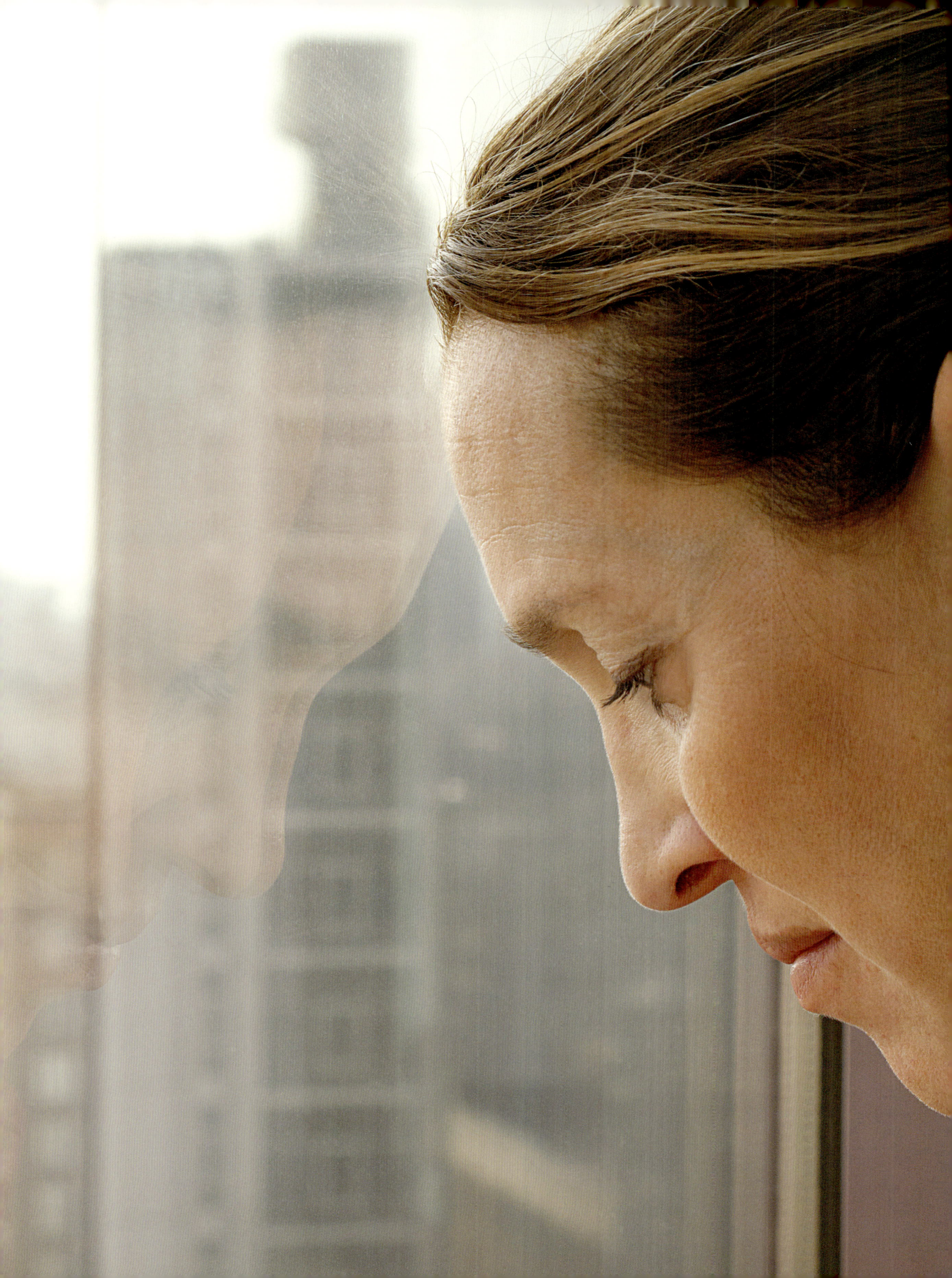

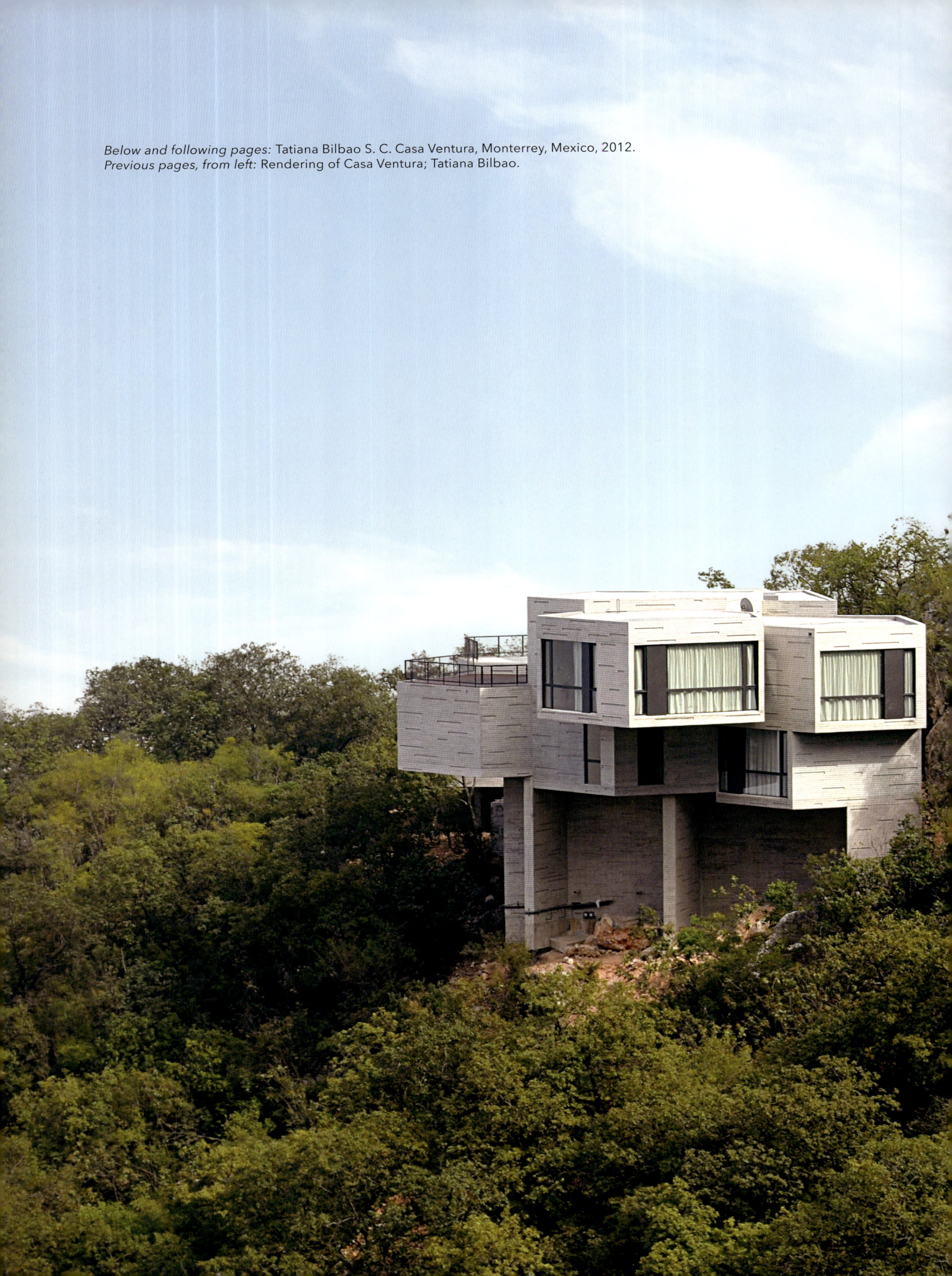

Below and following pages: Tatiana Bilbao S. C. Casa Ventura, Monterrey, Mexico, 2012.
Previous pages, from left: Rendering of Casa Ventura; Tatiana Bilbao.

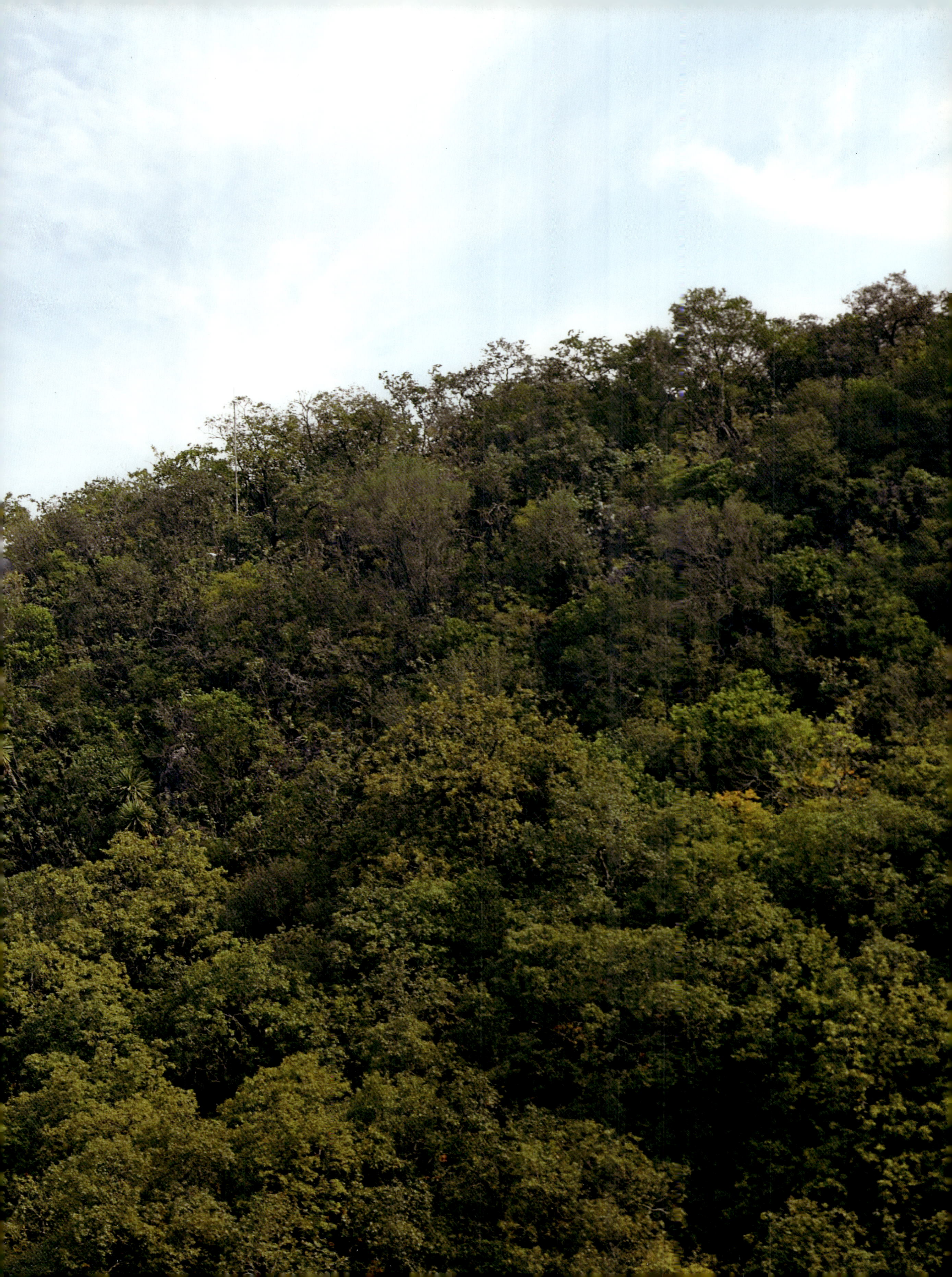

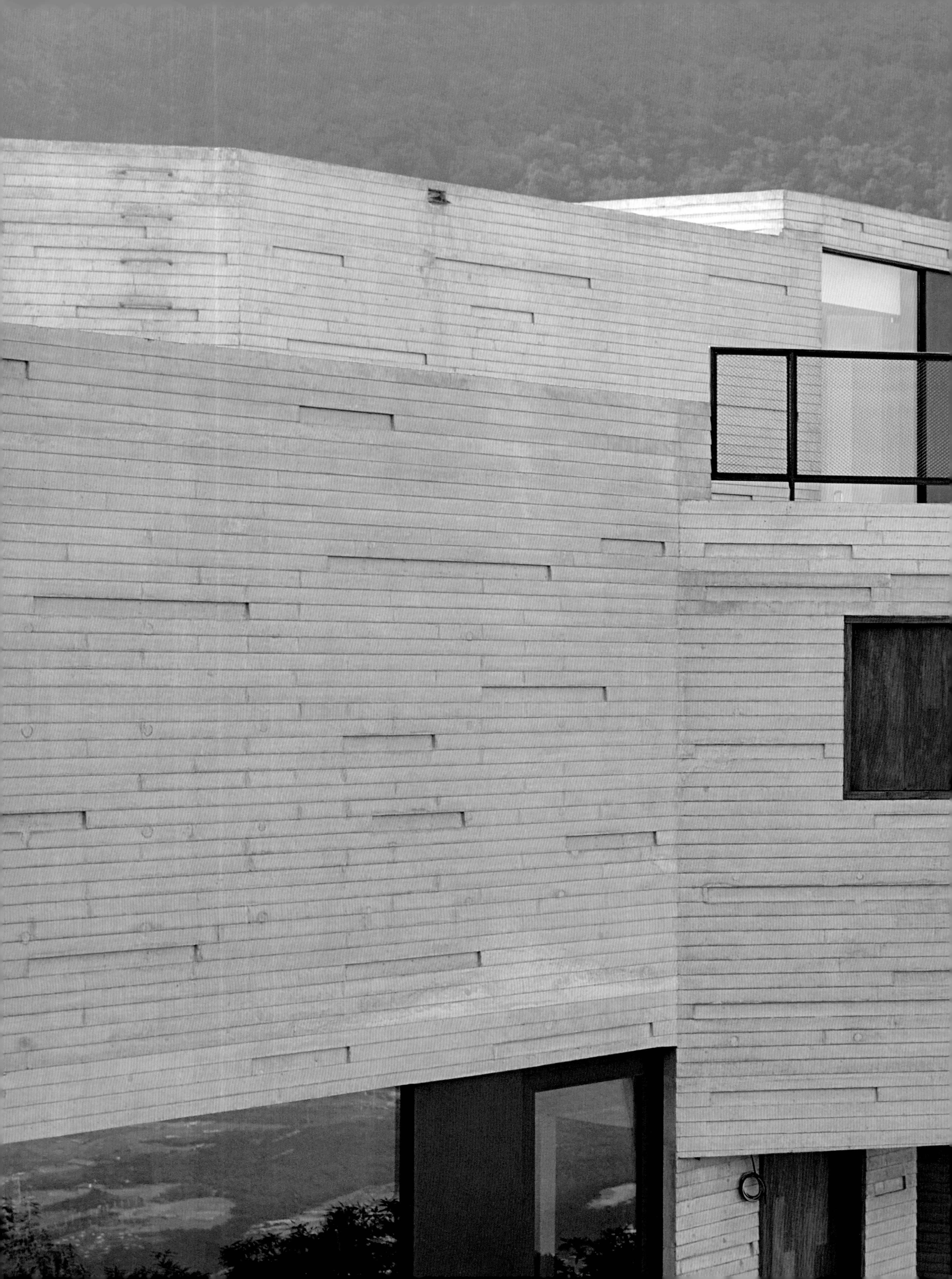

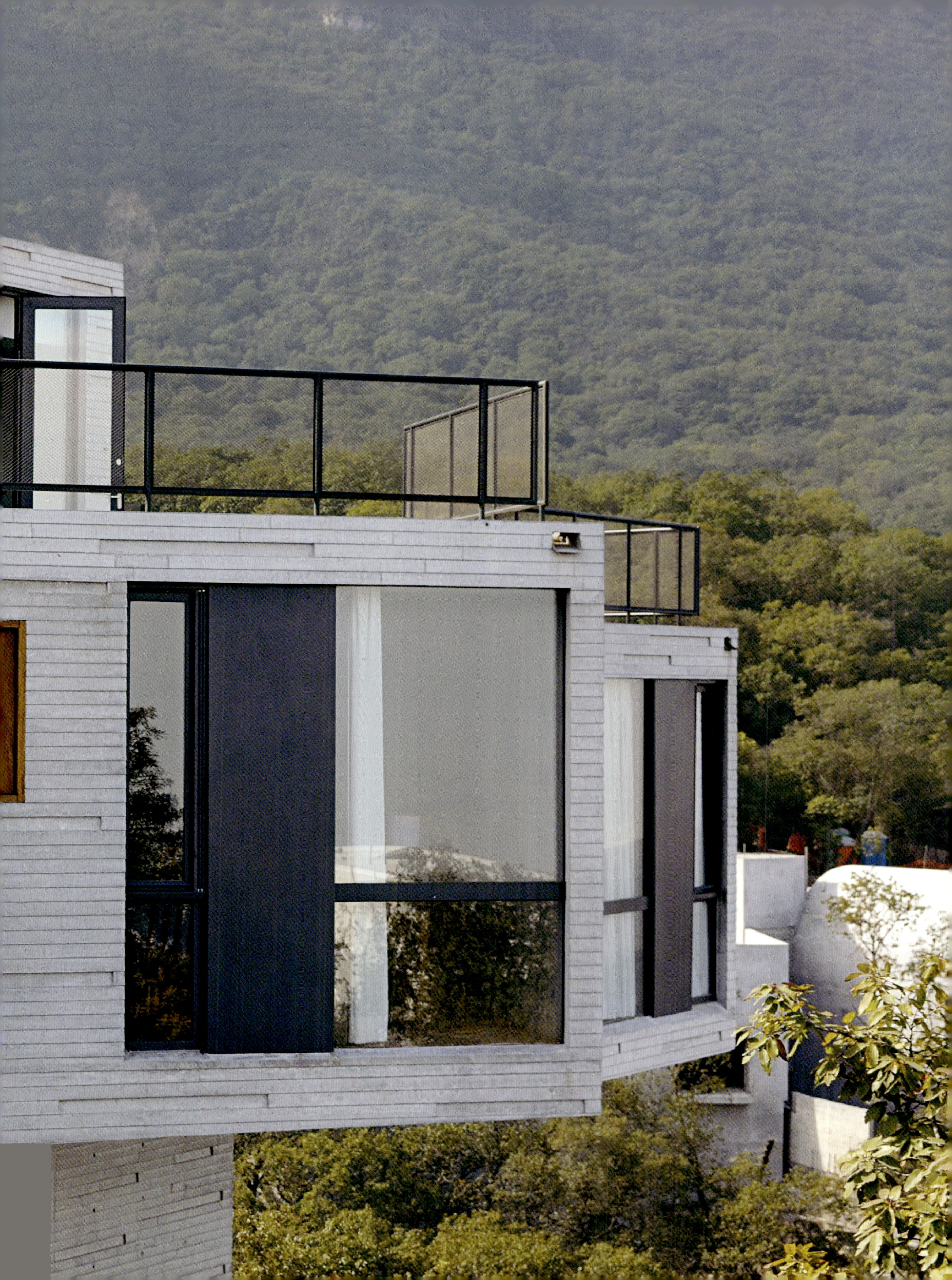

DAVID CHIPPERFIELD

When the Fundación Jumex Arte Contemporáneo wanted to move its exhibition space from the Jumex juice factory in the suburbs to a more institutional context in Mexico City, it turned to British architect Sir David Chipperfield, the man responsible for the Hepworth Wakefield art gallery in West Yorkshire (2011) and an extension to the St. Louis Art Museum (2013), among many other internationally renowned exhibition spaces. For the small, 2,500-square-meter lot in the Plaza Carso in Polanco, directly across from the Museo Soumaya, Chipperfield designed a three-story, 1,600-square-meter structure topped by four triangular skylights that bathe the top floor in natural light. Clad in locally sourced white travertine, the structure resembles a ritualistic statue from some bygone era—or the flowing hair of the video game character Sonic the Hedgehog. It immediately became a recognizable landmark in the downtown area, drawing visitors in to see exhibitions curated from the private collection of Jumex heir Eugenio López Alonso, which consists of four thousand works by the likes of Jeff Koons, Gabriel Orozco, and Donald Judd.

The Jumex is Chipperfield's first project in Latin America. Founded in 1984, his firm has offices in London, Berlin, Milan, and Shanghai, and is known for creating art galleries and retail spaces that revitalize neighborhoods. These include the numerous retail spaces Chipperfield has designed for Dolce & Gabbana since 1999 in locations as diverse as Los Angeles and Osaka, as well as the upcoming Musée des Beaux-arts, a modernist museum in Reims, France, that will rise from the fortifications of the medieval city, connecting—as all great architecture does—the historic with the future.

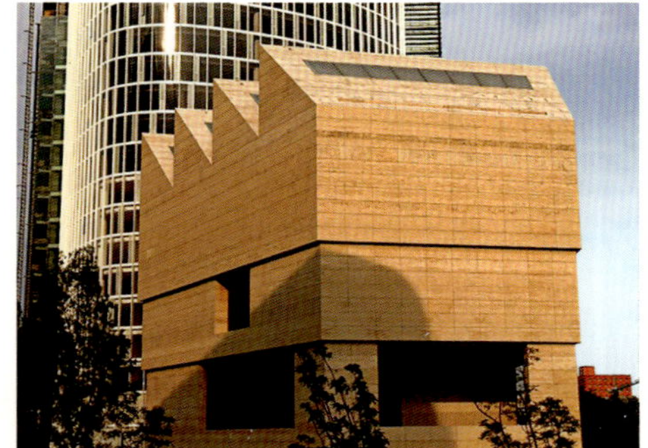

Left: David Chipperfield Architects. Museo Jumex, Mexico City, Mexico, 2013. *Right:* Sketch of Museo Jumex.

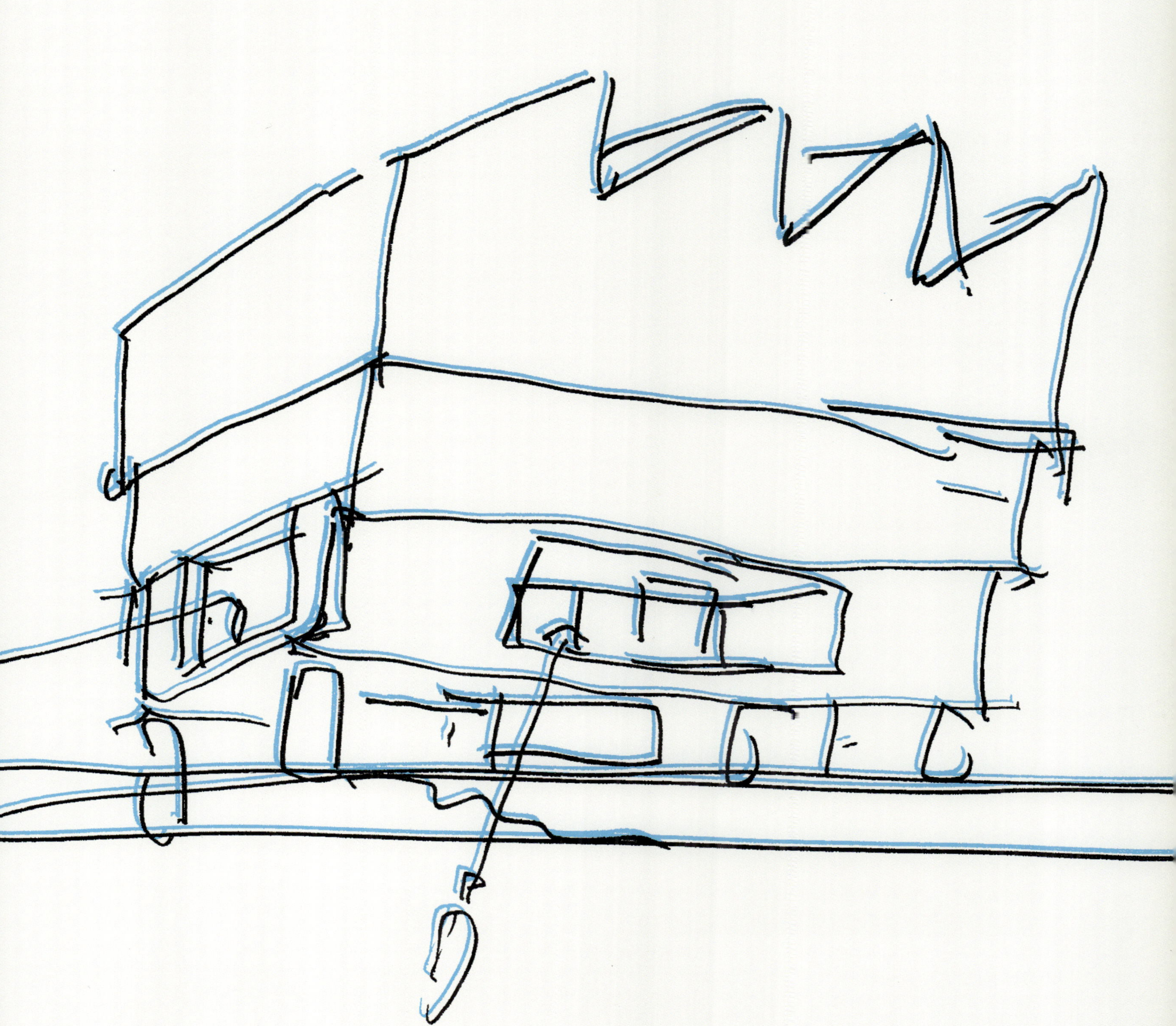

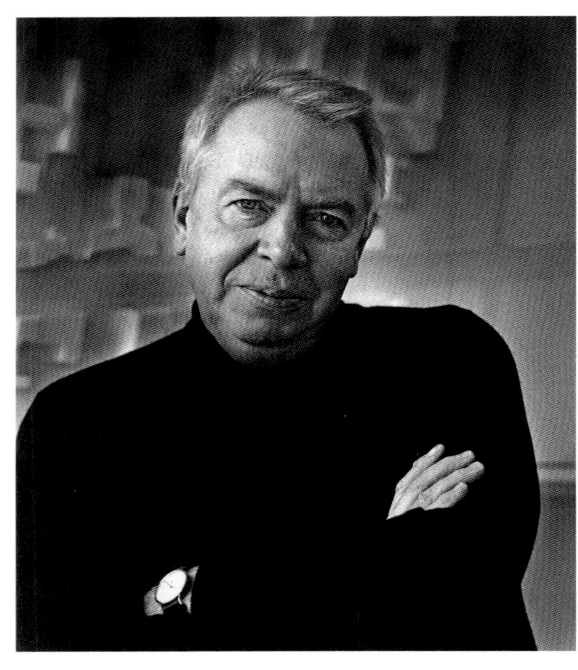

David Chipperfield.
Opposite: Interior of Museo Jumex.

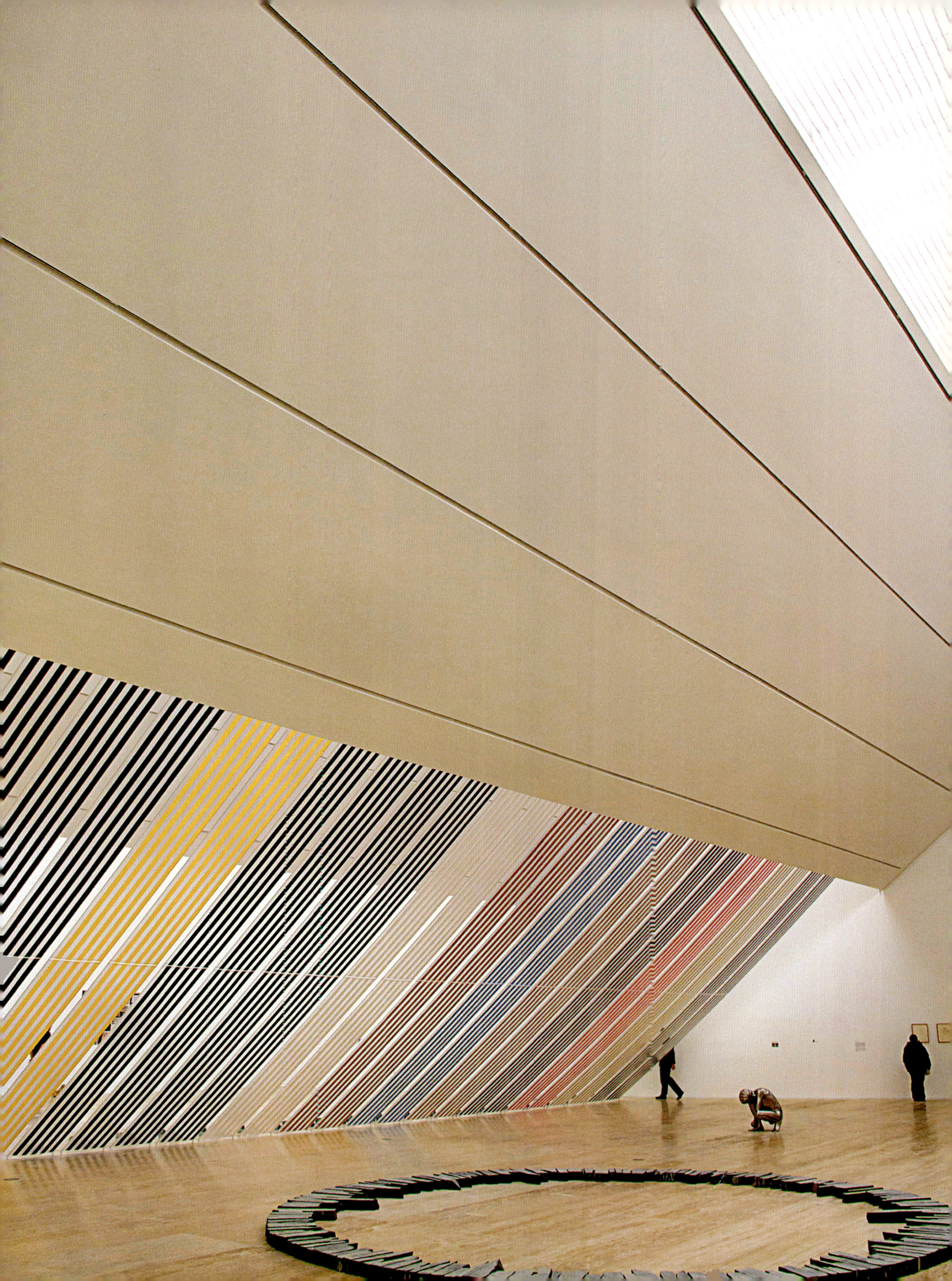

NEIL DENARI

Neil Denari is an architect with a formidable academic career—currently, he is the Vice Chair at the Architecture and Urban Design school at the University of California, Los Angeles—but it wasn't until 2011 that he completed his first commission for a freestanding building. The structure, HL23, is a fourteen-story condominium tower overlooking the High Line in New York City. Constructed from folded steel panels, which support windows that curve like a concave mirror over the manicured wilderness of the elevated walkway, the building is one of the most critically lauded residential structures to grace the New York skyline in the past decade.

Born in Fort Worth, Texas, in 1957, Denari received a bachelor's degree in architecture from the University of Houston in 1980, and a master's in architecture from Harvard in 1982. After graduate school, he lived and worked in Paris and New York before setting down roots in Los Angeles in 1988, where he taught at the Southern California Institute of Architecture and established the practice that is today known as Neil M. Denari Architects (NMDA).

After spending the majority of his career in the theoretical realm—where many of his machine-inspired ideas were manifested in drawings that have ended up in the permanent collections of seven major museums, including the Museum of Modern Art in New York—Denari is finally getting his chance to make his mark on the physical world. Along with a commercial building in Beverly Hills and an apartment complex in Vancouver, NMDA is currently working on the New Keelung Harbor Service Building in Taiwan: a mesh structure coiled at the base of the Keelung mountains that will service up to ten thousand cruise ship passengers a day. Not bad for an academic from California.

Neil Denari.

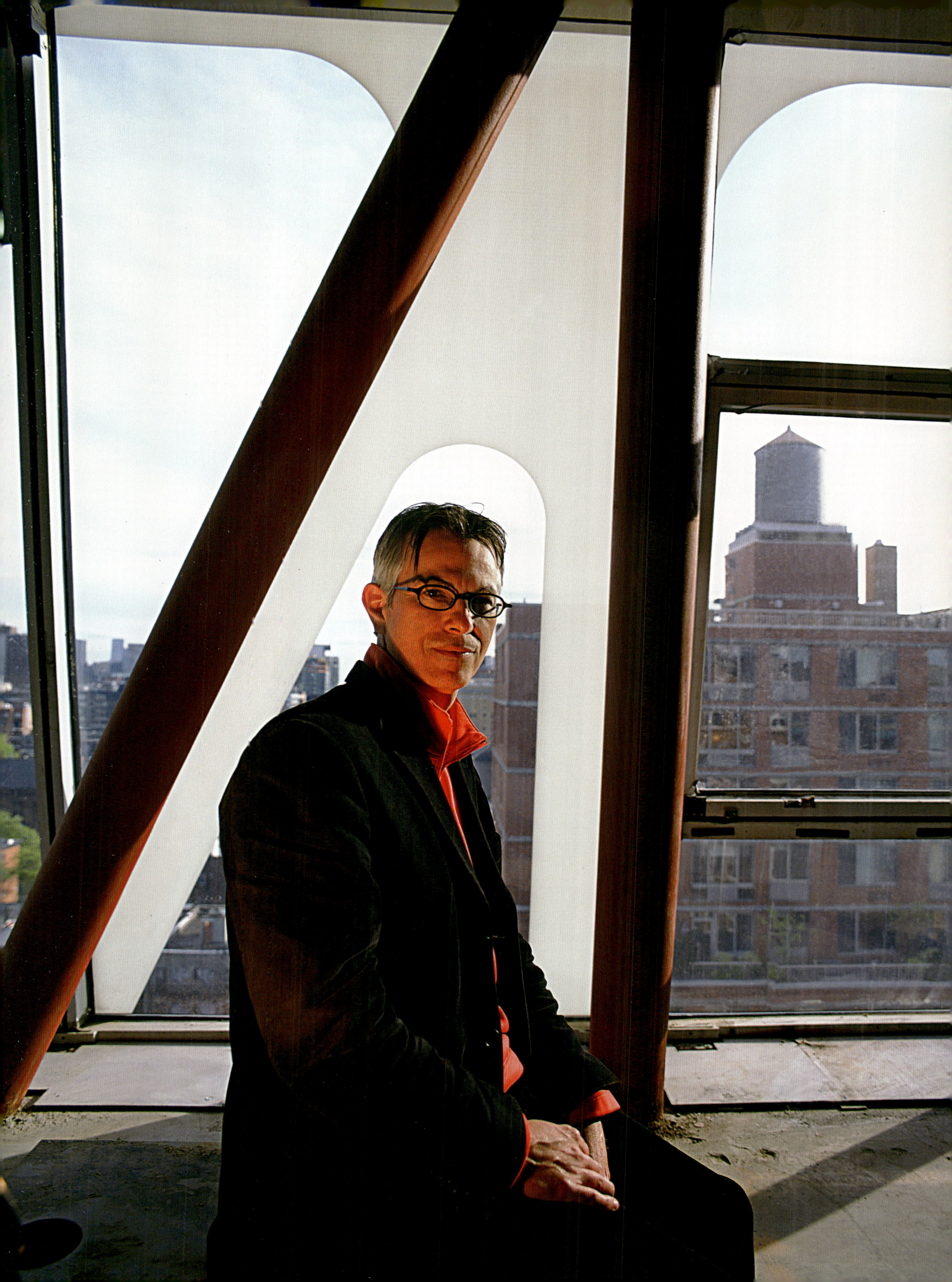

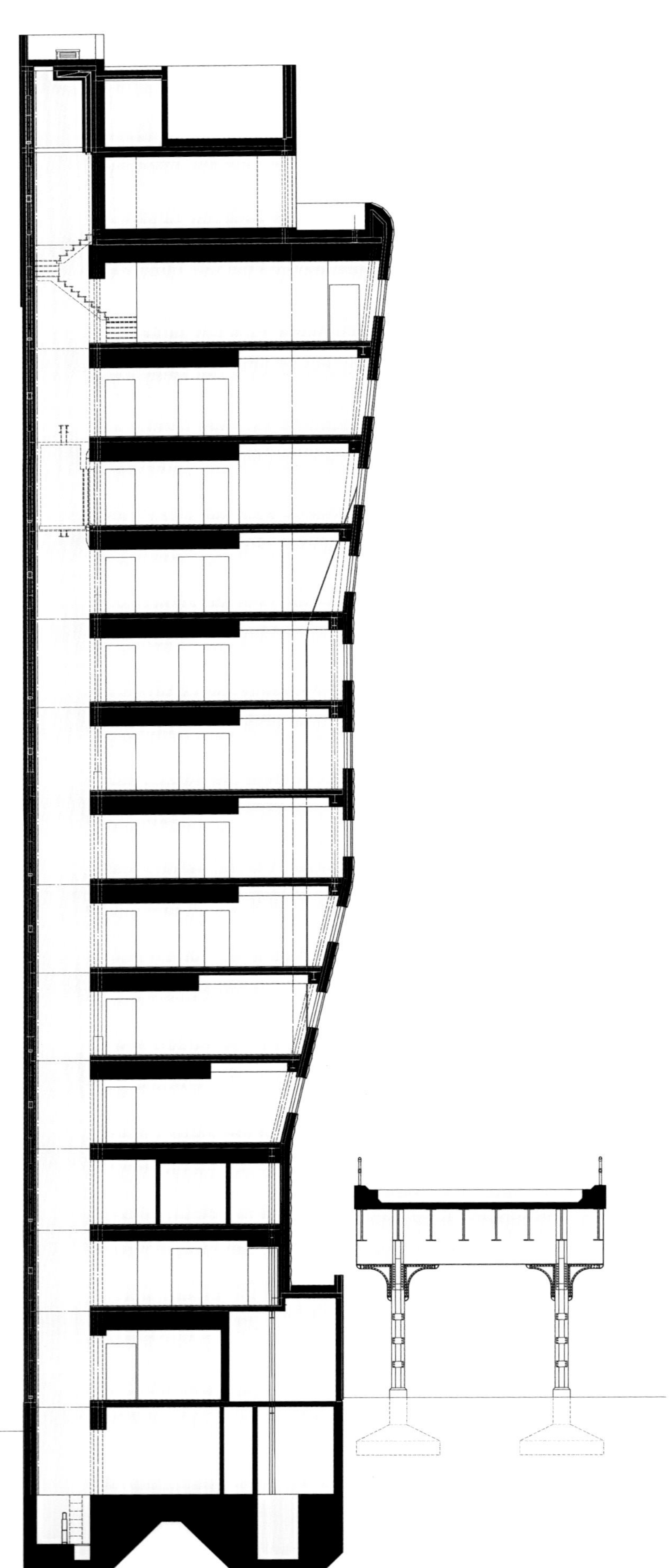

Rendering o⁵ High Line 23 building.
Opposite: Neil M. Denari Architects. High
Line 23 condominium building, New York
City, 2011.

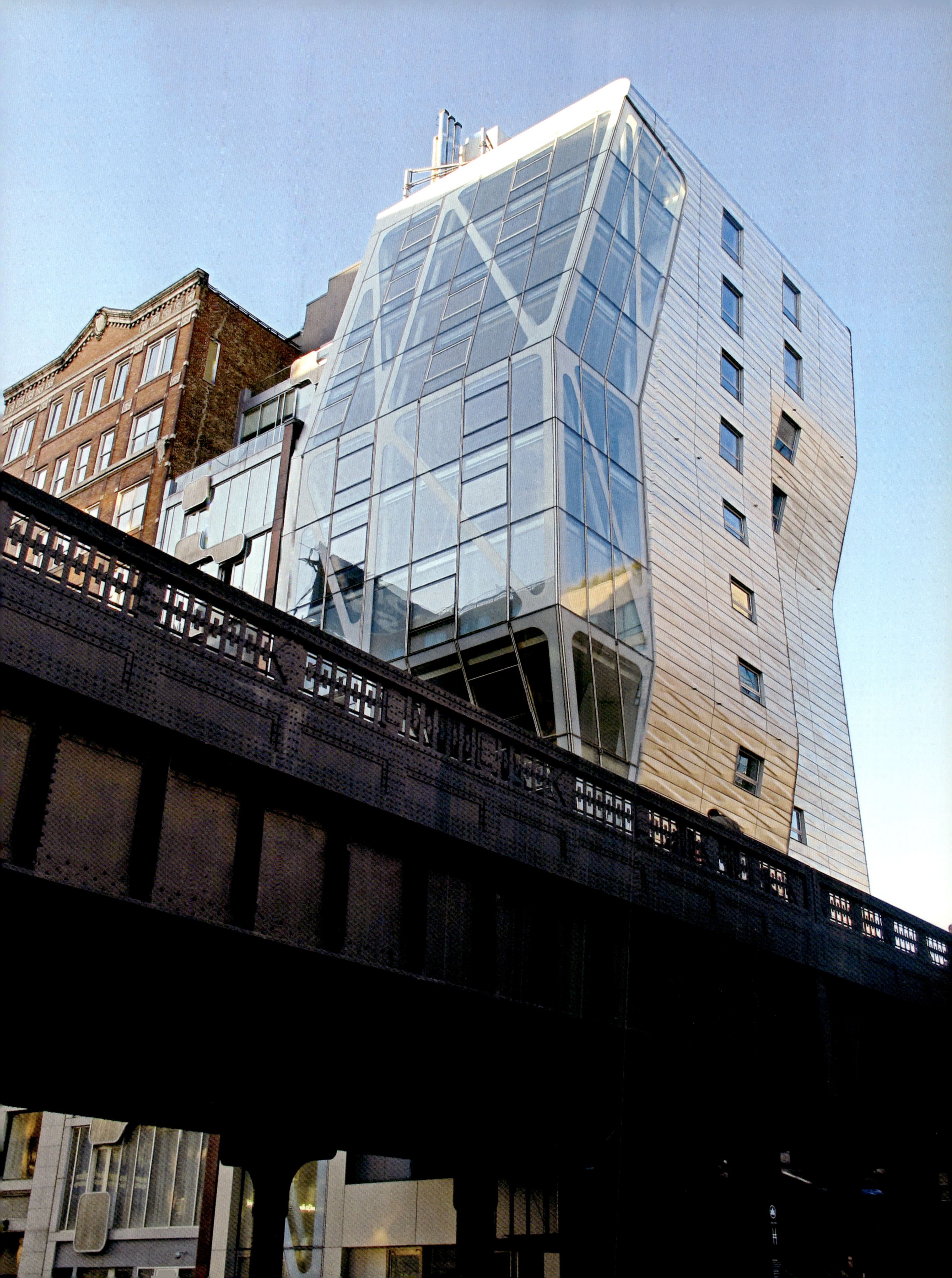

MASSIMILIANO FUKSAS

Walking into Terminal 3 at Shenzhen Bao'an International Airport in Shenzhen, China, feels less like entering a transit space than it does being completely immersed in a prismatic crystal. Consisting of thousands of hexagonal skylights arranged in a honeycomb pattern, which casts dancing patterns on the polished tiled floors and stainless steel counters of the interior, the design by Italian architecture firm Studio Fuksas aims to uplift the moods of the 45 million passengers estimated to pass through the terminal on an annual basis. Although this experience, from the outset, can look highly technological and cool in tone—from the exterior, the terminal resembles a spaceship or an ice formation—the architects insist that they were looking at the natural world when designing the structure, most particularly at the manta ray: a gigantic, silvery fish marked by two winglike shapes on either side of its body.

Creating pattern and texture with light—and in the process, activating not only the mind, but also the body—is characteristic of the work of Massimiliano Fuksas, whose international practice was founded in Rome in 1981 by Fuksas and his wife, Doriana Mandrelli. Other projects include the Georges-Freche School of Hotel Management (2012) in Montpellier, France, whose facade is marked by anodized aluminum punctured by five thousand triangular windows, and the Foligno Church (2009) in Italy, a monolith given form by light entering windows shaped in irregular geometric patterns. Light is one of the most potent materials in this elegant firm's arsenal, with which they redefine style in our technologically dominated environment.

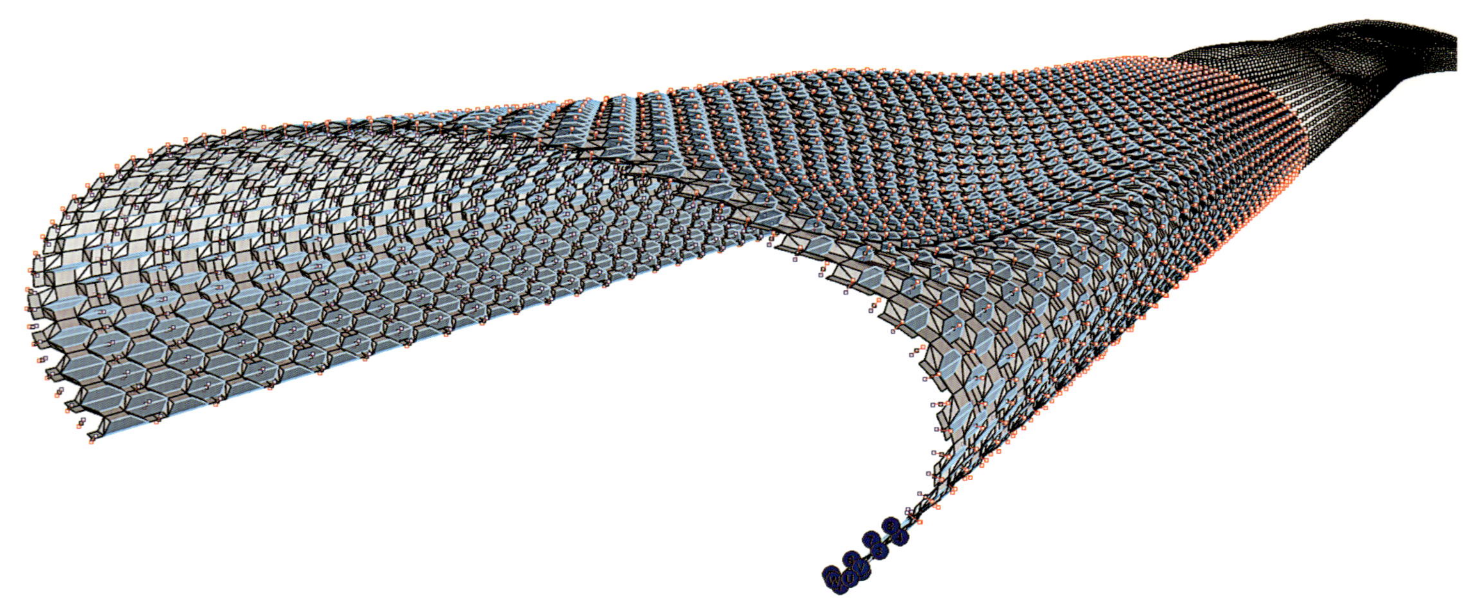

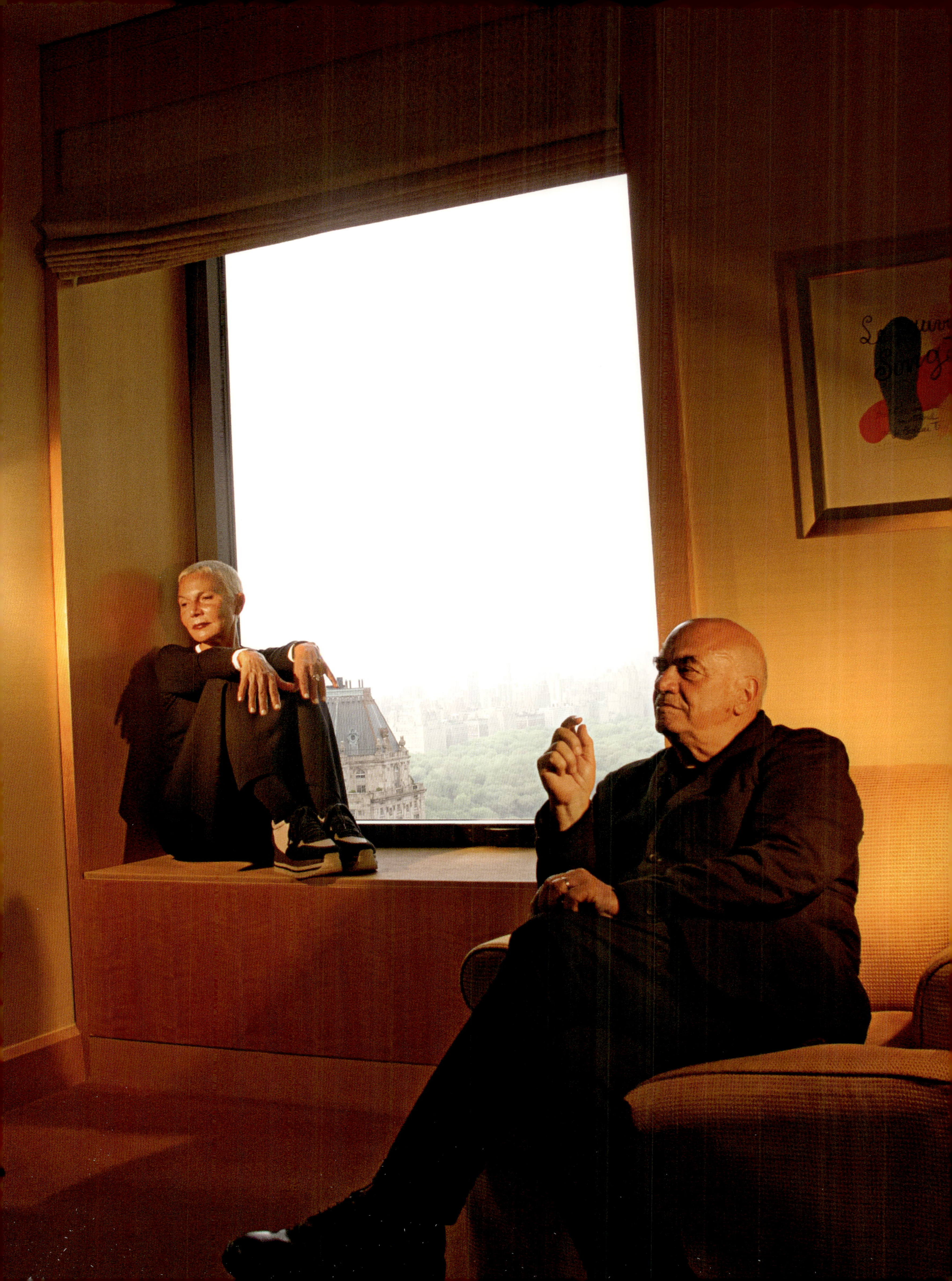

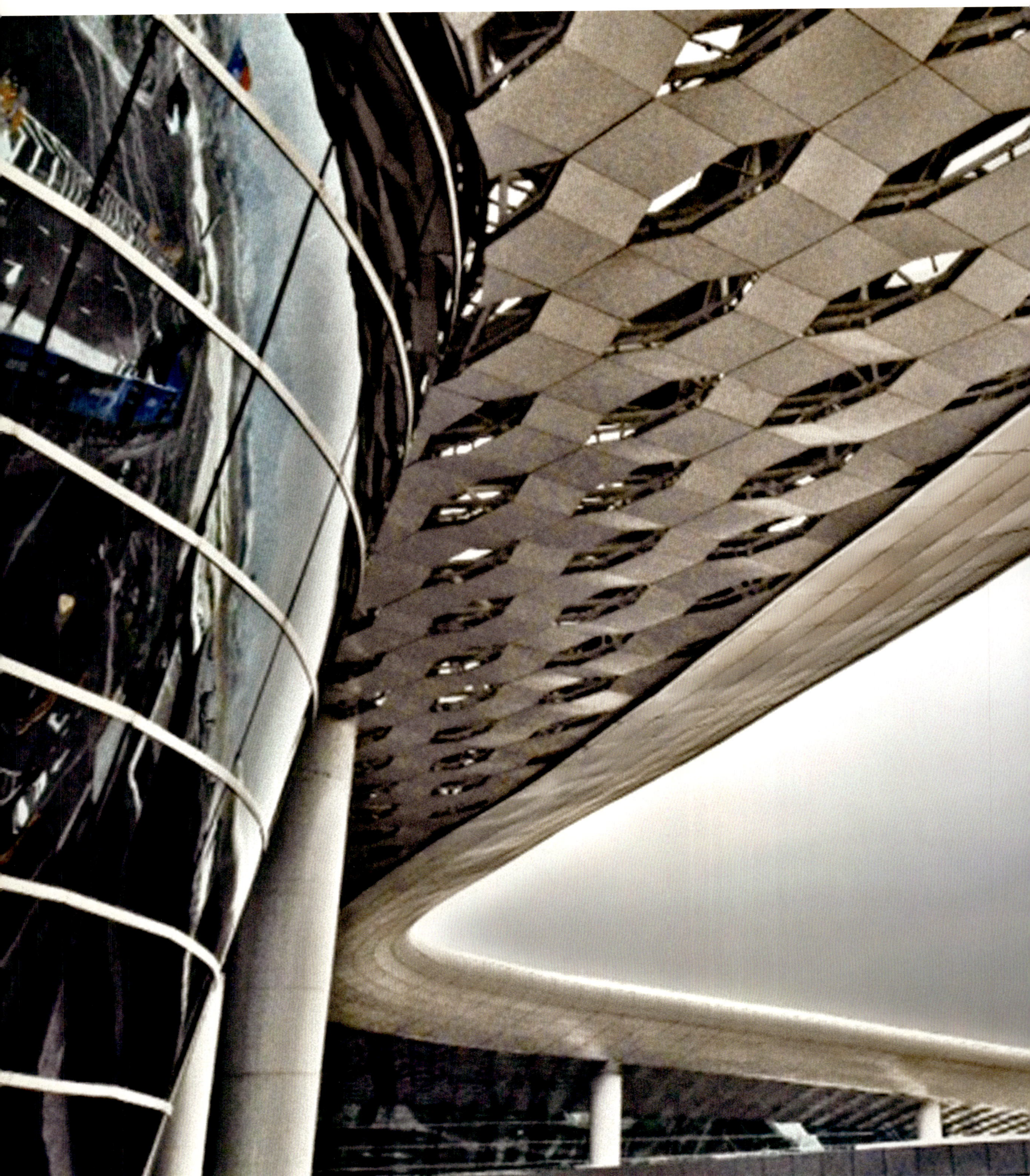

Left and following pages: Studio Fuksas. Terminal 3 at Shenzhen Bao'an International Airport, Shenzhen, China, 2013.
Previous pages, from left: Rendering of Terminal 3 at Shenzhen Bao'an International Airport; Massimiliano Fuksas and Doriana Mandrelli of Studio Fuksas.

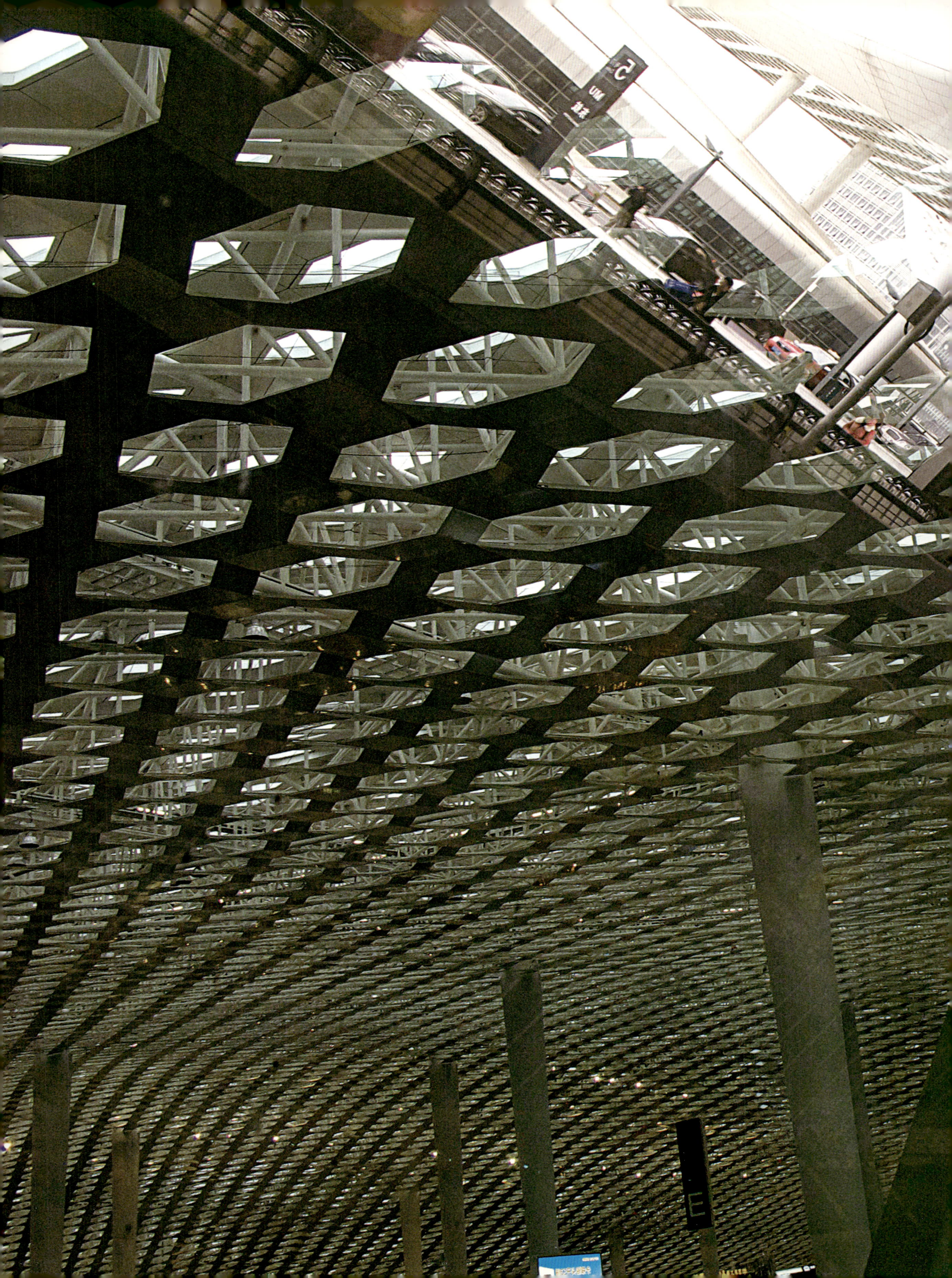

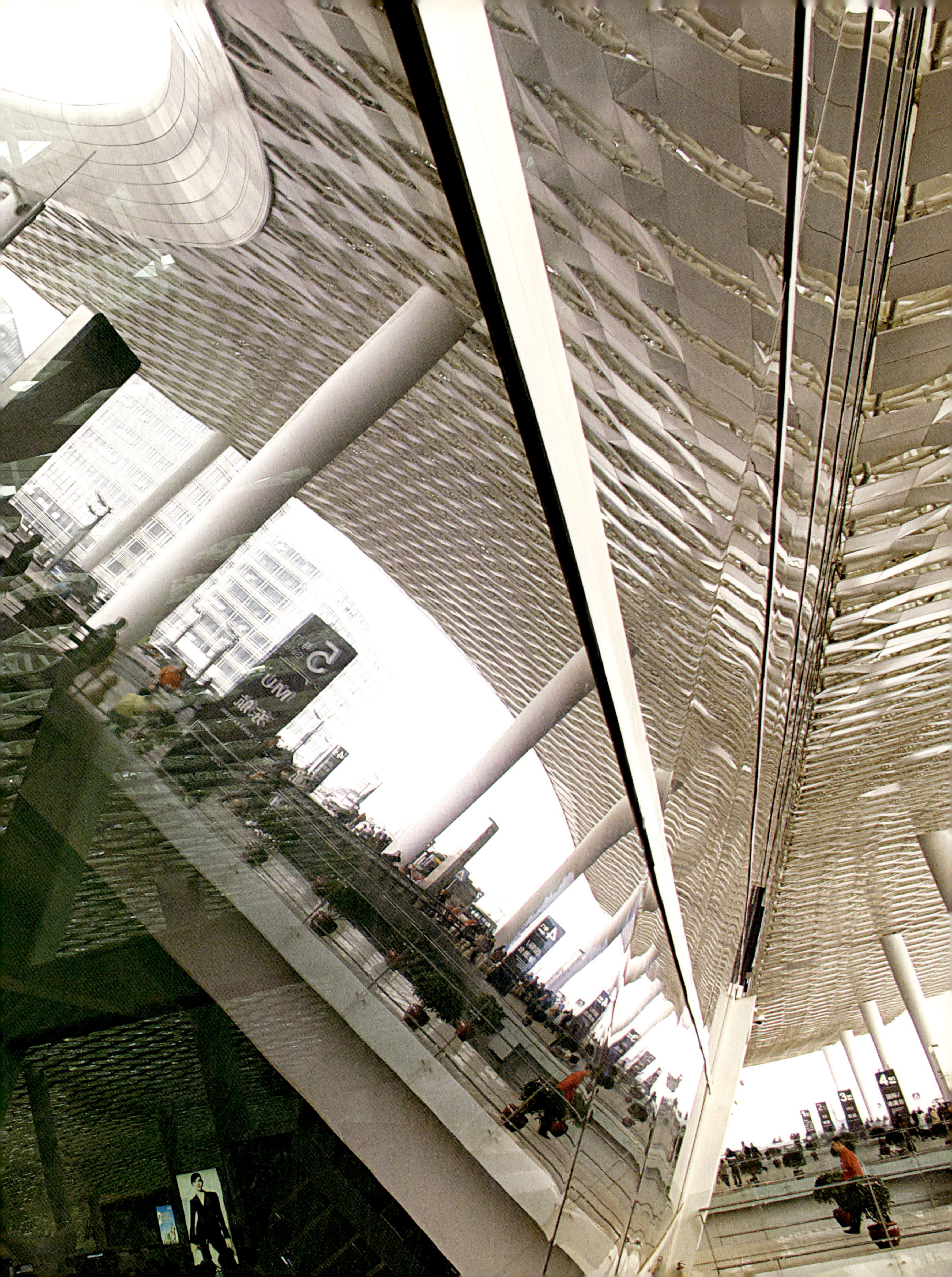

JEANNE GANG

AQUA TOWER

In Chicago, a town that boasts some of the most iconic skyscrapers in the world, the fifty-year-old Jeanne Gang has already made her mark on the skyline with the Aqua Tower, an eighty-two-story building that resembles sheaths of paper gently balanced on top of each other. Housing a hotel, apartments, condominiums, and offices, the 1.9-million-square-foot structure, marked by its irregular curved terraces, also boasts an 80,000-square-foot green terrace atop its plinth, which comes replete with an outdoor pool and a running track. It has received a number of prestigious awards, including the 2009 Skyscraper of the Year from Emporis and the 2010 Honor Award, Distinguished Building, from the AIA Chicago. To date, it is the tallest building in the world to have a woman as the lead architect.

With Studio Gang, the collective of architects, designers, and innovators she founded in Chicago in 1997, Gang has conceived of projects marked not only by their aesthetic beauty, but also for their attention to sustainability and the communities in which they reside. Such projects include the SOS Children's Villages Lavezzorio Community Center (2008), a structure where foster parents are trained on the South Side of Chicago, and planned communities such as Hyderabad 02, a development that reconstructs the traditional Indian courtyard house into a twenty-five-story tower. The recipient of the 2011 John D. and Catherine T. MacArthur Foundation Fellowship for her "optical poetry," Gang has projects in the works in locations as far-flung as Taipei, Mexico City, and Shanghai.

Jeanne Gang.

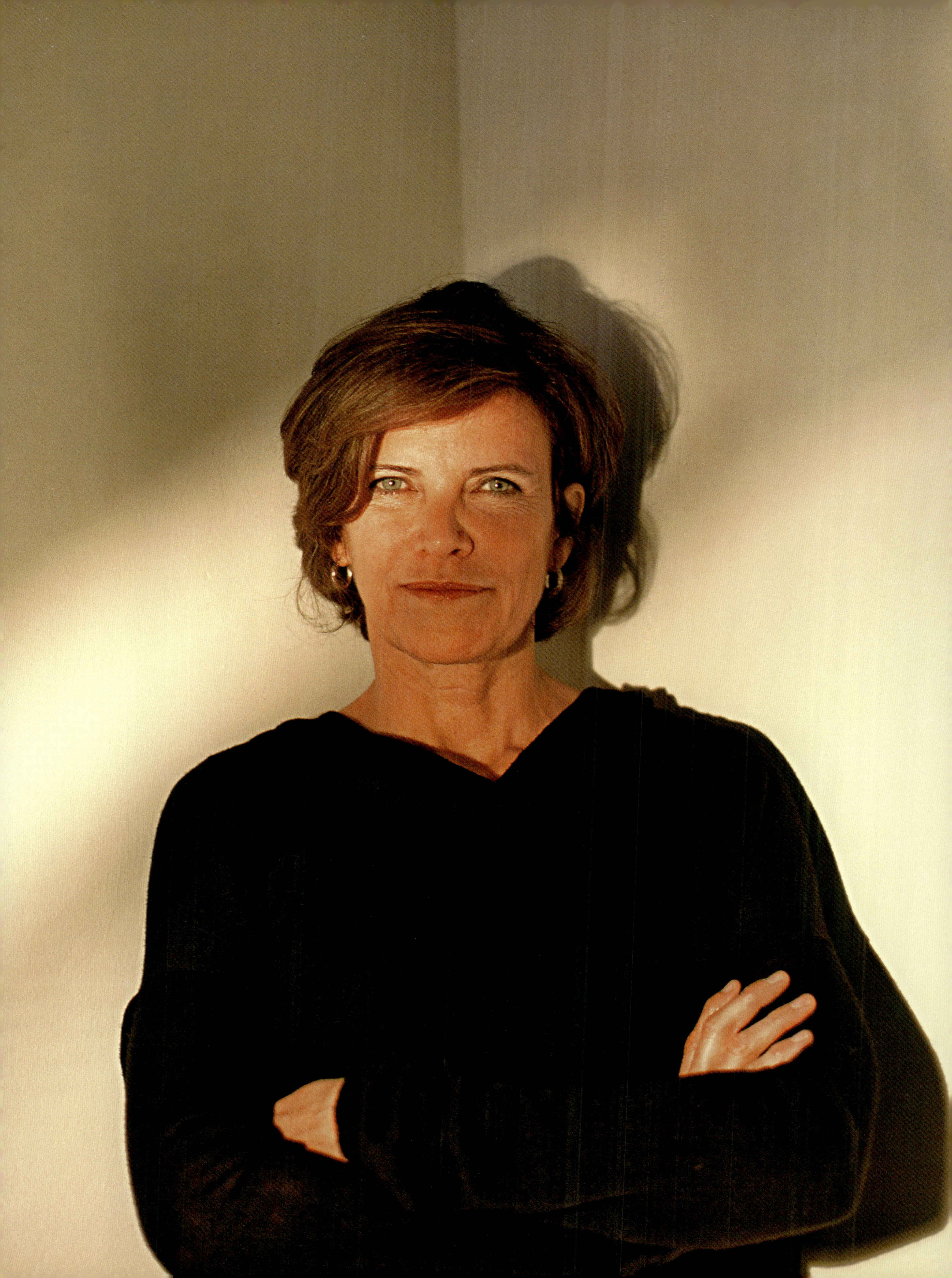

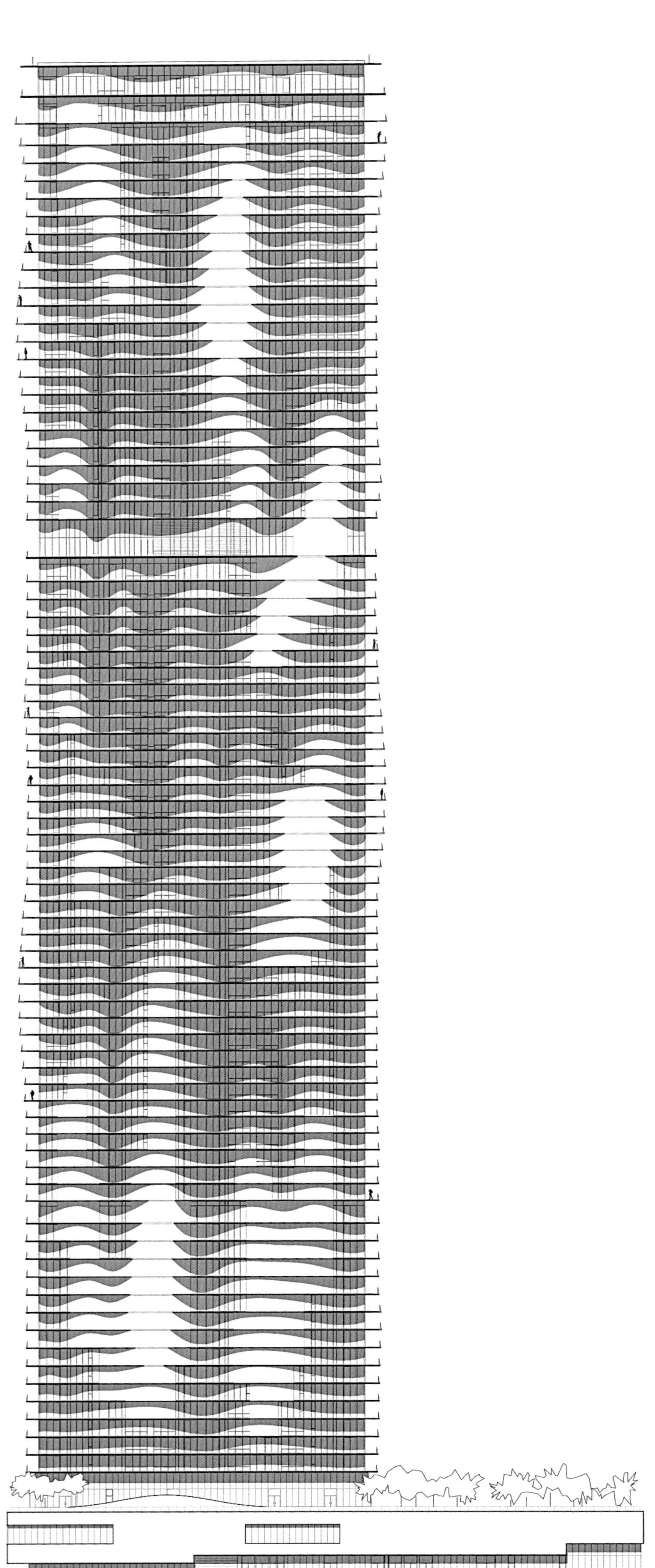

Rendering of the Aqua Tower.
Opposite: Studio Gang Architects.
Aqua Tower, Chicago, Illinois,
2009.

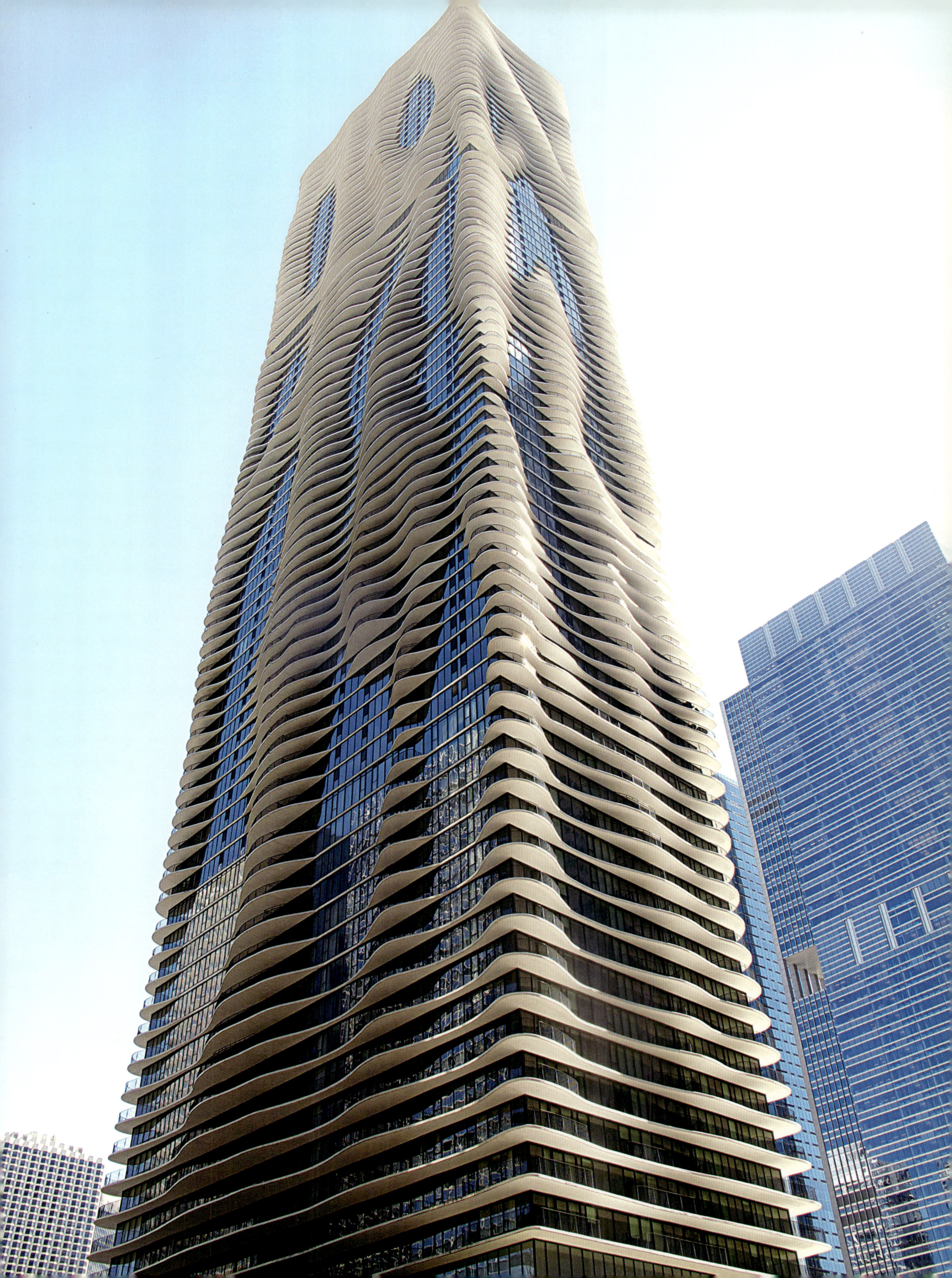

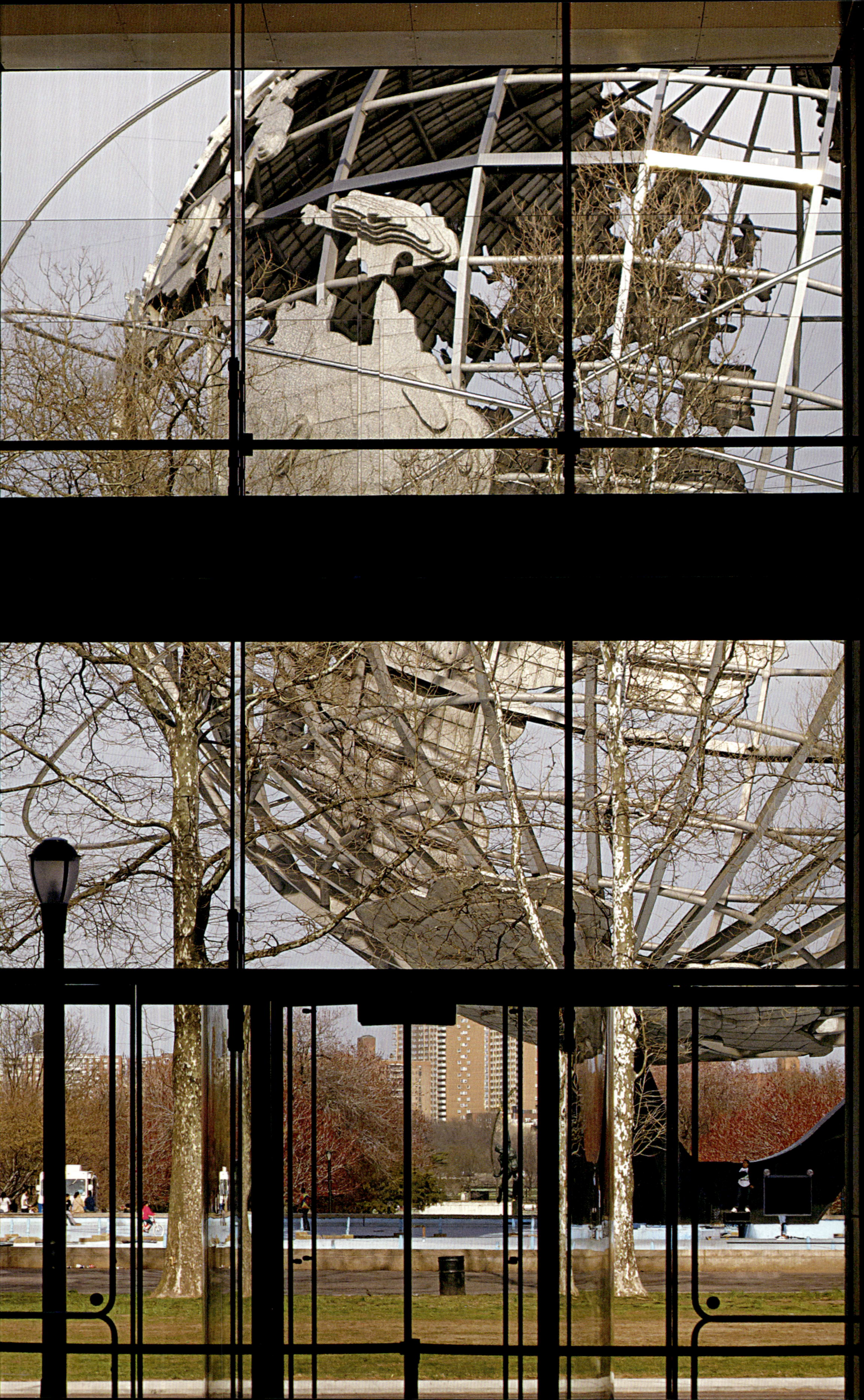

GRIMSHAW ARCHITECTS

As part of a general effort to revitalize a borough in New York long derided by natives, the Queens Museum unveiled the first phase of renovations to its Flushing Meadows site. Designed by Grimshaw Architects, a firm founded by Sir Nicholas Grimshaw in 1980, the structure is marked by a multimedia facade that allows commissioned works of art to be projected on the exterior walls. The display—which is visible from the Grand Central Parkway, one of the many arteries used by daily commuters into the center of the city—sparks interest in an institution that aims to make a mark in the thriving cultural landscape of New York City. On the interior, a hanging glass lantern diffuses natural light in such a way that it invites the public to congregate in a central lounge area. The Queens Museum, in essence, does not want to be merely a gallery—it wants to be a destination for the community.

The structure is characteristic of the internationally renowned firm, which has offices in New York, London, Melbourne, Sydney, and Doha. Along with designing many high-tech museum projects, including the Patricia and Phillip Frost Museum of Science in Miami (slated to be finished in 2015) and the National Space Centre in Leicester, England (2001), it is known for creating works that define the landscapes in which they reside. One such structure is the Eden Project (2001) in Cornwall, a series of adjoining biomes created from inflated hexagonal and pentagonal plastic cells that generates enough electricity for five thousand households. Like Grimshaw's other projects, it offers a model for how architecture can affect positive change along with creating a unique built environment.

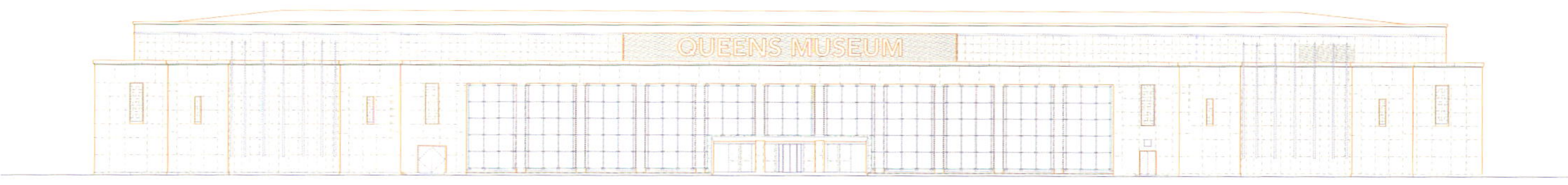

Rendering of the Queens Museum.
Opposite: Grimshaw Architects. Queens Museum, Queens, New York, 2013.

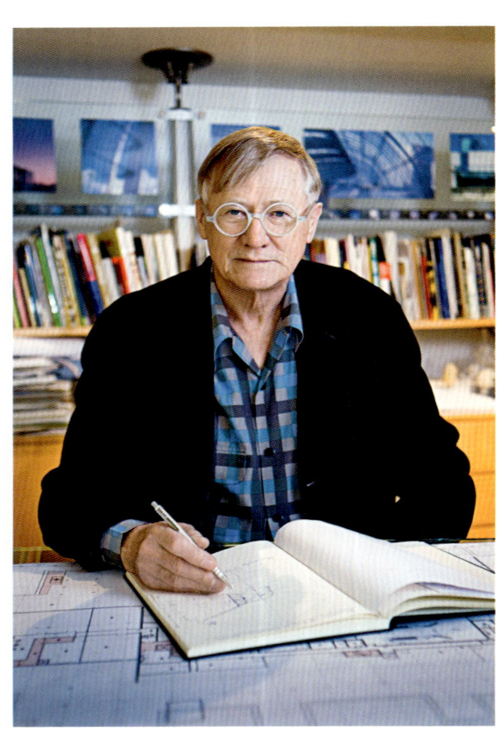

Nicholas Grimshaw of Grimshaw Architects.
Opposite: Interior of the Queens Museum.

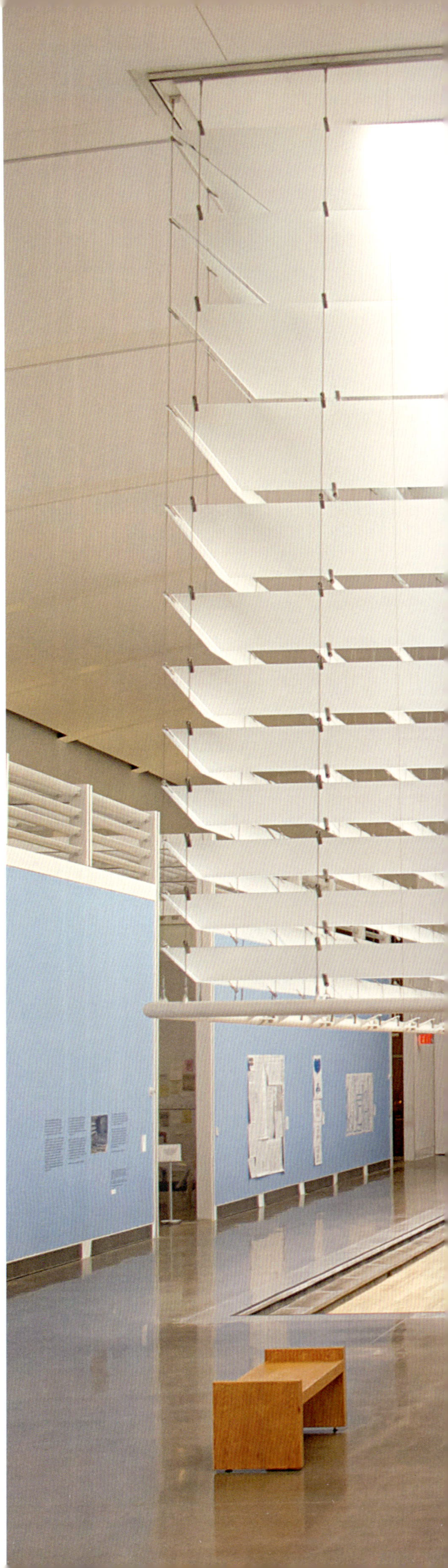

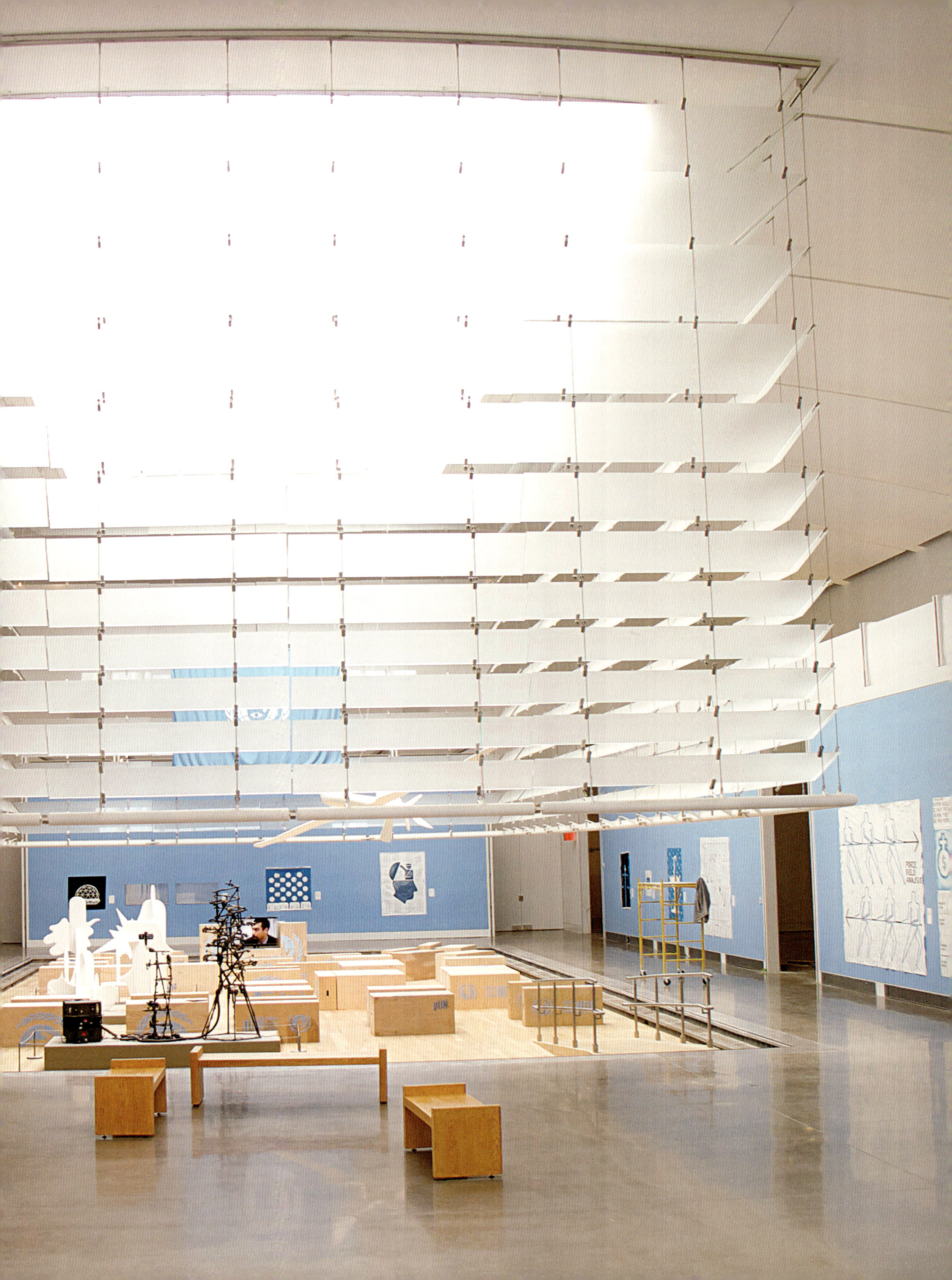

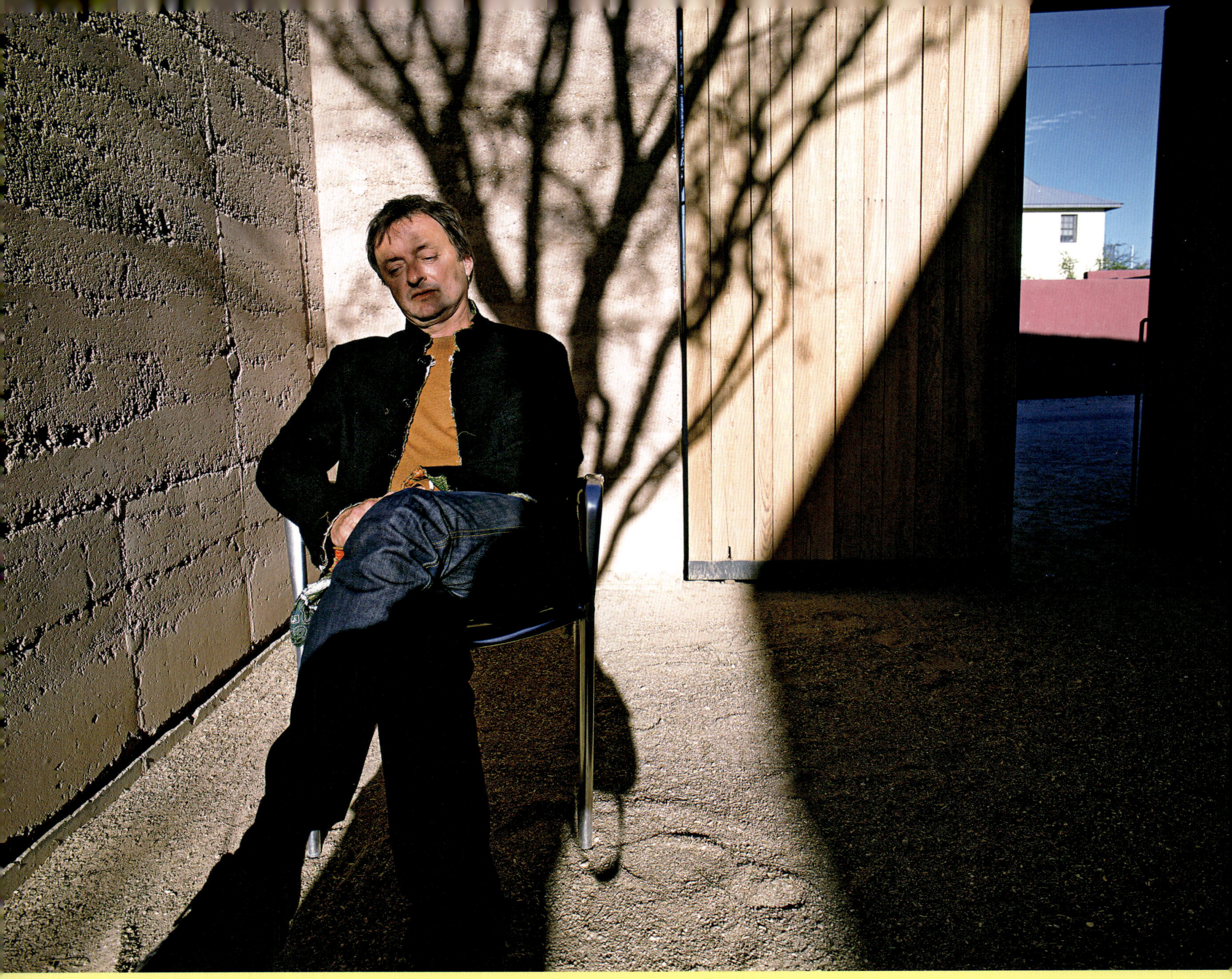

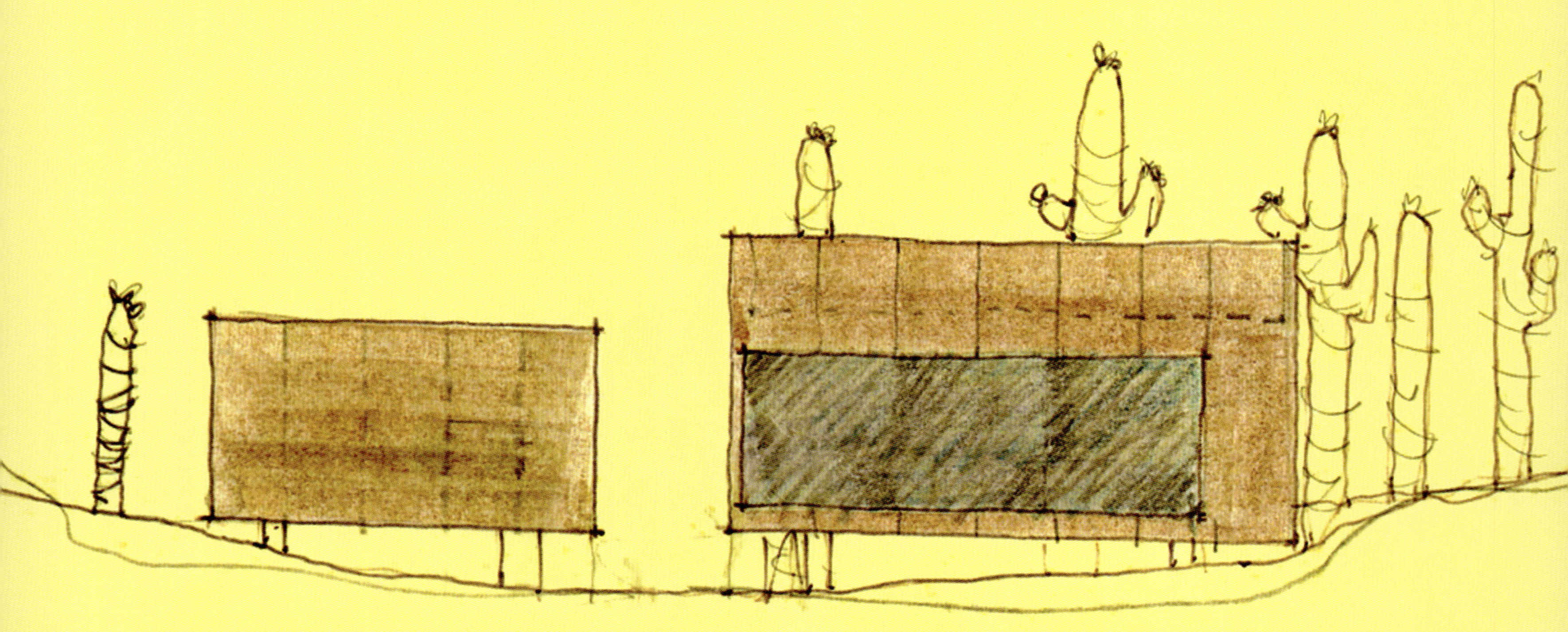

RICK JOY

For Rick Joy, the desert is not merely a type of landscape—it is also a quality of light and atmosphere that inspires much of his work. Ever since establishing his firm in Tucson, Arizona, in 1993, many of his projects are located in the desert. And even those that are not, such as the Woodstock Farm (2010) in Vermont, are informed by the observational skills he has learned over the years from reading the arid landscape he calls home. Joy does not merely build on top of the natural world—he designs in communion with it.

Notable of all of his residential projects is the Desert Nomad House, a set of three rusted steel cubes that rest like nesting birds, or an art installation by Donald Judd, at the base of a mountain range a few miles west of Tucson. Although they form less than fifteen hundred square feet all together, Joy utilizes the landscape in such a way that the living space seems expansive. Each of the three cubes services a different function. A master bedroom cube faces west toward the mountain, which glows bright orange as the sunrise creeps down its facade. The living room has expansive views over downtown Tucson. And a third living quarter, used alternately as an office, pushes up against the side of the mountain itself, which creates a terrarium of sorts in a picture window. From a distance, the structure looks like a natural outcrop of the valley—a rock formation left behind by the machinations of the earth. Like much of Joy's work, it looks wild and settled all at once.

Top: Rick Joy.
Bottom: Sketch of the Desert Nomad House.
Following pages and pages 64-65: Rick Joy Architects.
Desert Nomad House, Tucson, Arizona, 2005.

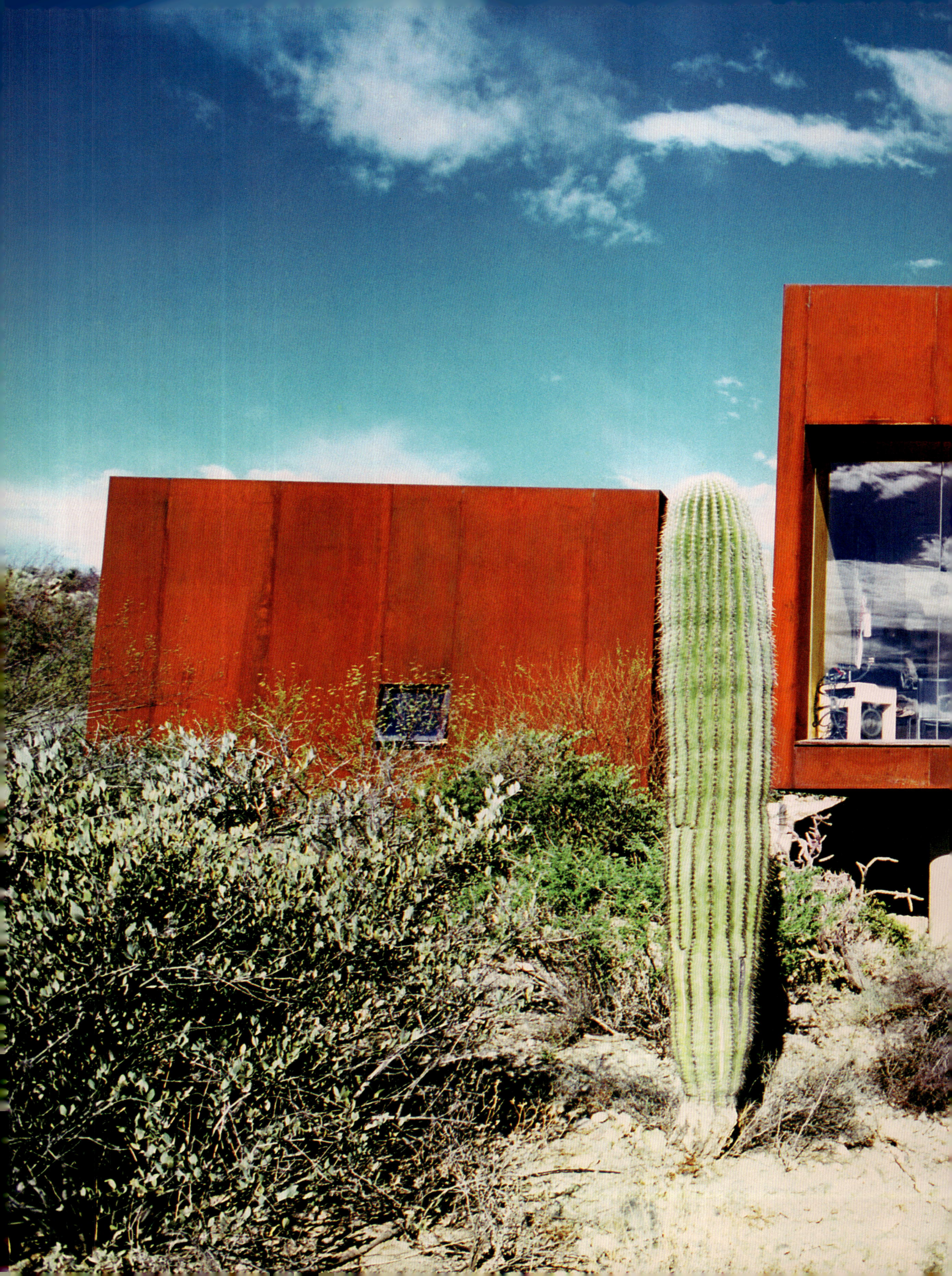

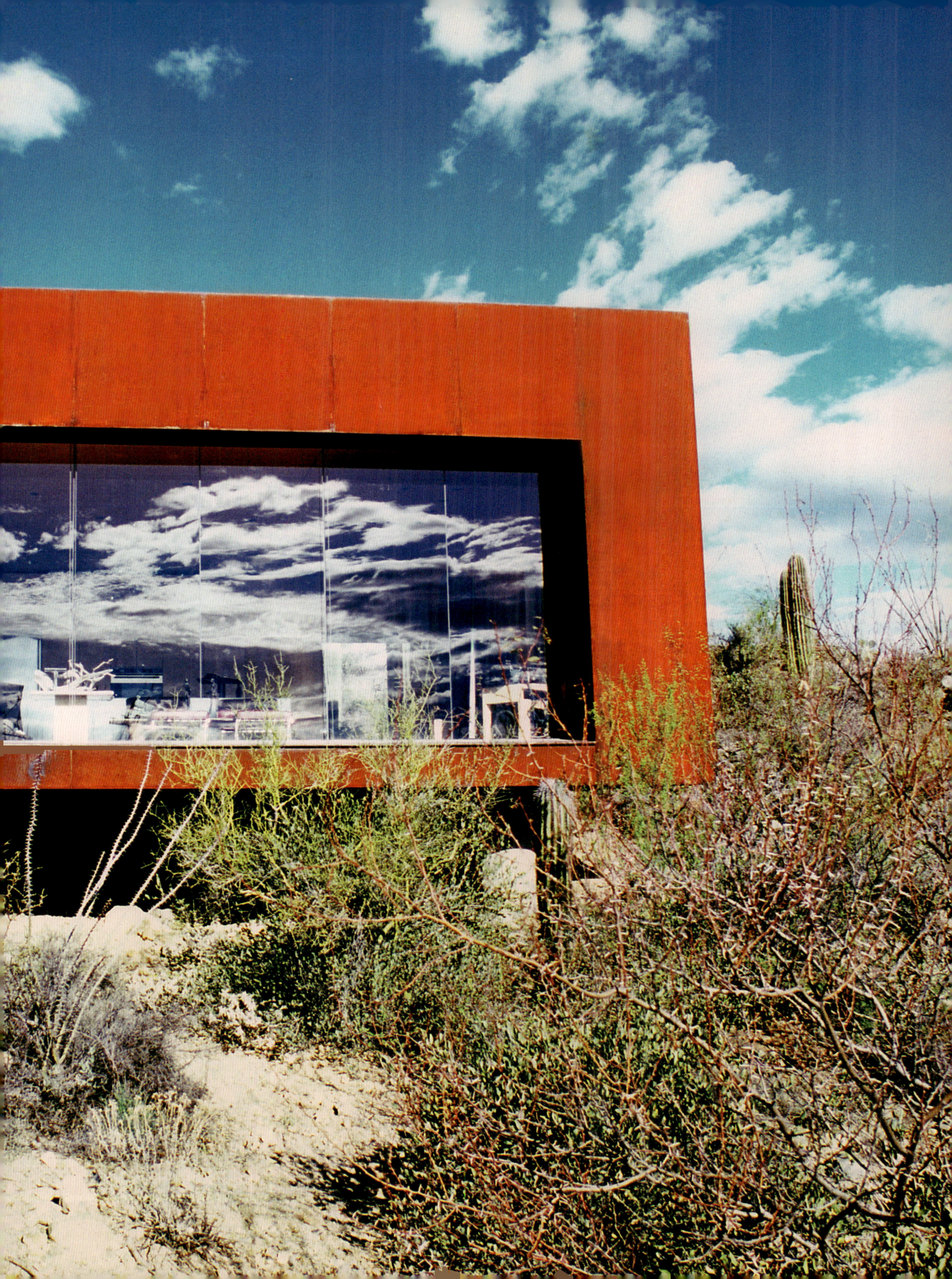

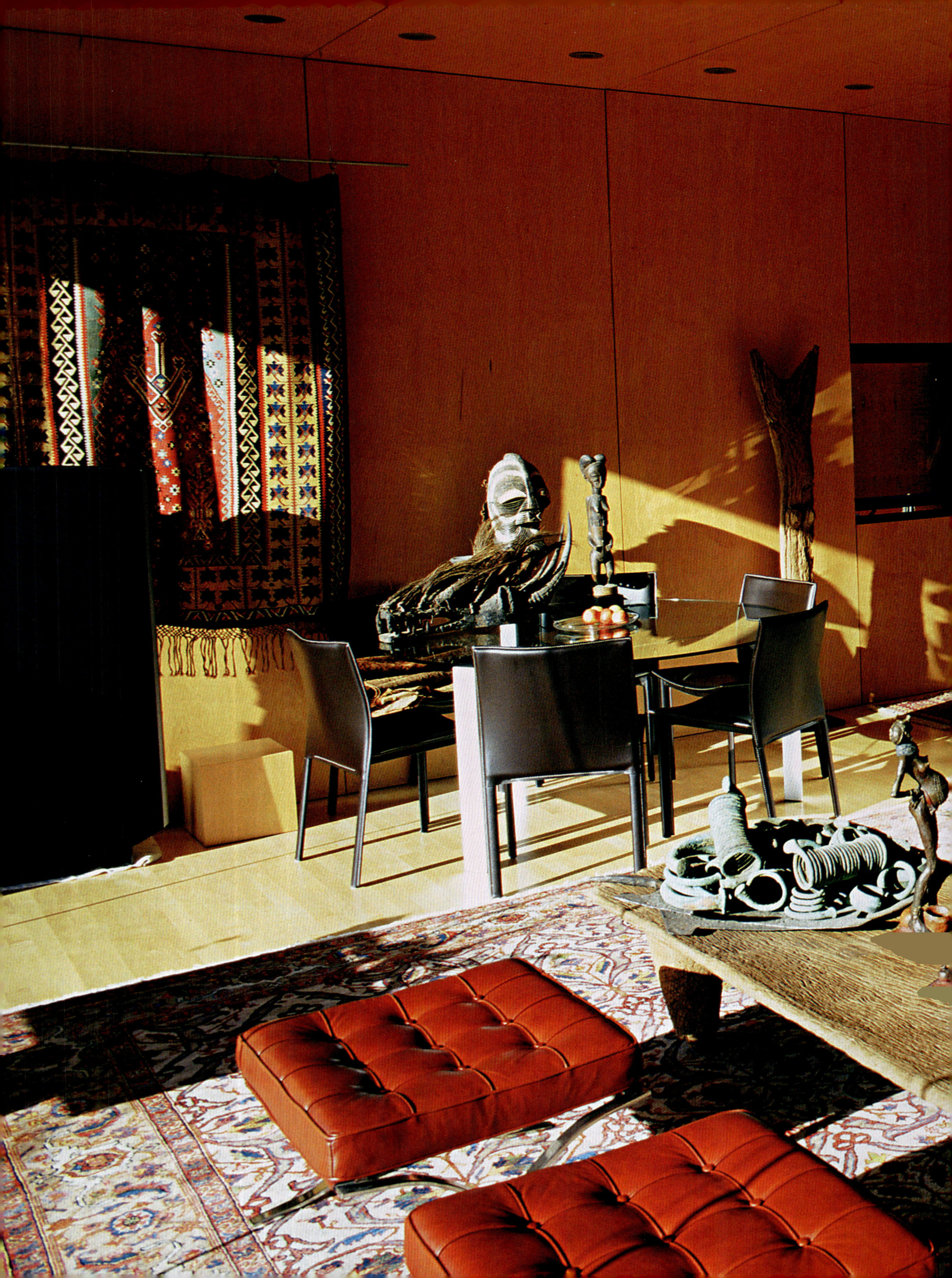

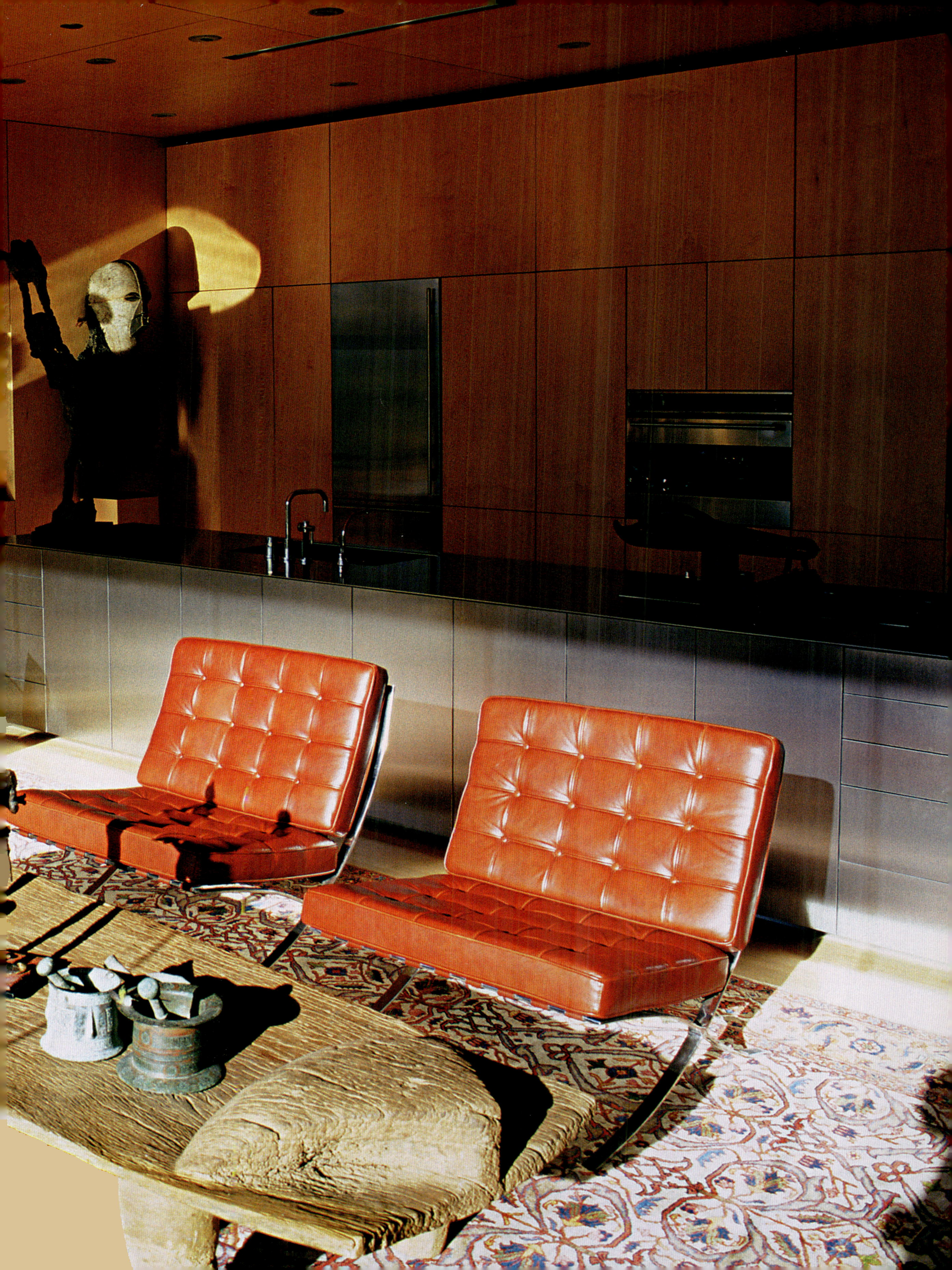

KENGO KUMA

Stating that his goal as an architect is to reinterpret the Japanese tradition of framing nature in the built environment using twenty-first century materials, Kengo Kuma, whose firm has offices in both Tokyo and Paris, is known for creating permanent structures that are marked by a spatial immateriality. These buildings include the Xinjin Zhi Museum in Chengdu, China, which consists of a particle-like facade constructed of tiles hung from wire, and the FRAC Marseille, a cultural center marked by an enamel glass wall that hangs like a veil over the structural framework.

Although he maintains a strong presence in Japan, where he is a professor at the Graduate School of Architecture at the University of Tokyo, Kuma has received increasing acclaim in France in recent years, where in 2009 he was made an Officier de l'Ordre des Arts et des Lettres. In 2013, he completed the Conservatoire de Musique et de Danse Darius Milhaud in Aix-en-Provence, a new home for one of the oldest dance and music conservatories in Europe. Home to a five-hundred-seat auditorium and sixty-two teaching spaces that accommodate six disciplines—strings and keyboards, wind instruments and voice, drums, ancient and traditional music, jazz, and electro-acoustic music—the exterior consists of folds of metal that resemble an abstract work of Japanese origami. On the interior, open spaces clad in panels of pale wood allow the building to feel airy despite its solid geometric form.

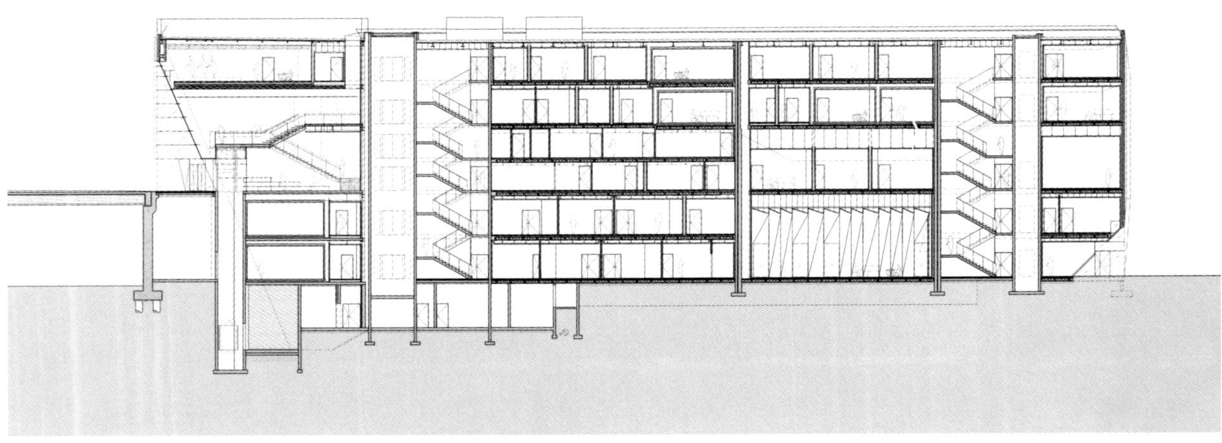

Rendering of the Aix-en-Provence Conservatory.
Opposite: Kengo Kuma.
Following pages and pages 70–71: Kengo Kuma and Associates. Aix-en-Provence Conservatory of Music, Aix-en-Provence, France, 2013.

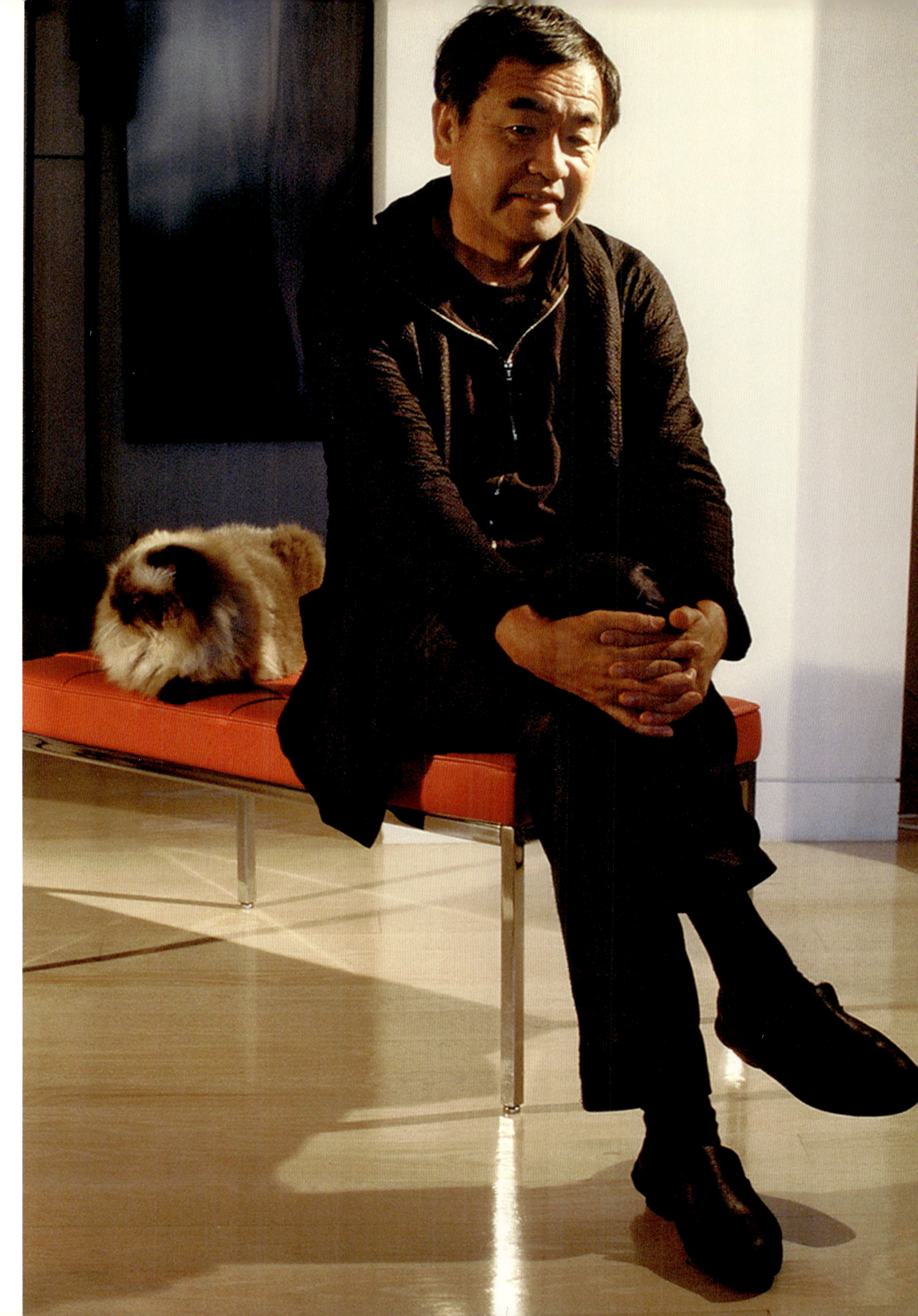

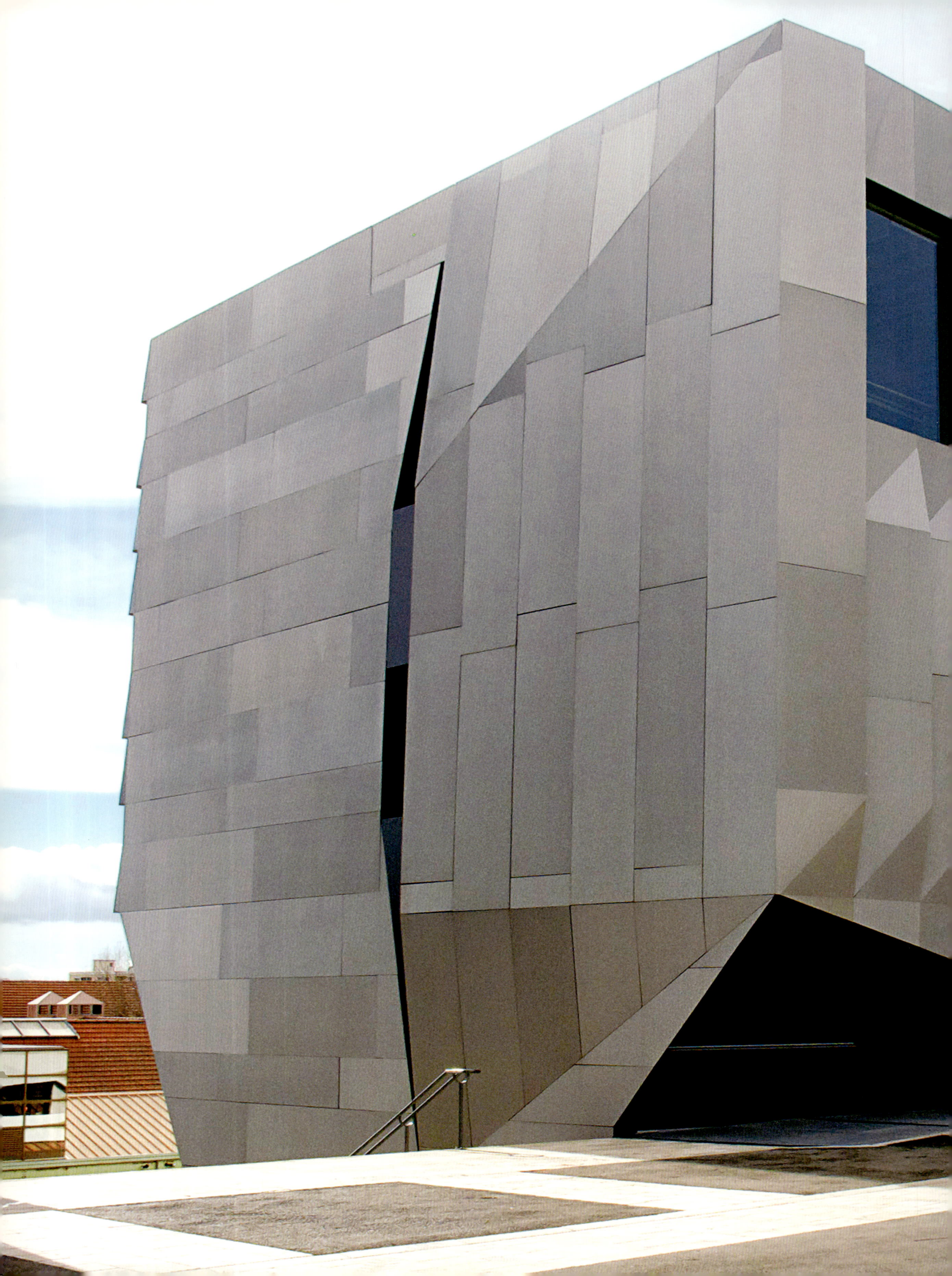

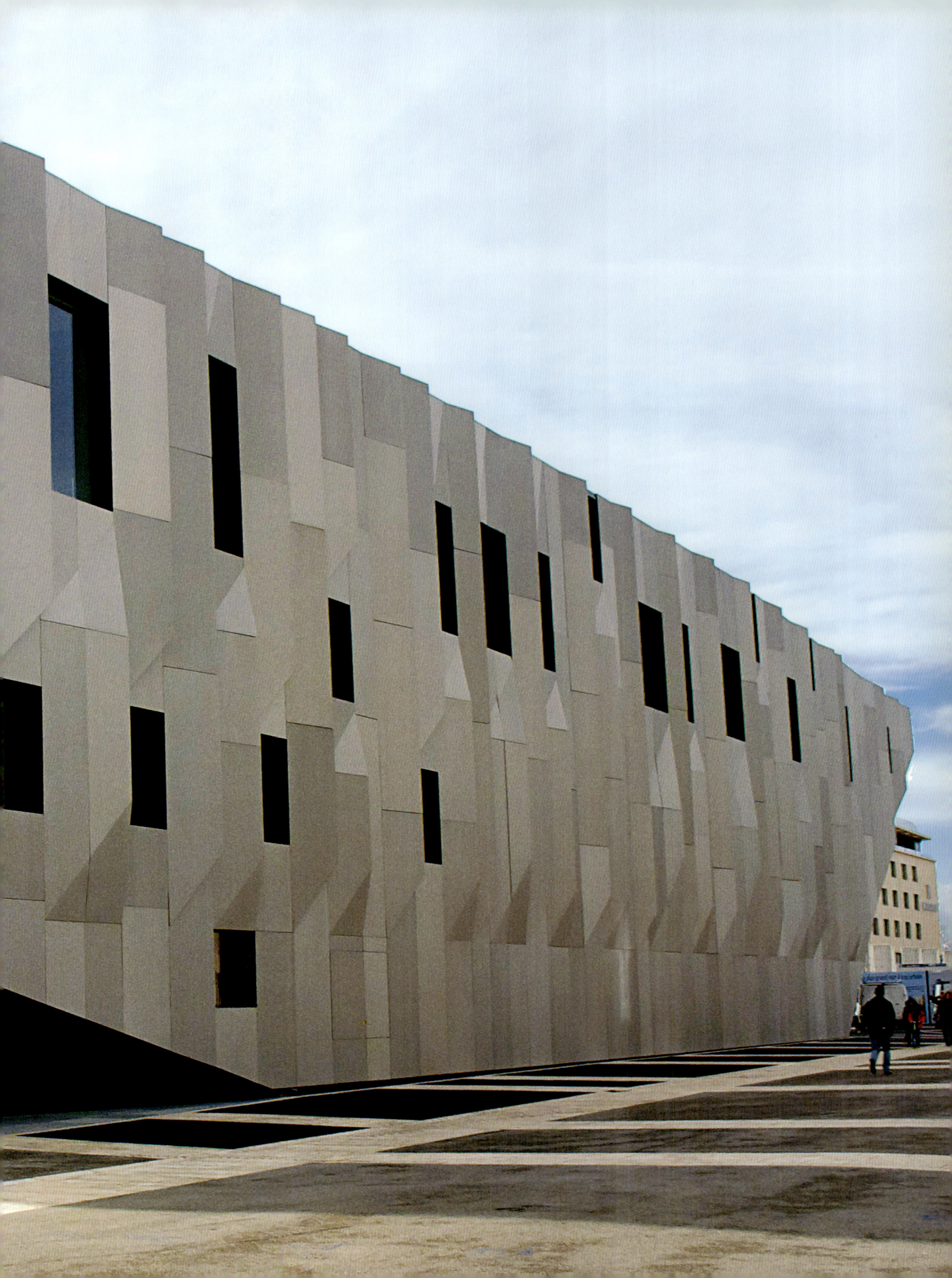

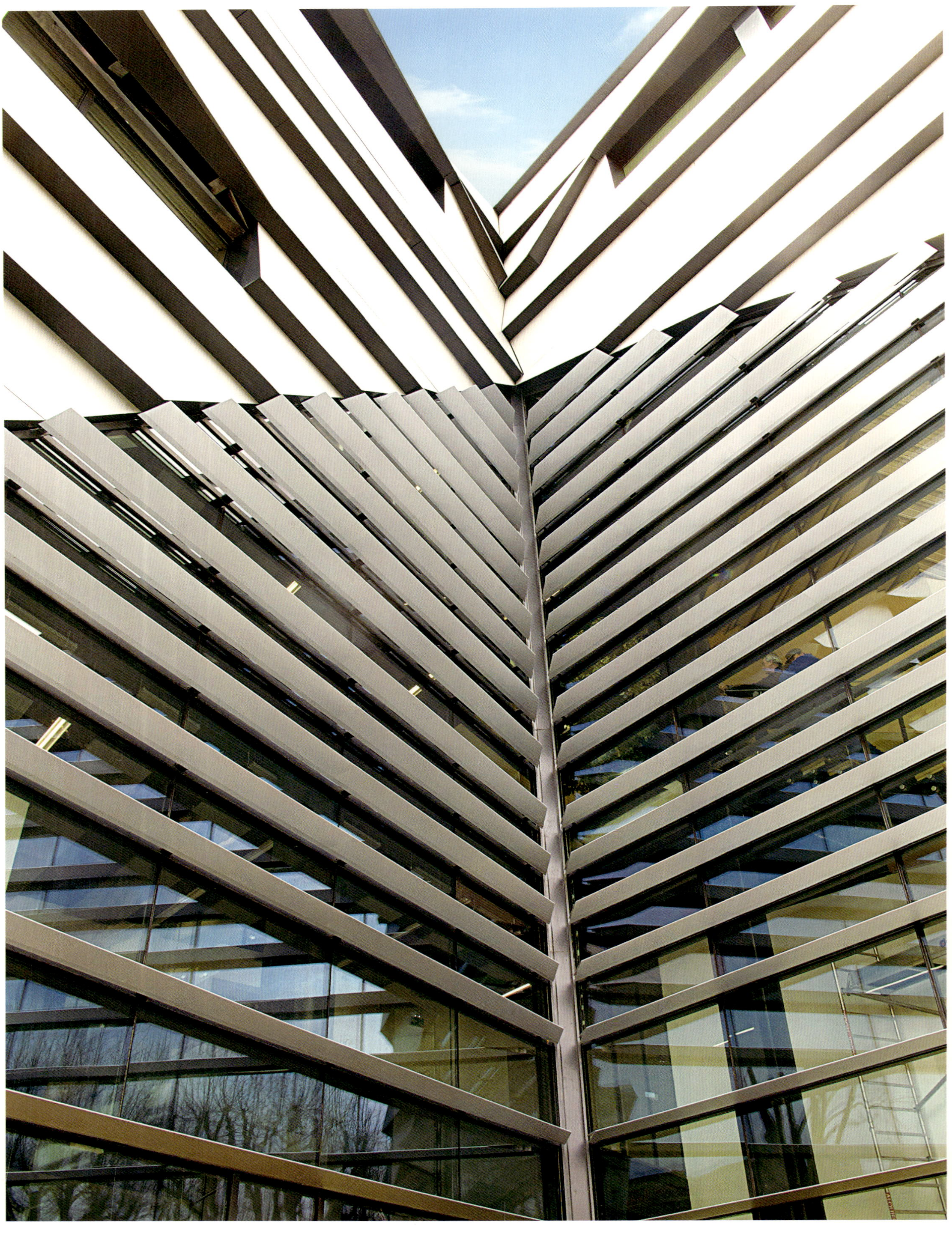

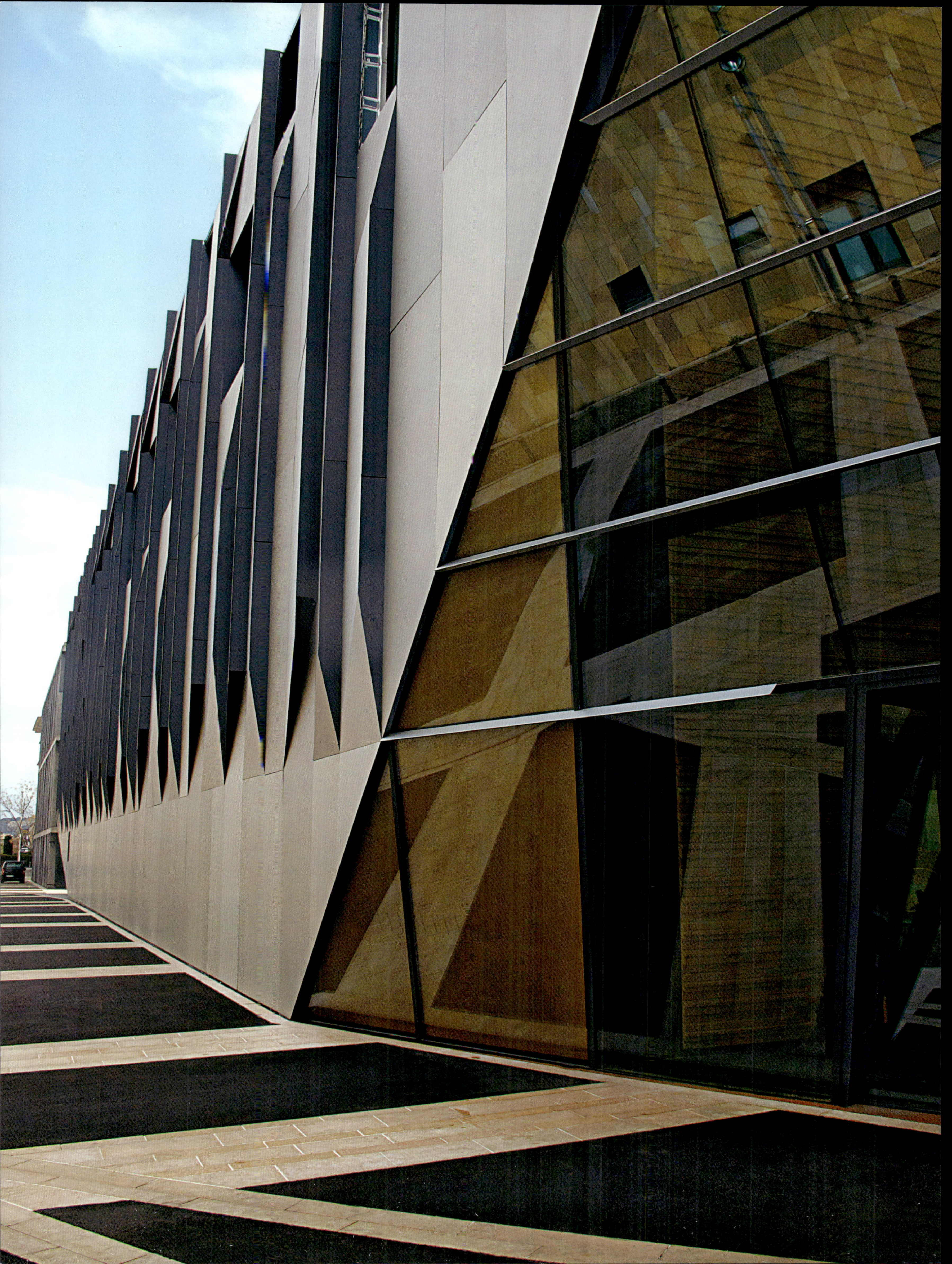

FUMIHIKO MAKI

The stakes were high for the architects involved in rebuilding the World Trade Center complex. Not only did they have to pay homage to the victims of the September 11th attacks, but they also had to contend with the scrutiny of the whole world. Fortunately, Pritzker-Prize-winning architect Fumihiko Maki, who designed Four World Trade Center—the smallest of the projected four towers on the sixteen-acre site—was more than up to the challenge. Born in 1928 in Tokyo, he studied at the University of Tokyo before receiving his Master of Architecture degree from Harvard in 1954. As a result of his education, Maki has spent most of his career gliding between the Eastern and Western worlds.

Maki's list of accomplishments is long and varied. Not only has he designed iconic buildings such as the Yerba Buena Center for the Arts (1993) in San Francisco and an extension for the MIT Media Lab (2009) in Cambridge, Massachusetts, he also founded the Metabolism Group, a 1960s Japanese architectural movement that equated mega-structures with the growth of organic matter and was widely influential in the realm of Japanese design.

Four World Trade Center is one of many projects Maki has worked on in Manhattan in recent years—others include 51 Astor Place and an expansion of the United Nations building. A sheath of mirrored glass cleaved in half toward the top, it is one of the more environmentally friendly skyscrapers yet completed in the twenty-first century, featuring fresh air drawn from vents at the top of the structure, as well as an abundance of natural light. It is the first in a series of steps toward recovery in one of the most iconic urban landscapes in the world.

Fumihiko Maki.

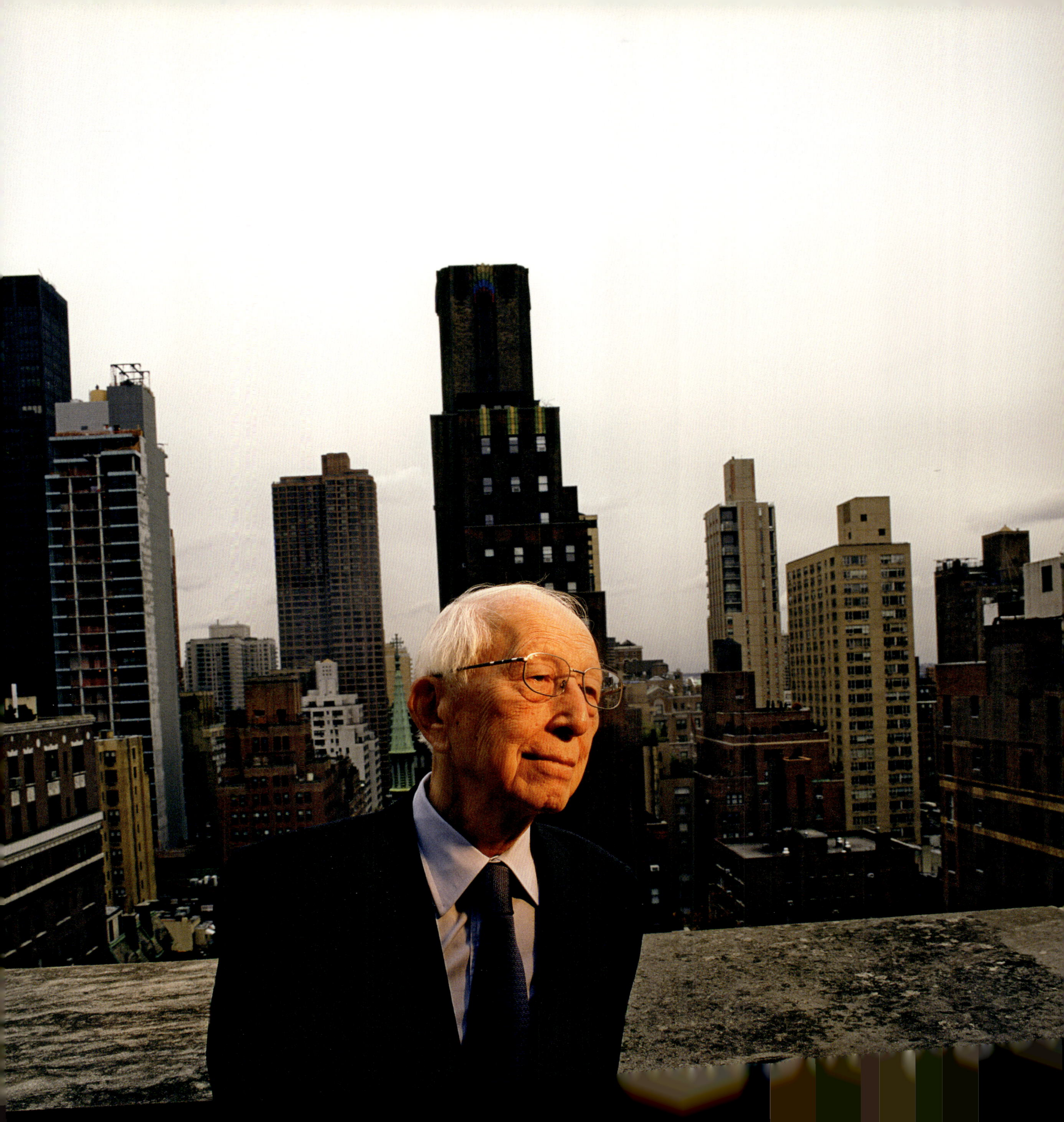

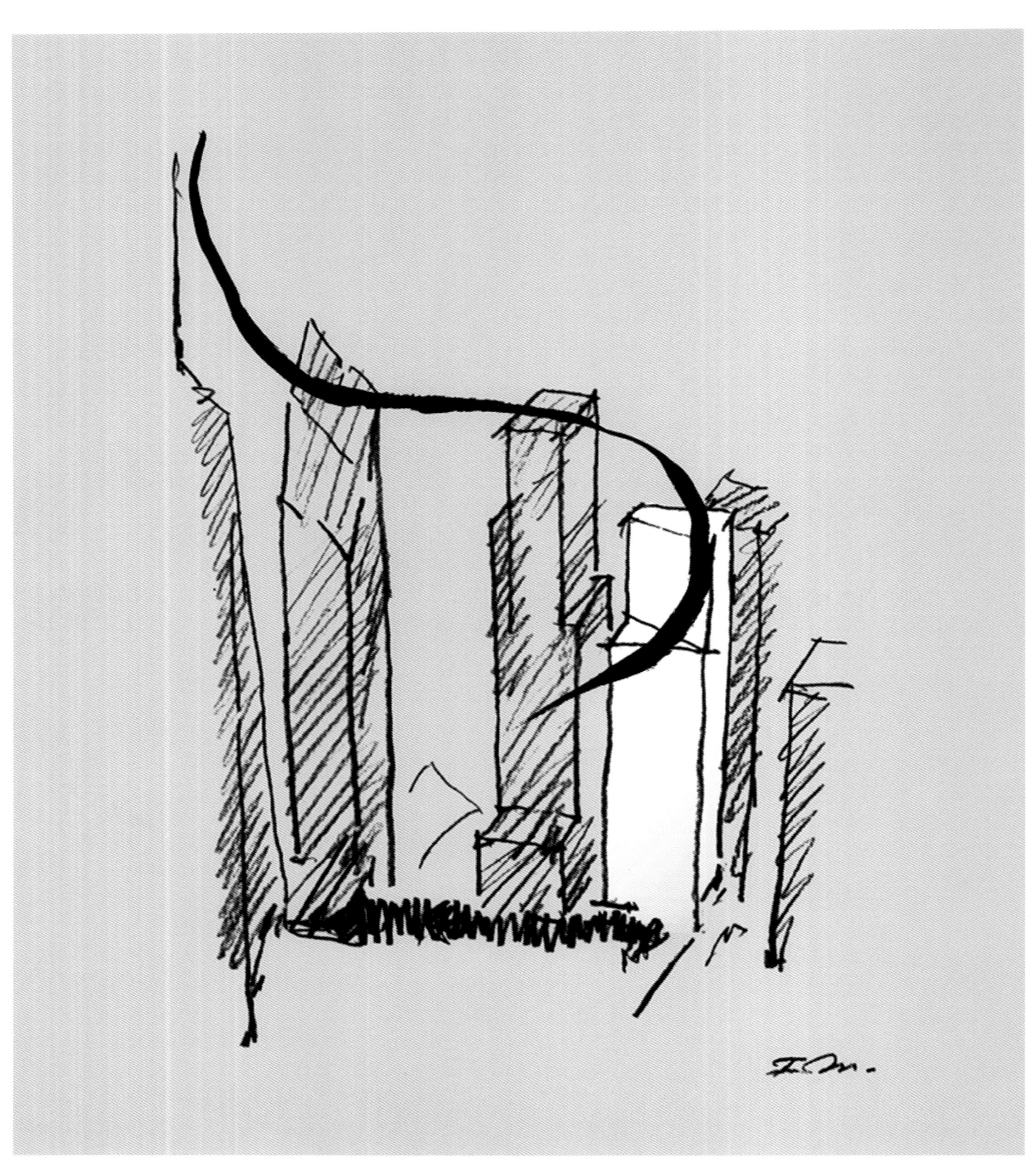

Sketch of Four World Trade Center.
Opposite: Maki and Associates. Four World Trade Center, New York City, 2013.

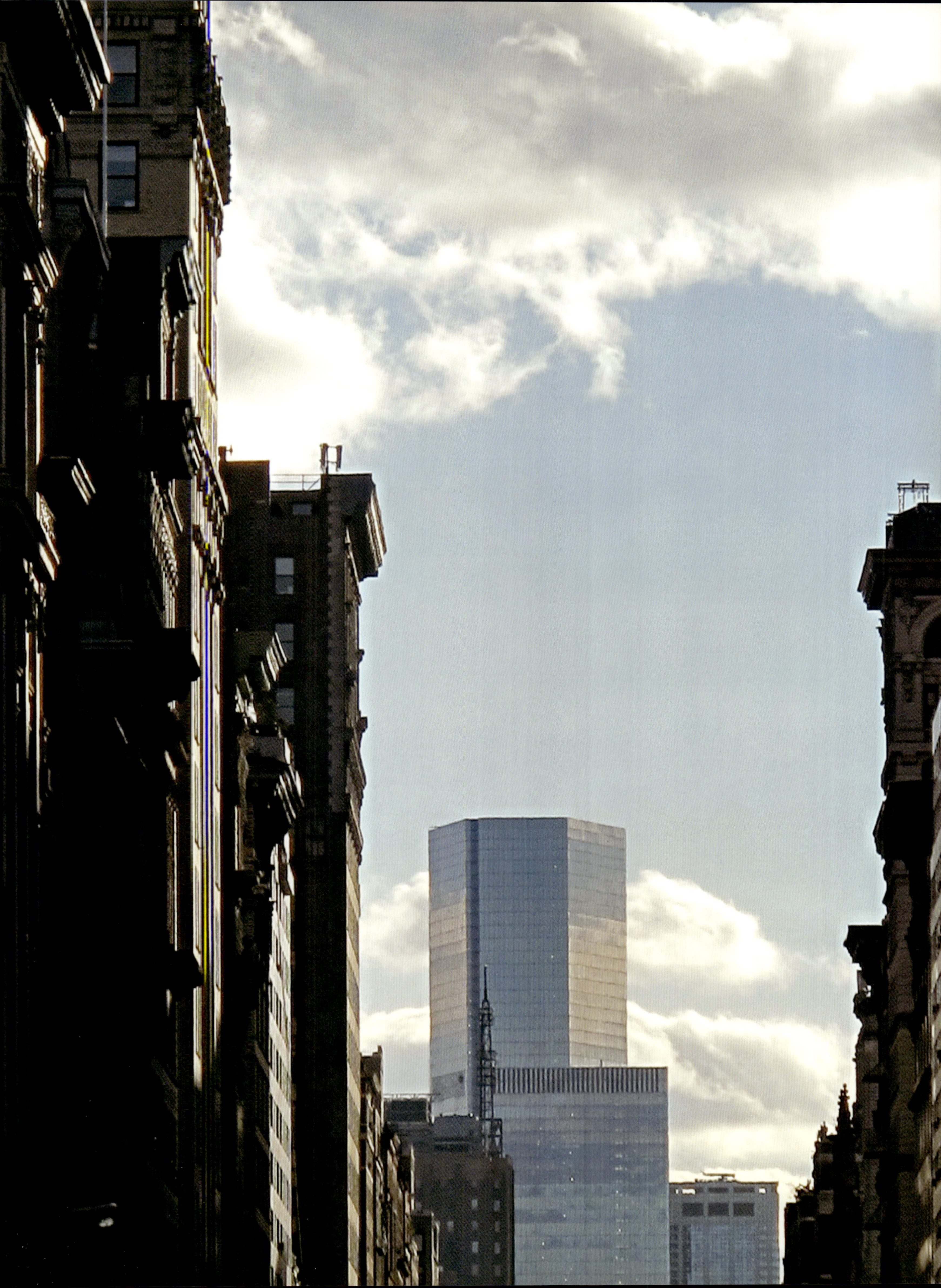

MICHAEL MALTZAN

When designing a home for a serious art collector, the architect must consider not only how the client himself will live in the home, but also how his art will live there along with him. Such was the case with the Ovitz Residence, a 28,000-square-foot home designed by Michael Maltzan for former Hollywood agent and art collector Michael Ovitz. Referring to it as a "villa" rather than a mansion, given that it was inspired by Venetian architect Andrea Palladio's sixteenth-century Italian country houses, the structure is a series of interconnecting boxes covered in a skin of perforated steel. Both its size and layout translate to power and prestige, meant to impress the owner's guests, many of whom visit just to see his art collection—which includes works by Willem de Kooning, Jean Dubuffet, Jasper Johns, Robert Rauschenberg, Mark Rothko, and Pablo Picasso, to name just a few artists.

Building houses for art collectors is where Maltzan has made his mark—along with the Ovitz home, he has also constructed houses for Beverly Hills art collectors Alan Hergott and Curt Shepard, as well as for artists Lari Pittman and Roy Dowell. Despite his rarefied client list, Maltzan is equally interested in constructing housing projects for the urban poor in Los Angeles' blighted neighborhoods. These include the New Carver Apartments (2009), a barrel-shaped tower just thirty-five feet from Interstate 10, which provides privacy, views, and even a small backyard space for its formerly homeless residents. For Maltzan, the skills of the architect are elastic—just as easily applied to the less fortunate as they are to the wealthiest members of our society.

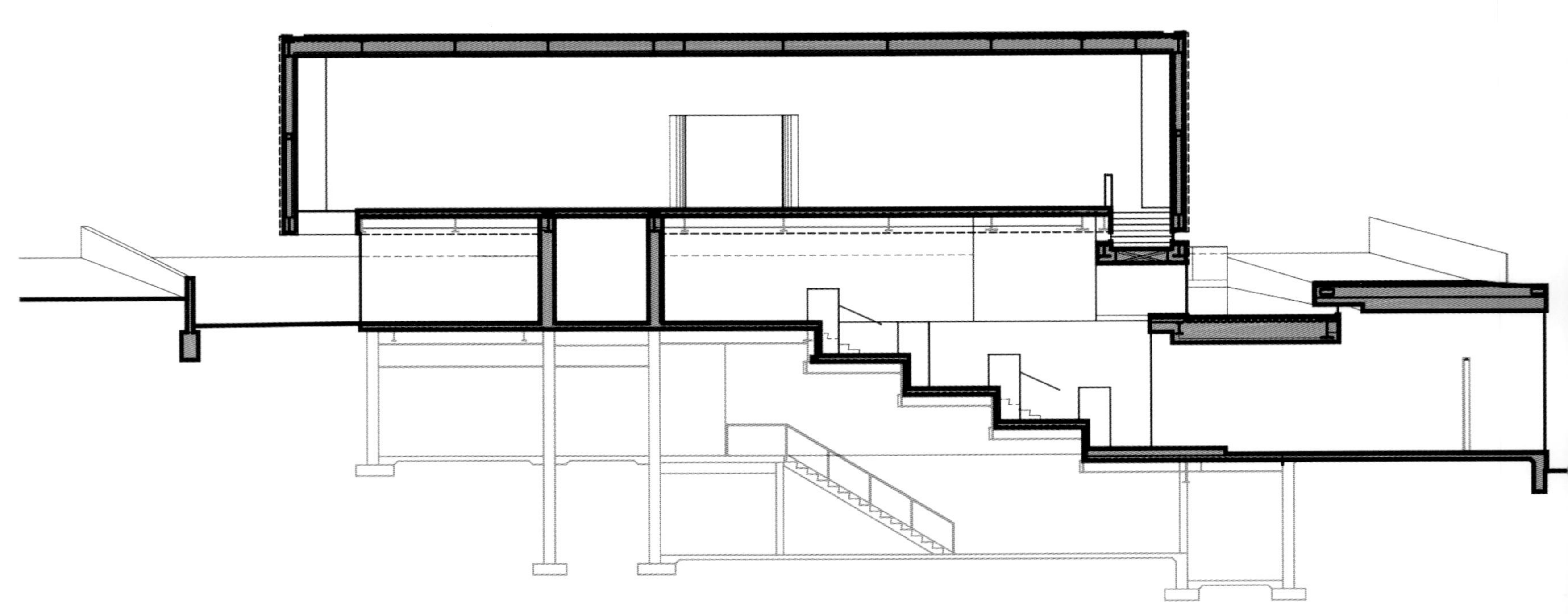

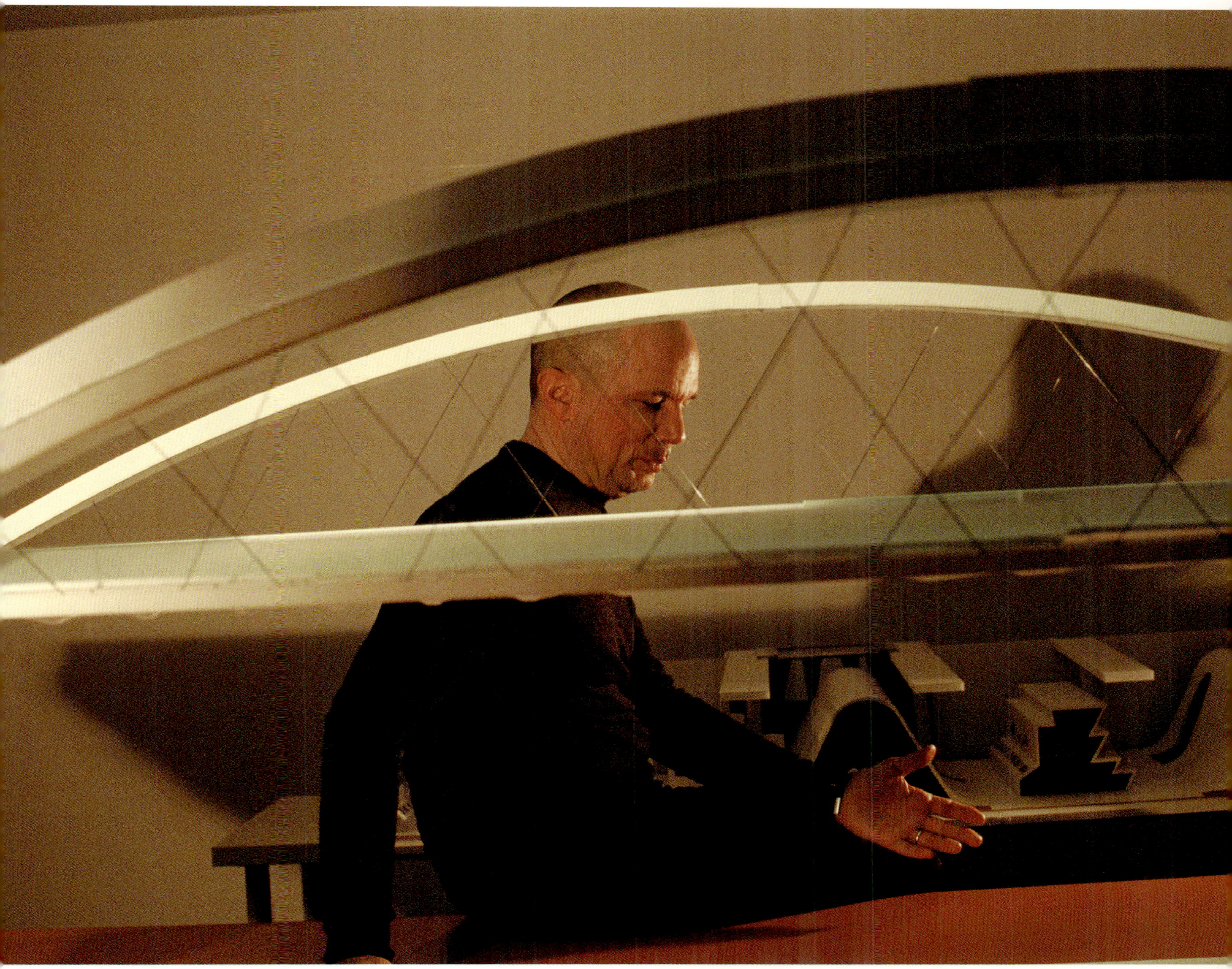

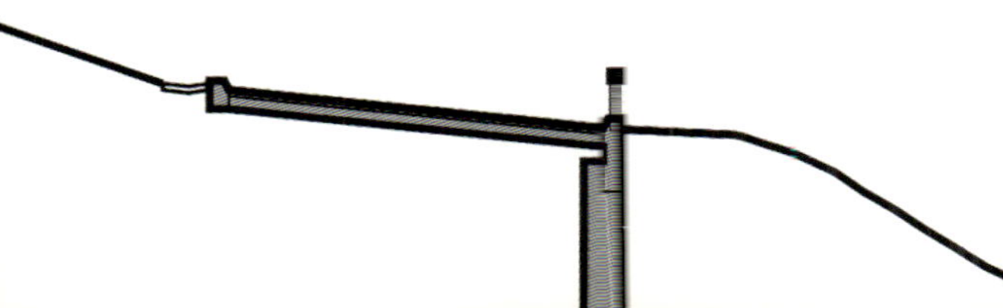

Michael Maltzan.
Opposite: Rendering of the Ovitz Residence.
Following pages and pages 80–81: Michael
Maltzan Architecture. The Ovitz Residence,
Beverly Hills, California, 2010.

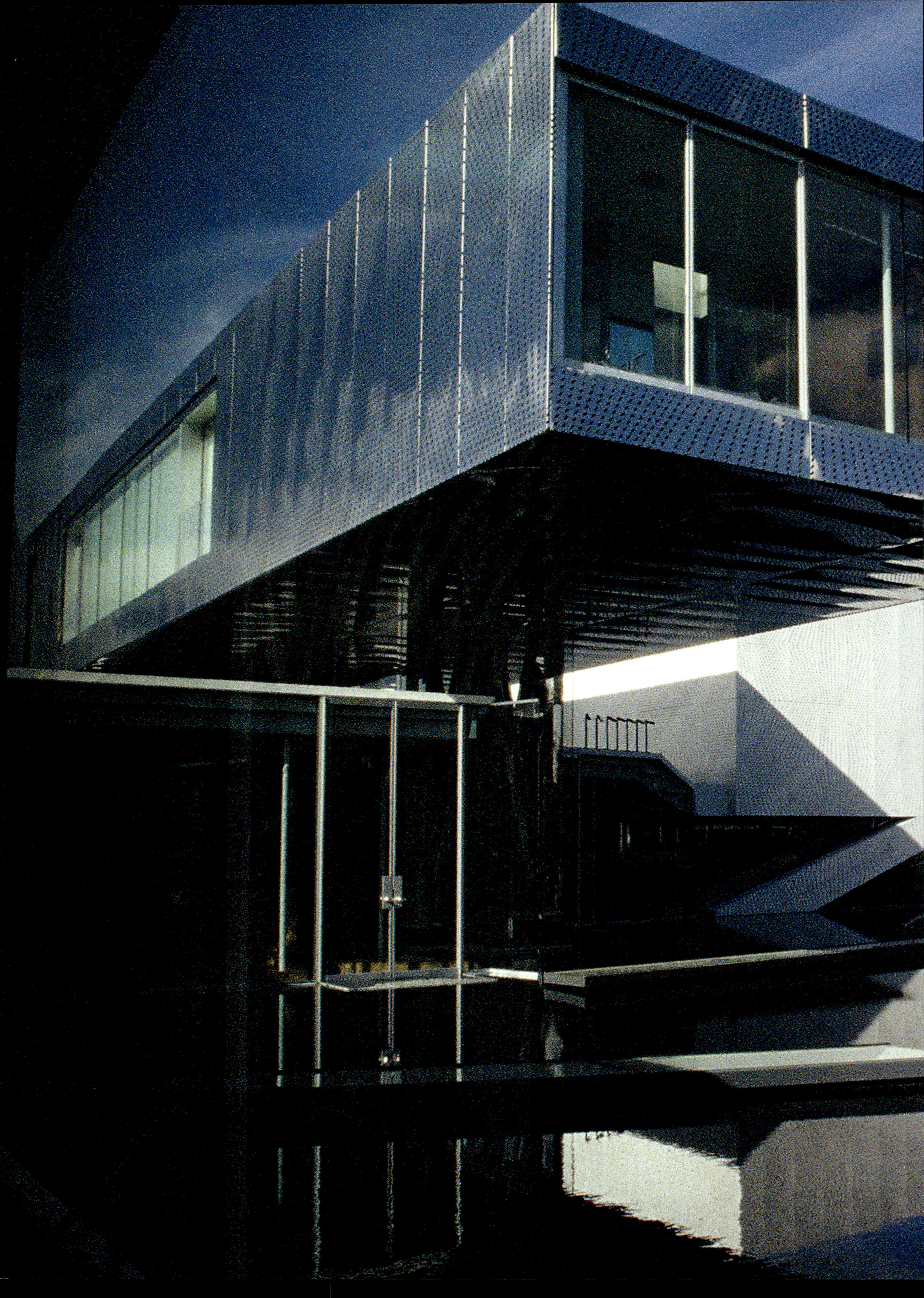

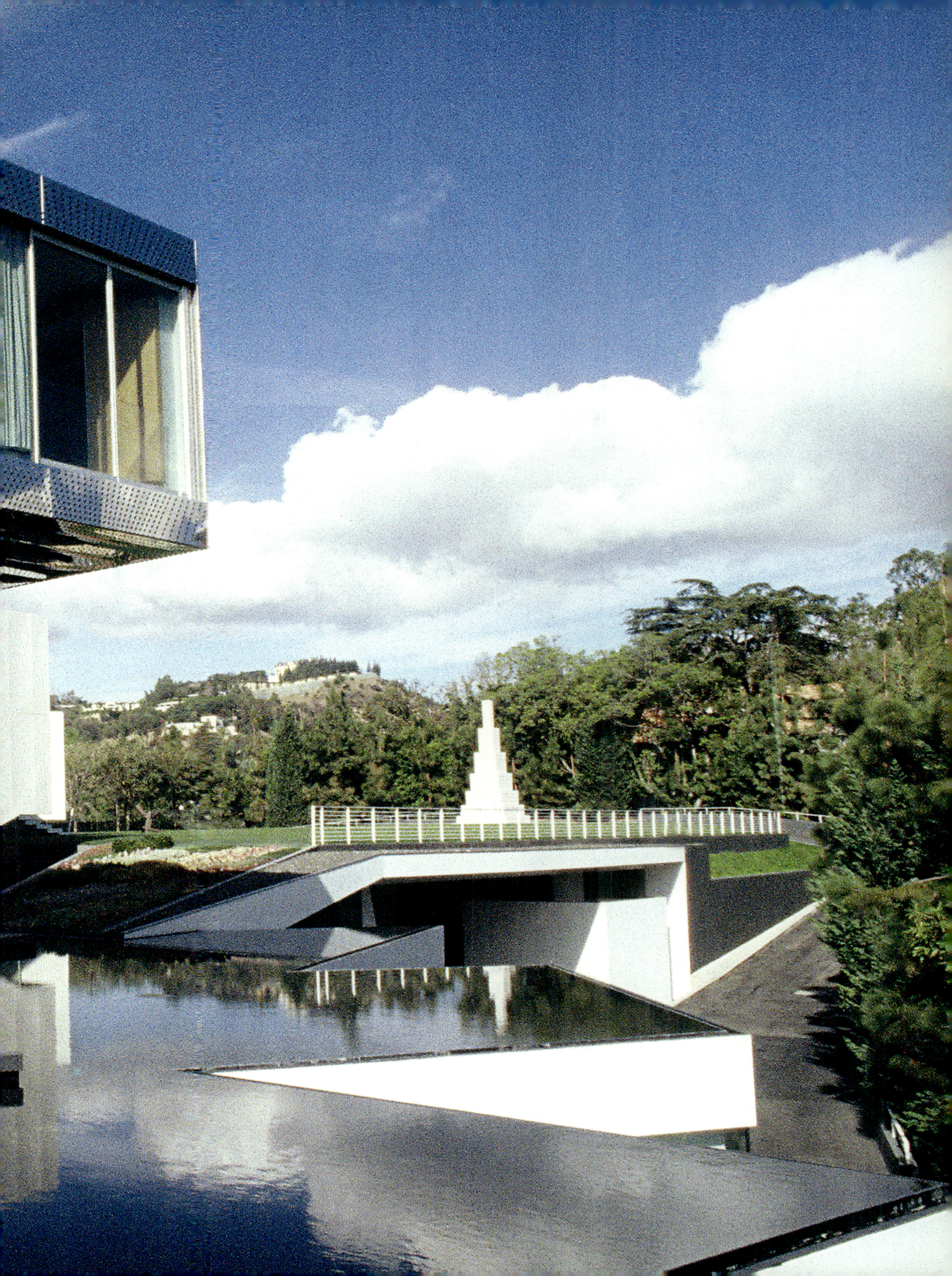

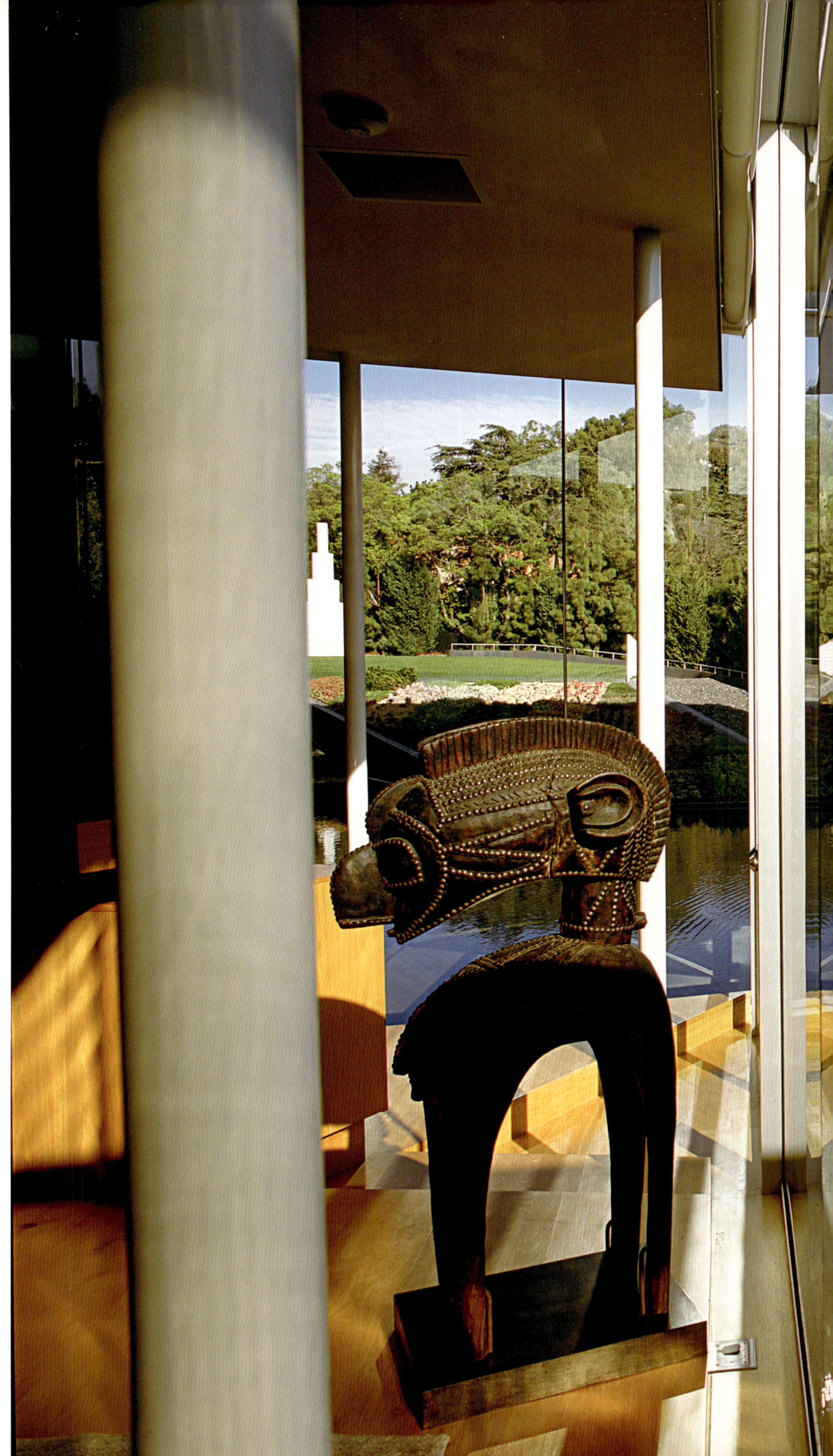

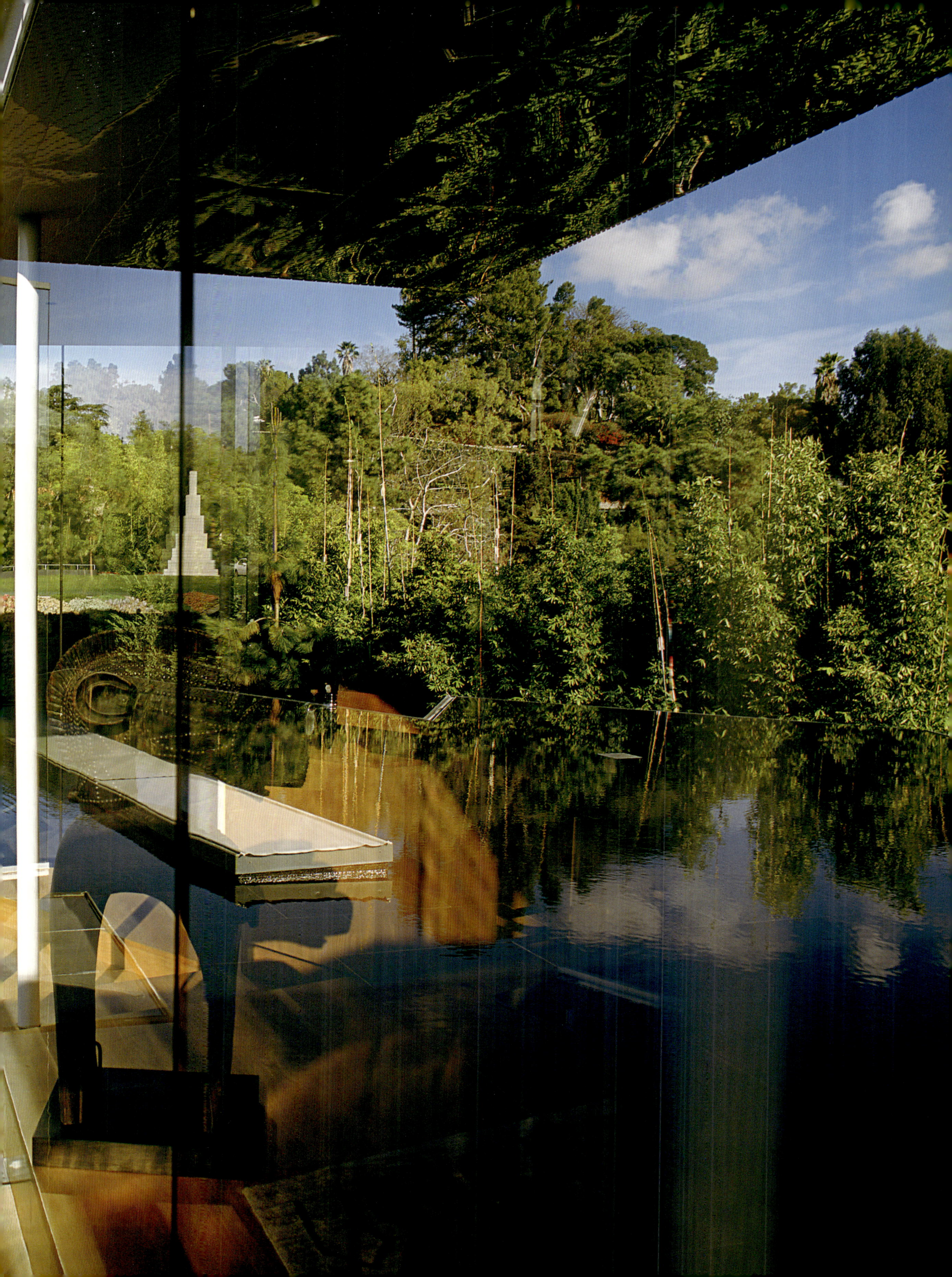

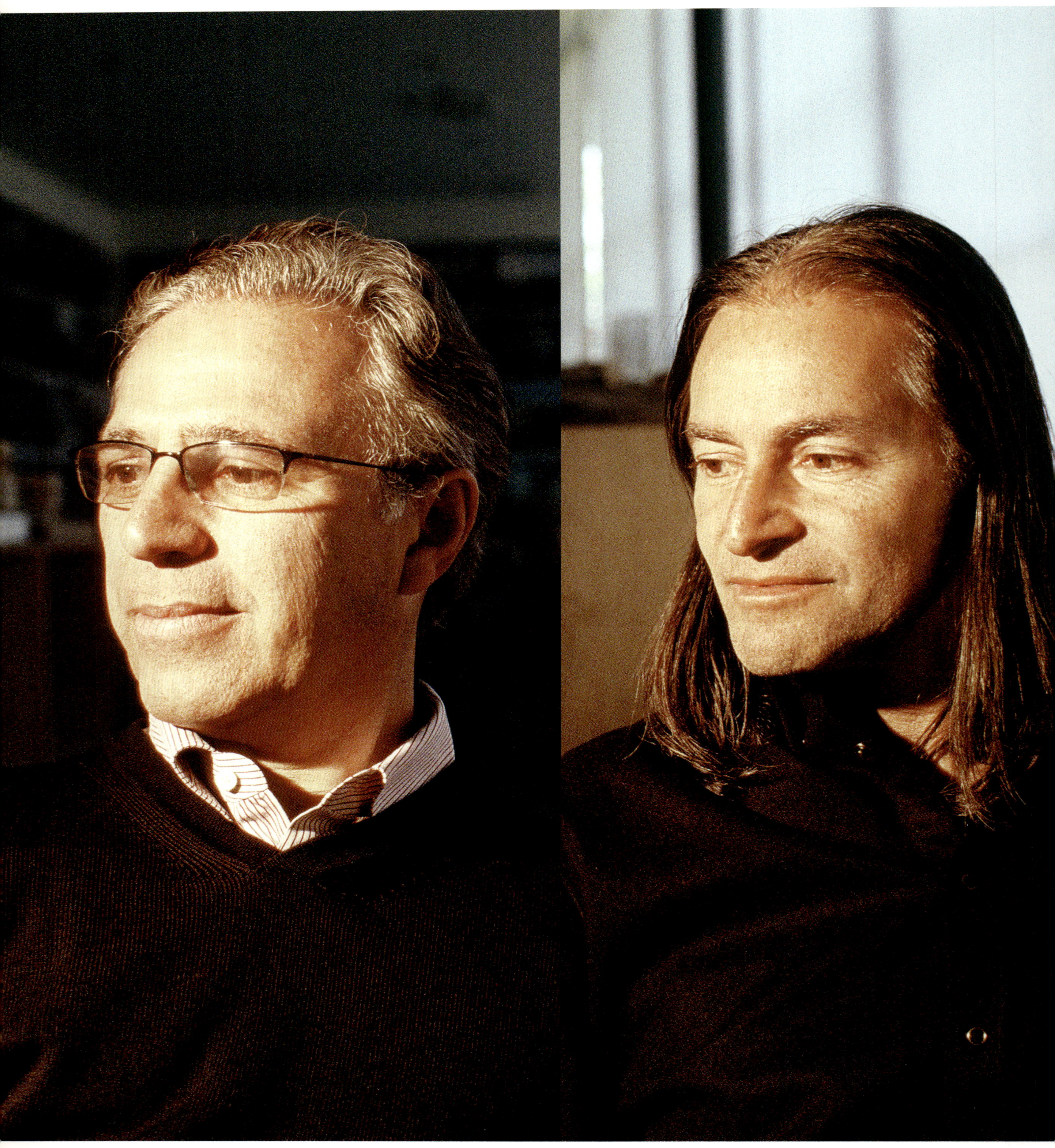

MARMOL RADZINER

Like the California modernists it so admires—such as Richard Neutra, whose famed Kaufmann House (1946) it recently renovated—California firm Marmol Radziner is involved from a project's conception down to the smallest details of its execution. Founded in 1989 by Leo Marmol and Ron Radziner, the firm employs not only architects, but also contractors, cabinet makers, metal fabricators, and site supervisors, allowing for continuity through the process of constructing the neo-modern, landscape-conscious homes that have landed them numerous honors, including being named the American Institute of Architects California Council's Firm of the Year in 2004.

One such home is the Trousdale Residence (2013), a 4,200-square-foot home perched on a terraced lot in a private community in Beverly Hills. Built for clients Skip Paul and Van Fletcher, who are themselves renowned in the design community for restoring homes by modernist architects such as A. Quincy Jones and Gardner Dailey, the four-bedroom structure consists of two wings tucked underneath the wide, flat roof of central structure that serves as a great room. Evoking subtle glamour through the use of natural materials such as cedar, ivory terrazzo, and sandstone, the single-story house exists very much in harmony with the gardens surrounding it. Crape myrtles line the open space between the great room and the master suite. The open lawn, which houses a heated outdoor deck and swimming pool, is encased in a canopy of California live oaks planted around the perimeter. From any vantage point, there is no clear divide between interior and exterior spaces—an effect accomplished thanks to the characteristically holistic approach of the firm, which served as the architect, landscape designer, and contractor for the project.

Plan of the Trousdale Residence.
Opposite: Leo Marmol and Ron Radziner of Marmol Radziner.

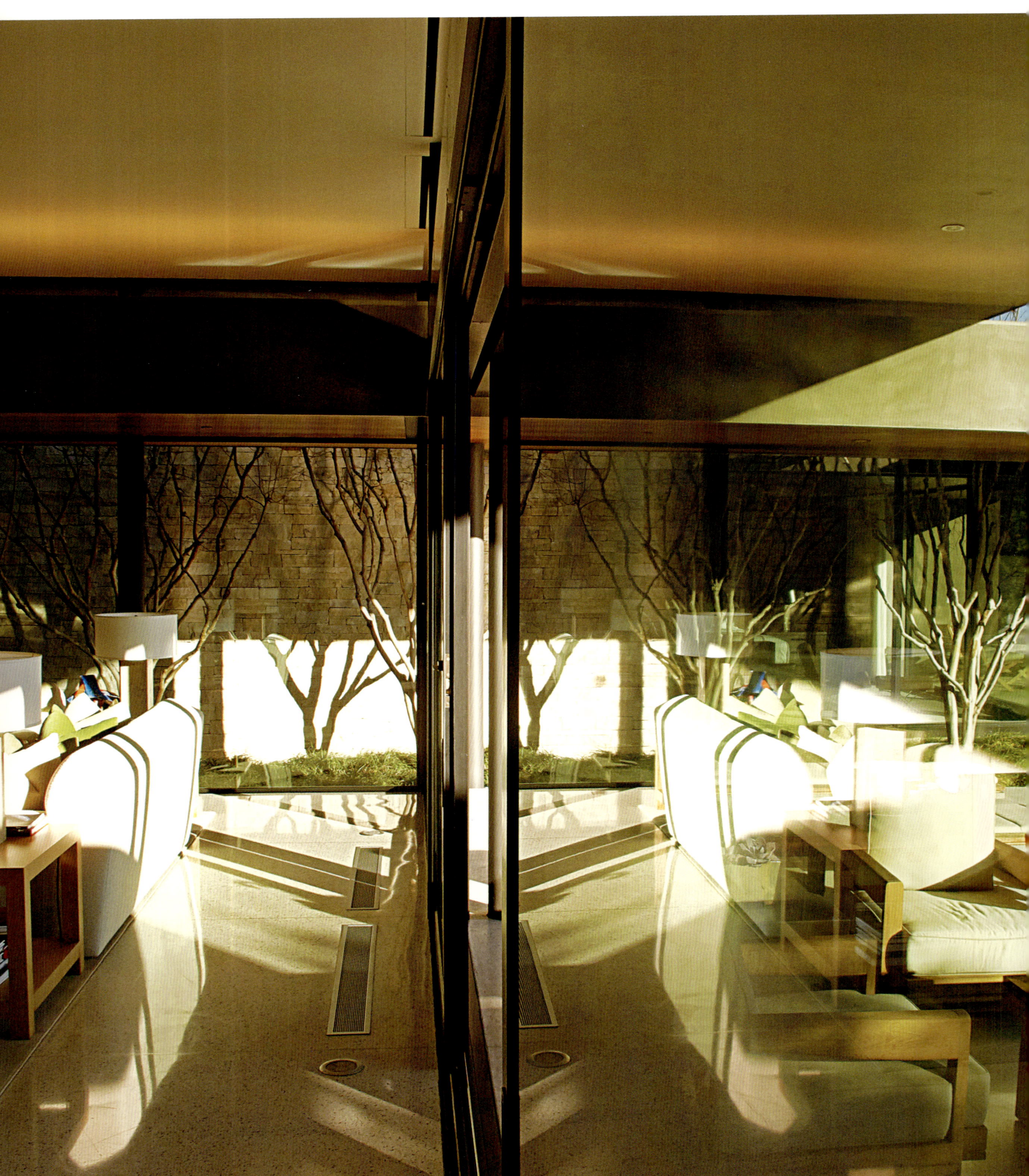

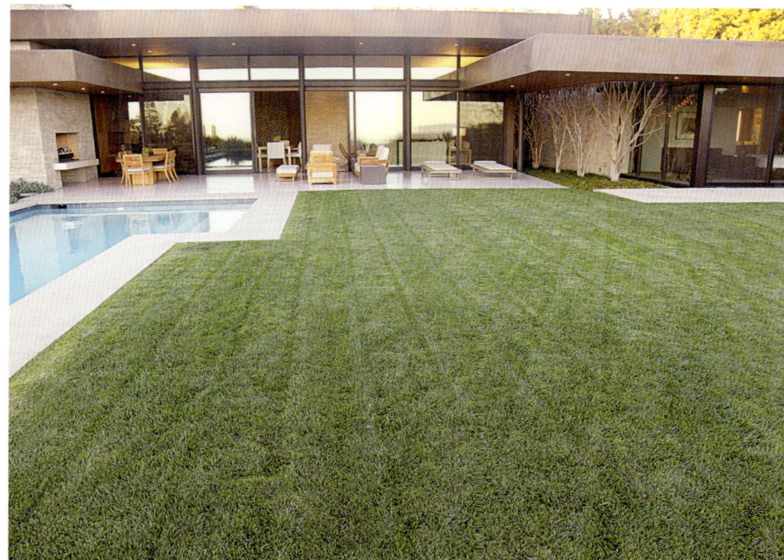

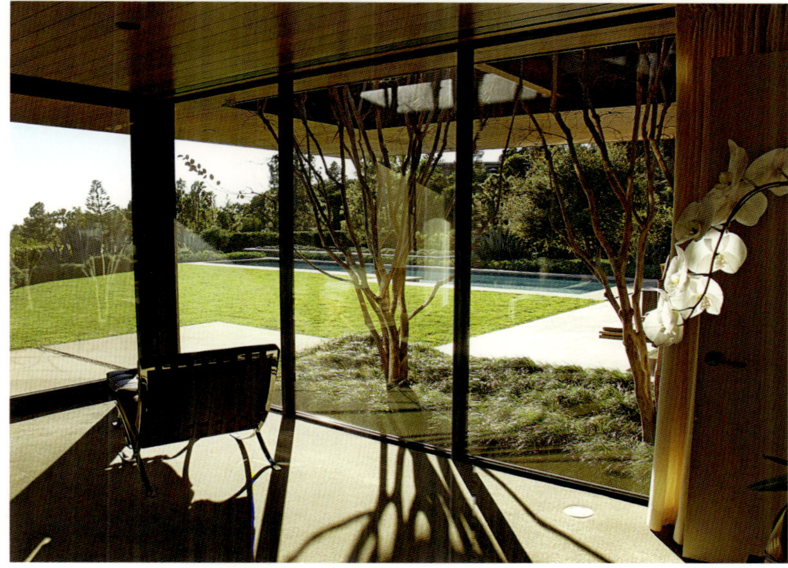

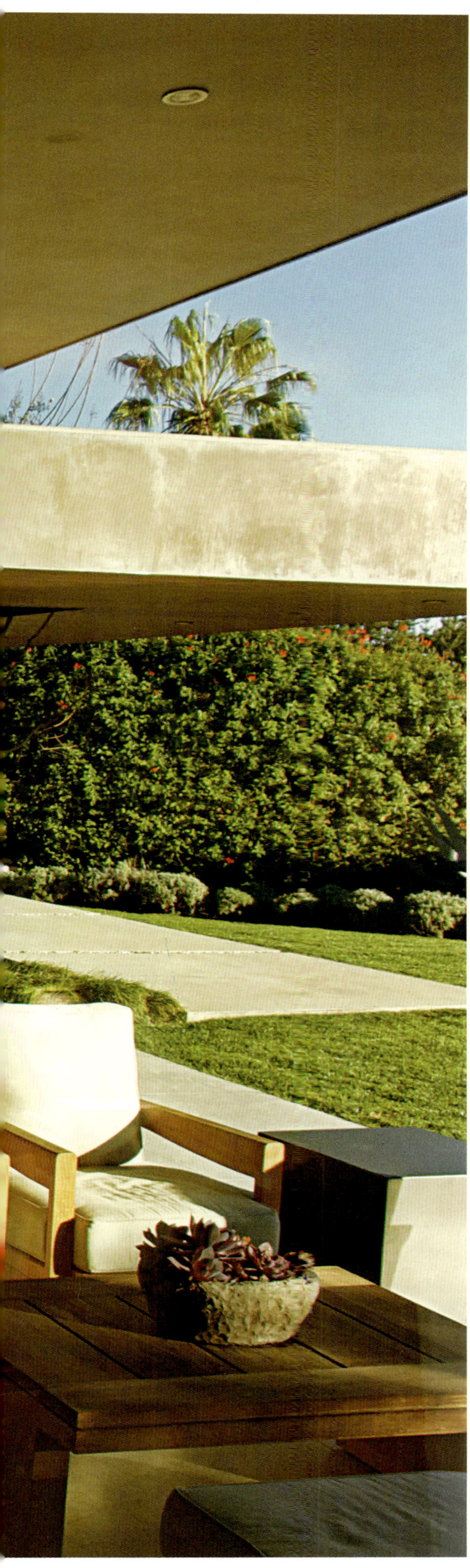

Marmol Radziner. Trousdale Residence, Beverly Hills, California, 2013.

JÜRGEN MAYER H.

SCHLUMP ONE AND ADA1

Unexpectedly, German architect Jürgen Mayer-Hermann is inspired by the encryption patterns used on the interiors of envelopes to ensure personal data protection—so much so, in fact, that he published a collection of them in *WirrWarr*, a coffee table book released in 2011. His affinity for the intricate designs can be found everywhere, from the carpets he creates to the interiors he designs with his firm, J. Mayer H. und Partner, Architekten, founded in Berlin in 1996.

But what comes to mind when looking at buildings by Mayer is not repetitive patterns found on envelopes, but rather those found in nature. For example, the Metropol Parasol (2011), a 16,000-square-foot public plaza he designed in Seville, resembles an outgrowth of fungus, or a honeycomb made by a swarm of gargantuan bees. And ADA1 (2007), an office building in the center of Hamburg, seems to take its inspiration from an amphibious body—at intervals along its white and black facade, oval windows jut out from the outer wall, like bulbous eyes on a fish out of water.

The monochrome color palette and viscous shapes of ADA1 were recycled in Schlump One, another office building in Hamburg. Originally constructed in the 1950s, the structure was renovated by Mayer in 2012. The organic language of the exterior, which recalls gel moving on a liquid surface or the drawings cf Keith Haring, repeats on the interior, making the whole building appear to be one continuous cellular structure. Inclusiveness is a feature of much of Mayer's work, given that he is often the interior designer as well as architect on many of his larger projects.

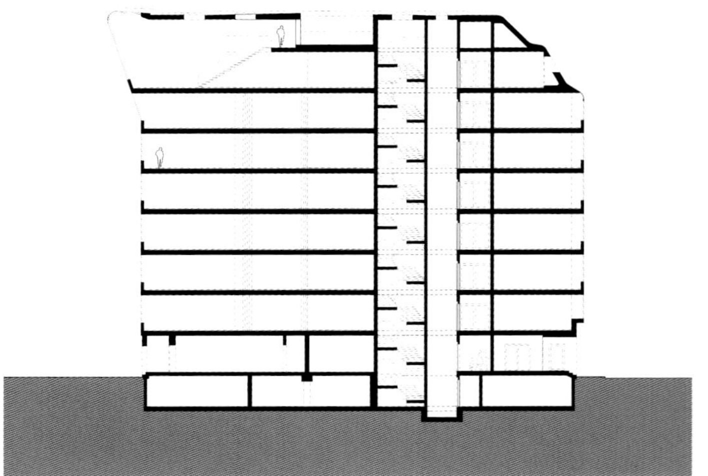

Rendering of Schlump One.
Opposite: Jürgen Mayer H.
Following pages: J. Mayer H. und Partner, Architekten.
ADA1, Hamburg, Germany, 2007.
Pages 90-91: J. Mayer H. und Partner, Architekten.
Schlump One, Hamburg, Germany, 2012.

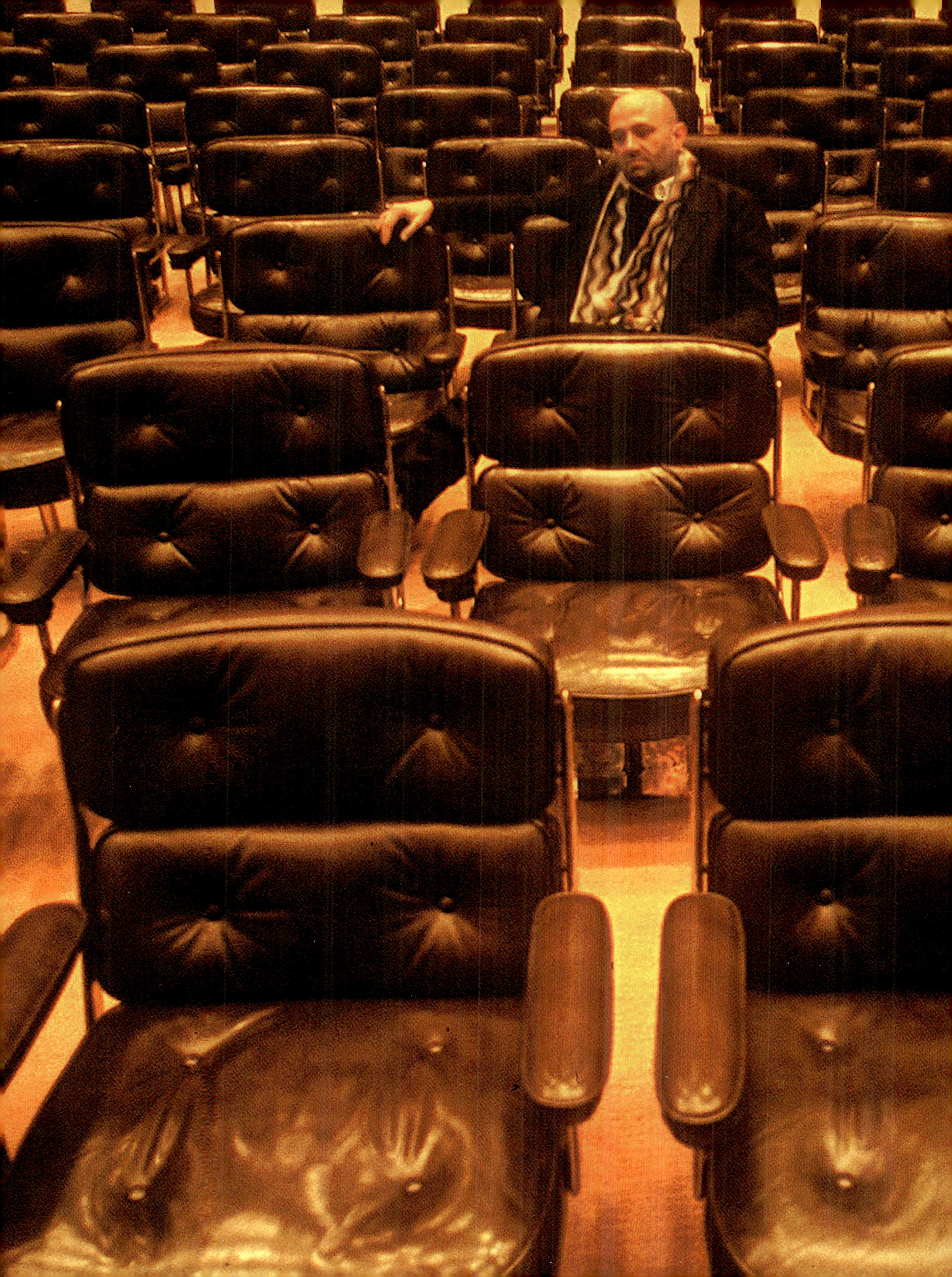

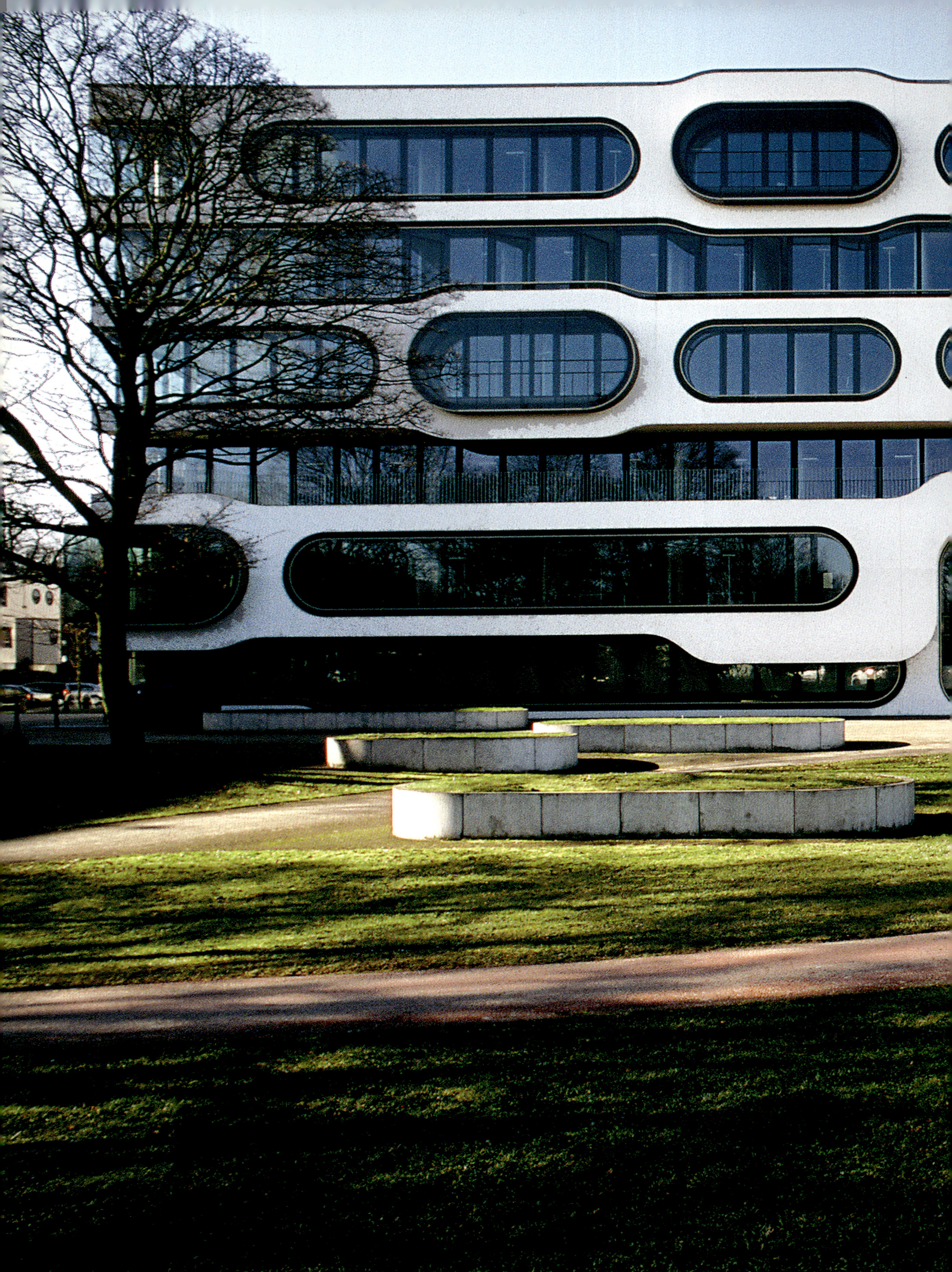

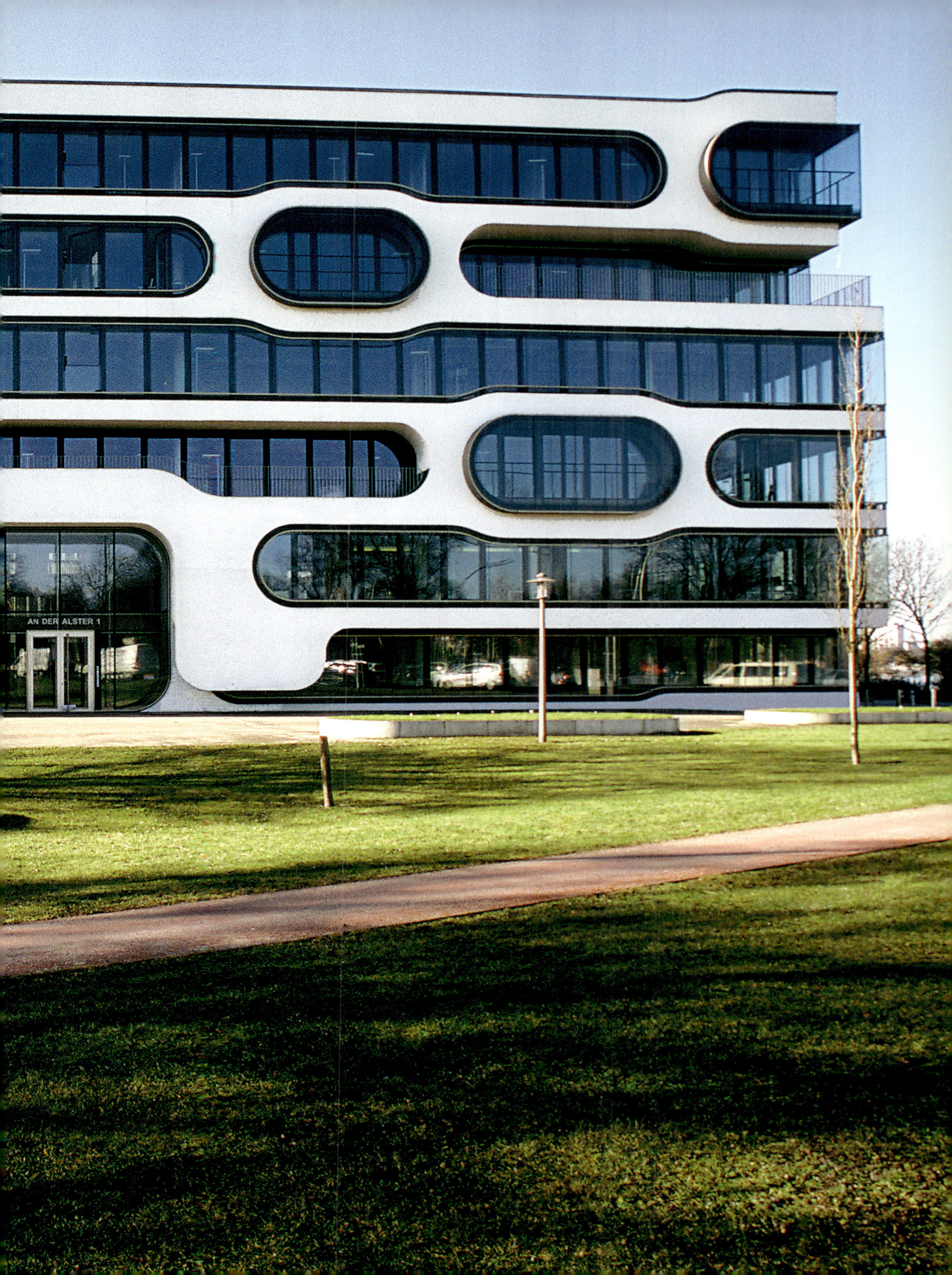

AN DER ALSTER 1

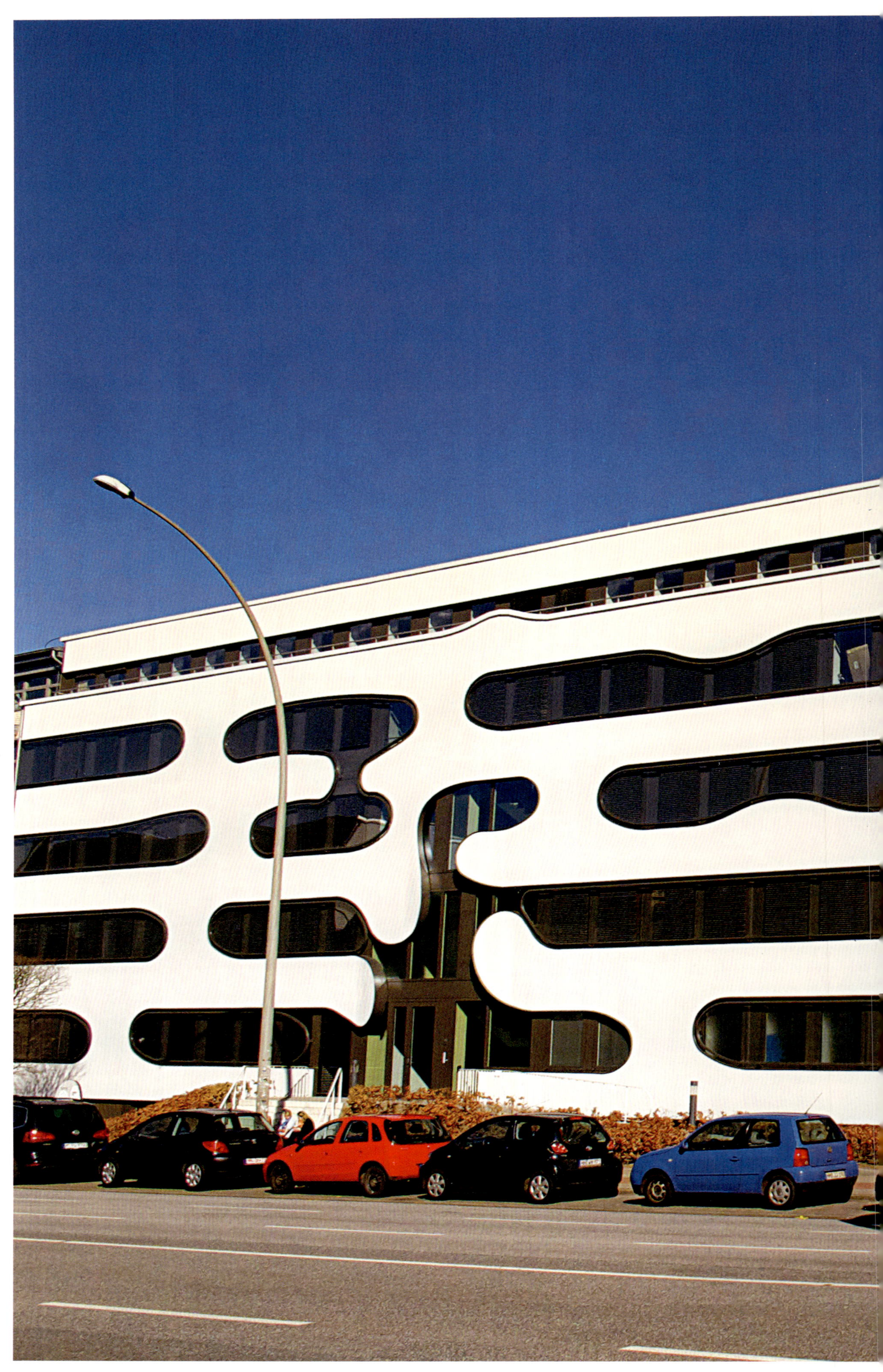

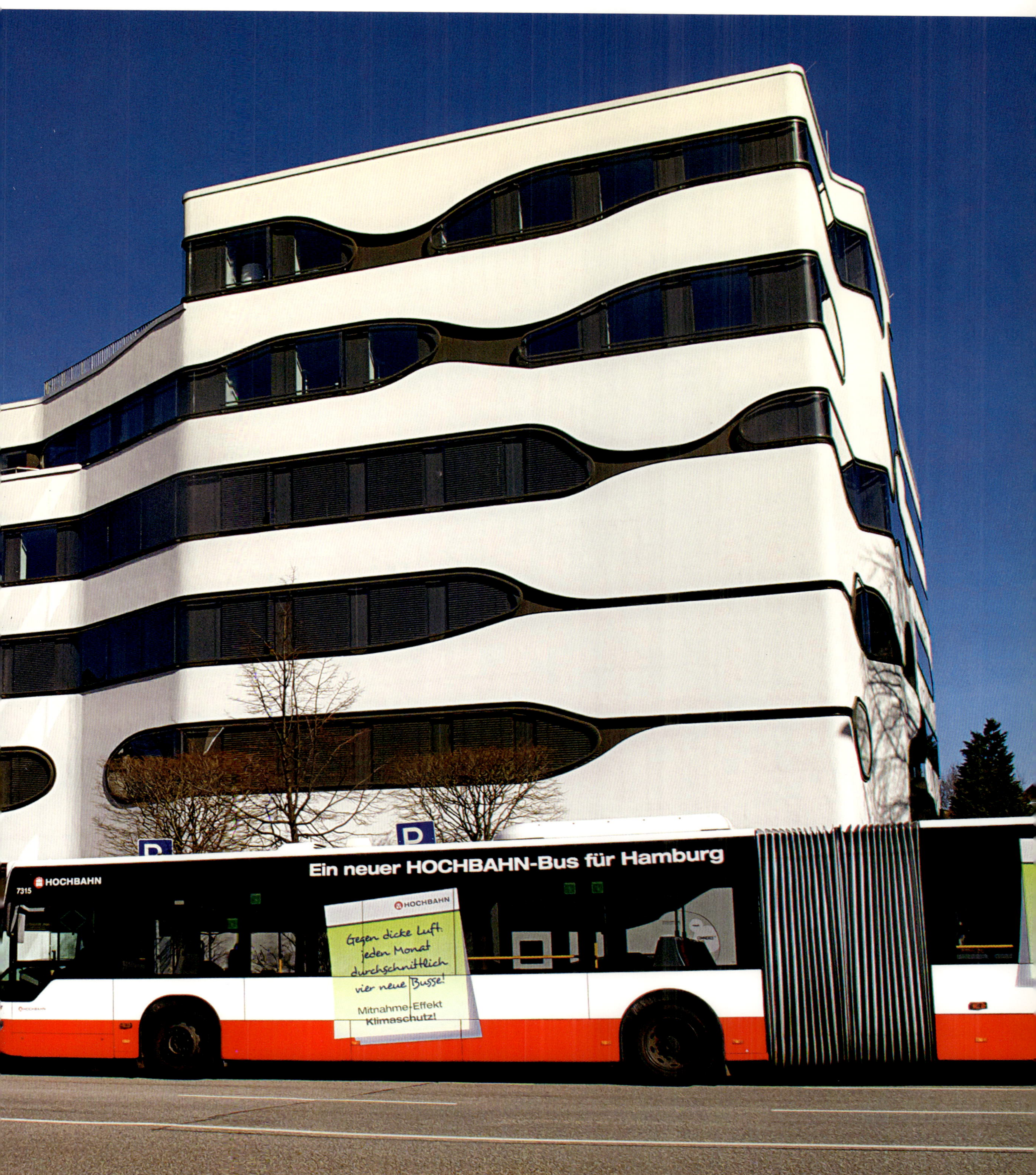
Ein neuer HOCHBAHN-Bus für Hamburg
HOCHBAHN
7315
HOCHBAHN
Gegen dicke Luft:
jeden Monat
durchschnittlich
vier neue Busse!
Mitnahme-Effekt
Klimaschutz!

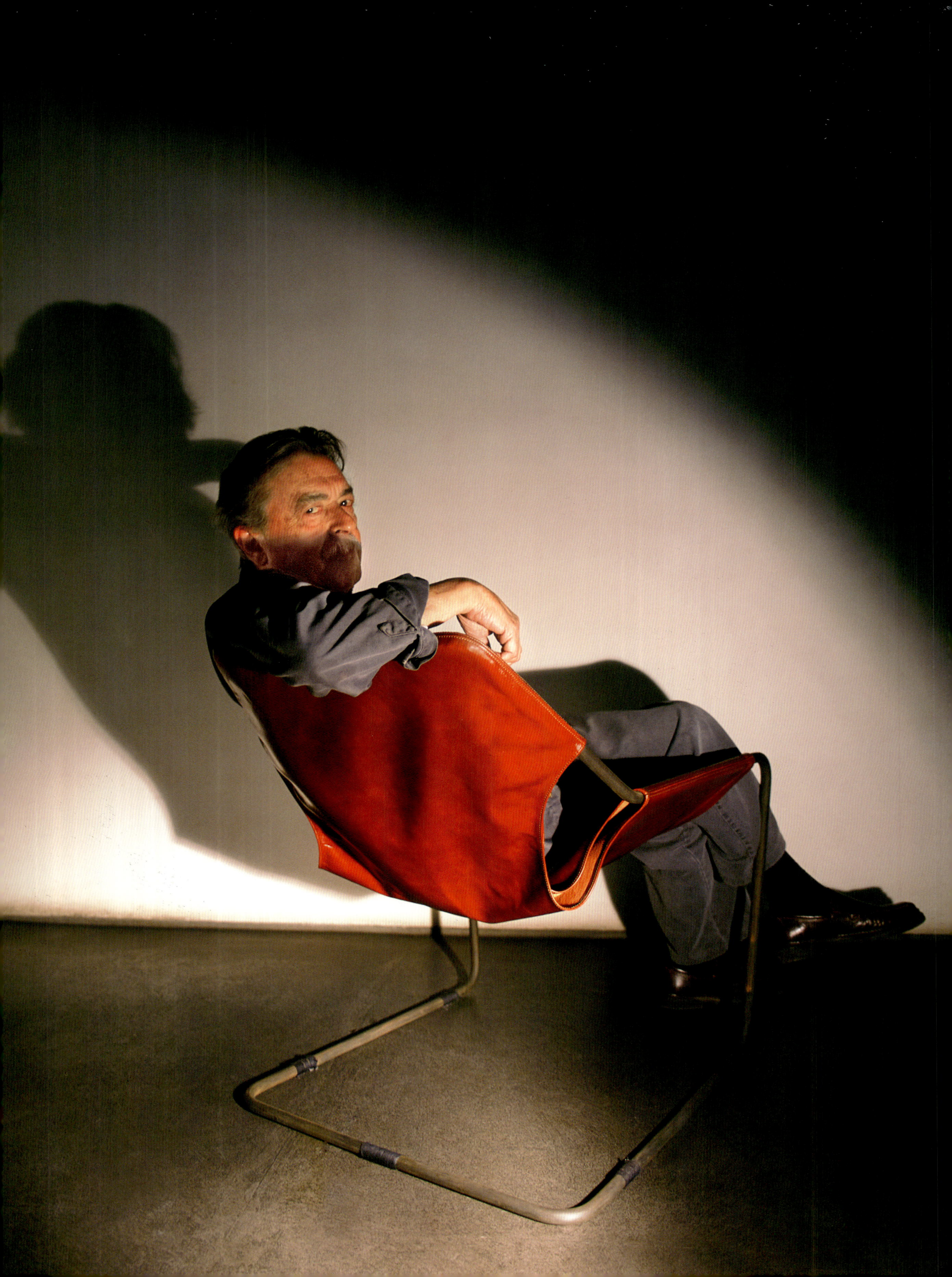

PAULO MENDES DA ROCHA

In the 1980s, when a 7,000-square-meter empty lot in São Paulo's Jardins district was scheduled to be transformed into a shopping mall, wealthy residents successfully lobbied to make it a public square instead. As a concession to double the space's value, they hired Brazilian architect Paulo Mendes da Rocha to create the Museu Brasileiro de Escultura (MuBE), a sculpture museum concealed almost entirely underground. In doing so, the residents received two gifts in one lot—a public park, and a cultural institution housing an art school.

MuBE, which was completed in 1995, is thus less a structure than it is a catacomb of cavelike spaces. With the exception of a single Brutalist outcropping along one edge of the lot which looks like a bridge and functions like a sculptural object, MuBE is almost entirely hidden underneath manicured gardens designed by Roberto Burle Marx, a Brazilian landscape architect.

Fans of Mendes da Rocha's work need not fear if they'd like to see more visible structures—the city of São Paulo is replete with his concrete creations, including the FIESP Cultural Center (1997), whose pyramid-shaped facade shows off thousands of twinkling LED lights that serve as an open-air art gallery, and the Chapel of Saint Peter (1987), a glass, concrete, and stone masterpiece whose religious activities revolve around a single enormous concrete column. His contributions to the built fabric of Brazil have led to his winning the Mies van der Rohe Prize for Latin American Architecture in 2000 and the Pritzker Prize in 2006.

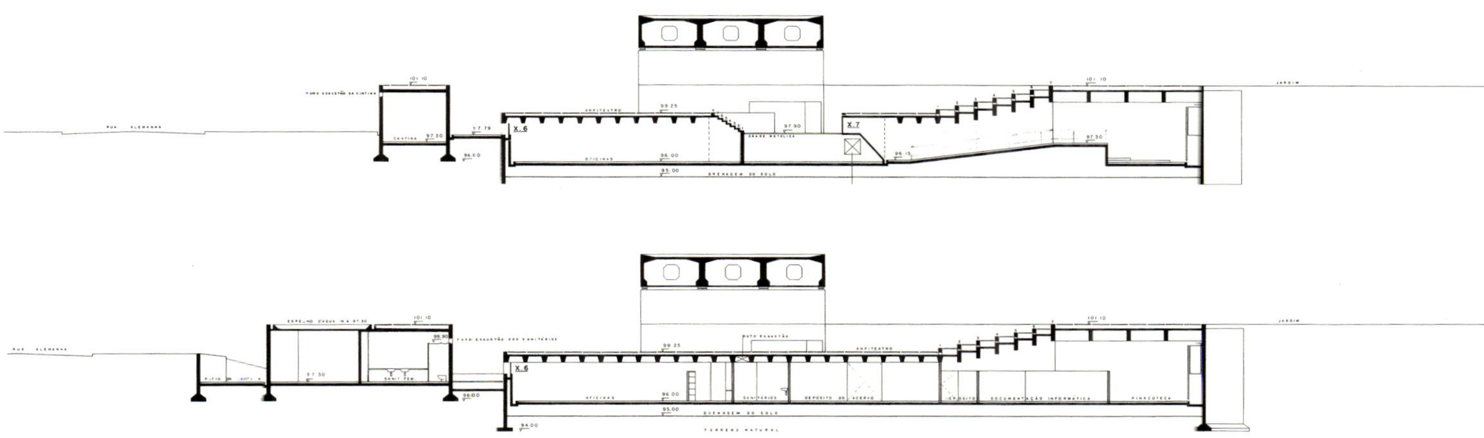

Renderings of the Museu Brasileiro de Escultura.
Opposite: Paulo Mendes da Rocha.
Following pages: Paulo Mendes da Rocha. Museu Brasileiro de Escultura, São Paulo, Brazil, 1995.

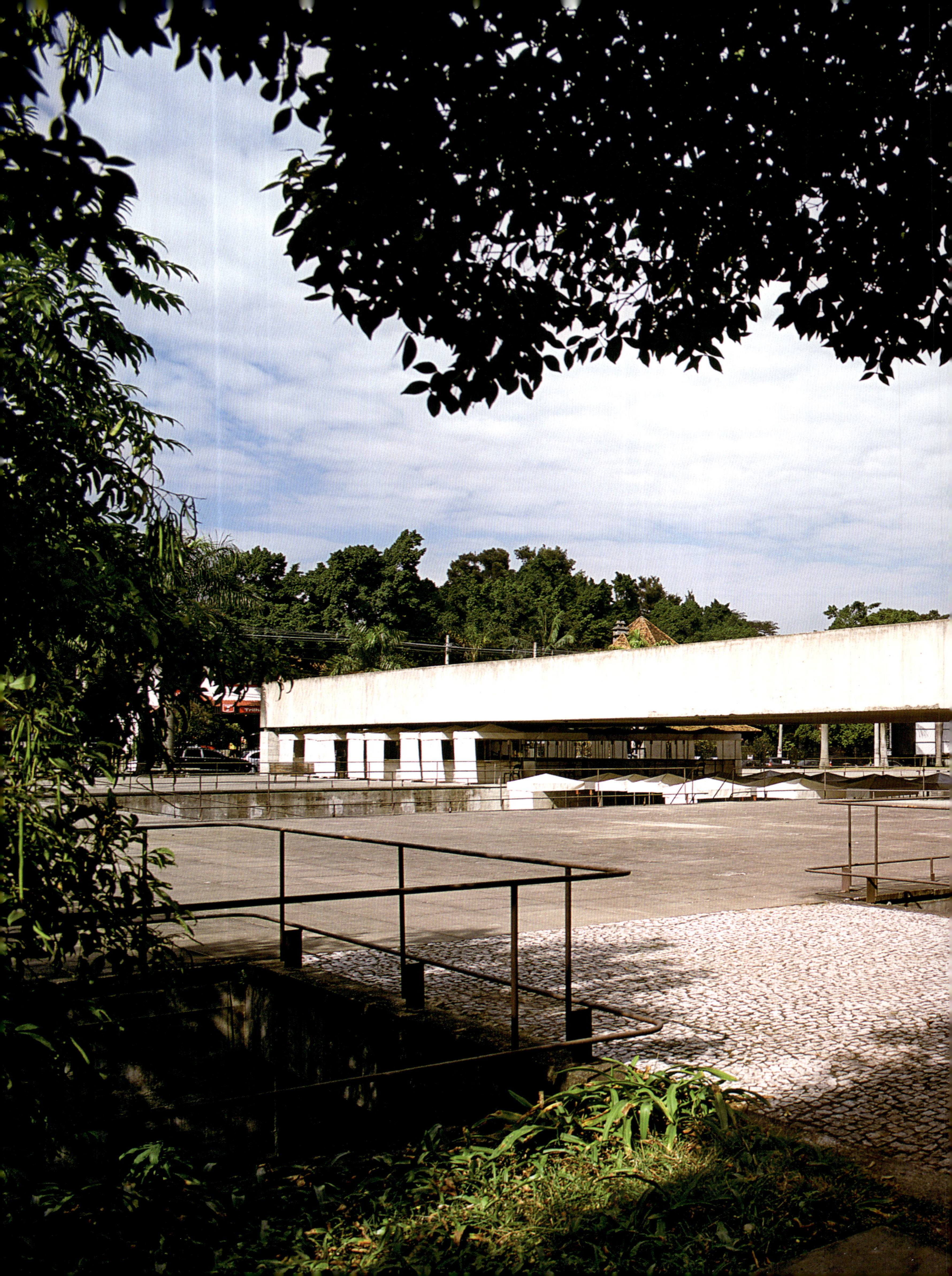

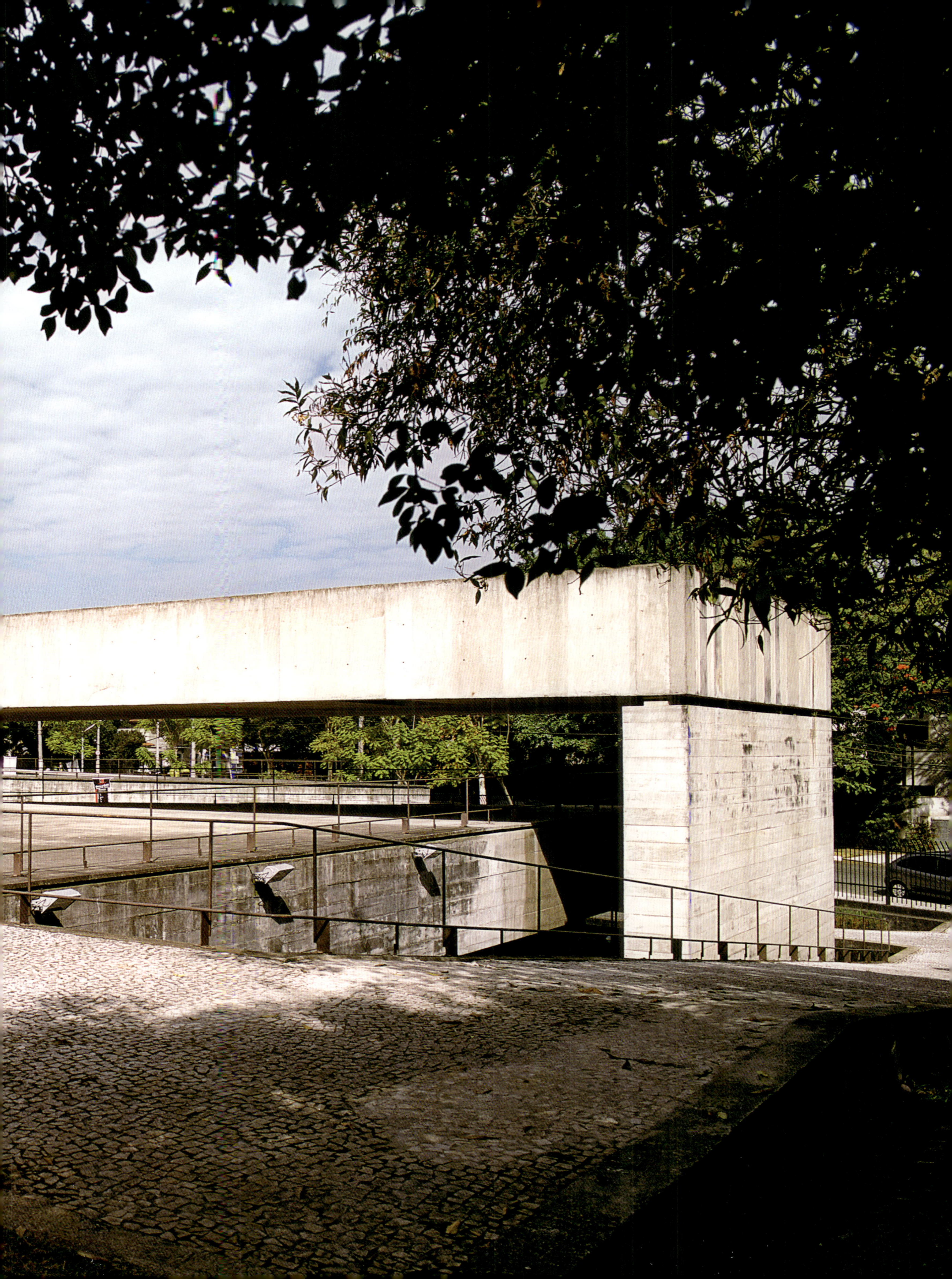

RAFAEL MONEO

It's no easy feat to build a new structure on a contained university campus—even less easy when this structure needs to be built over an existing gymnasium, as was the case with the Northwest Corner Building, a new science facility for Columbia University on 120th and Broadway. When considering the project, the architects—Rafael Moneo, Davis Brody Bond, and Moneo Brock Studio—added yet another restriction. They vowed to respect the original plans for Columbia University's Morningside campus, established when the site was originally developed by McKim, Mead and White in 1897. In order to do so, they had to restrict the width of the building to just sixty-five feet, and keep a respectful distance from the neighboring structure. The resulting creation, a rectangular tower marked on the campus side by a wall of glass windows and on the street side by a boxcar-like pattern of aluminum fins, opens the new structure onto the existing campus while at the same time keeping it contained from the surrounding neighborhood.

It is a feat characteristic of Moneo himself, a Spanish architect who won the Pritzker Prize in 1996 and the Prince of Asturias Award for the Arts in 2012. Stating that he respects, above all things, the sites where his buildings reside, he is known for his innovative designs, which include the Cathedral of Our Lady of the Angels (2002) in Los Angeles, California, and the Davis Museum and Cultural Center (1993) at Wellesley College in Massachusetts, as well as for his renovations of storied historic spaces, including extensions of both the Prado Museum and the Bank of Spain in Madrid.

Rafael Moneo.

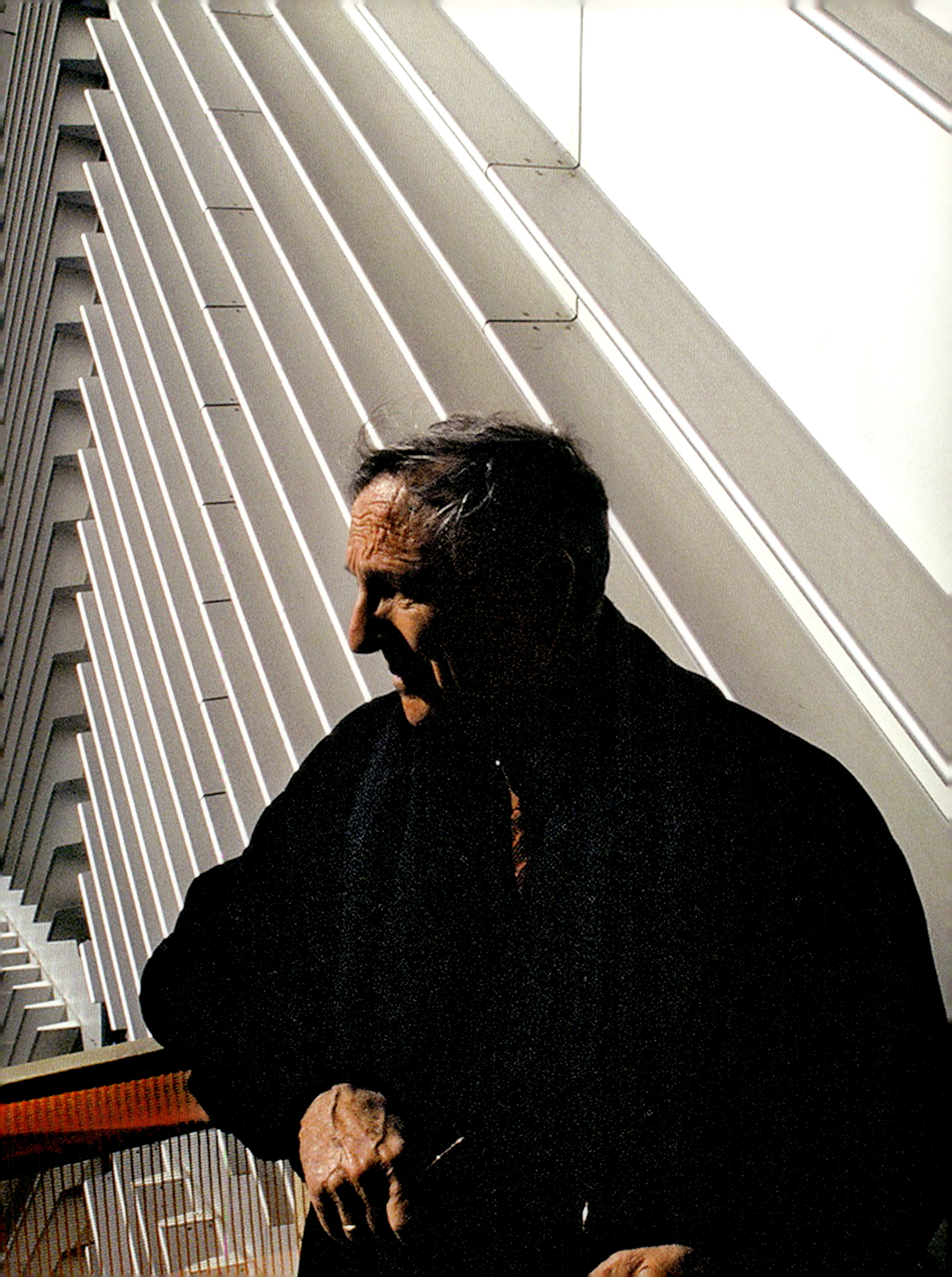

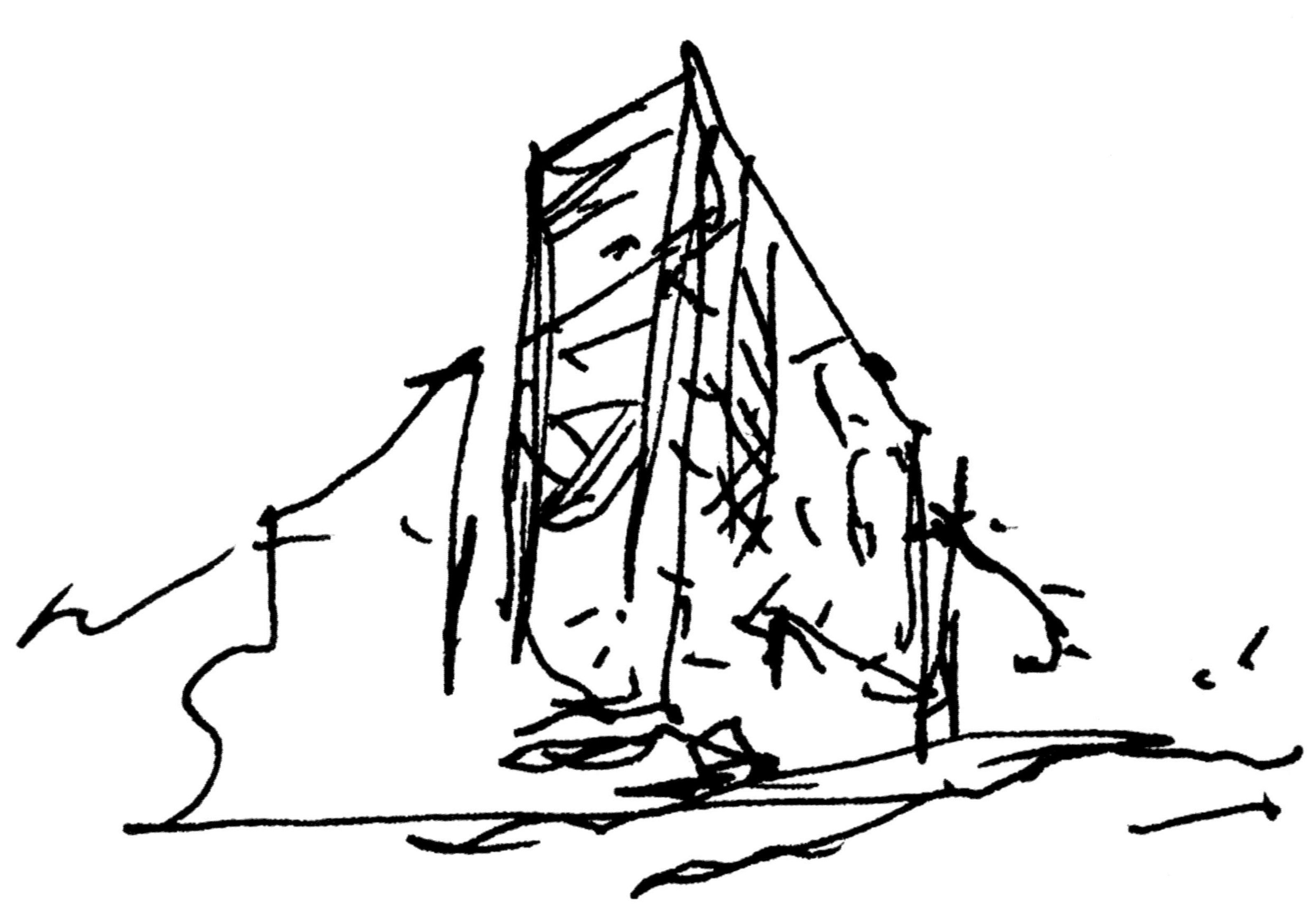

Sketch of the Columbia University
Northwest Corner Science Building.
Opposite: Rafael Moneo. Columbia
University Northwest Corner Science
Building, New York City, 2010.

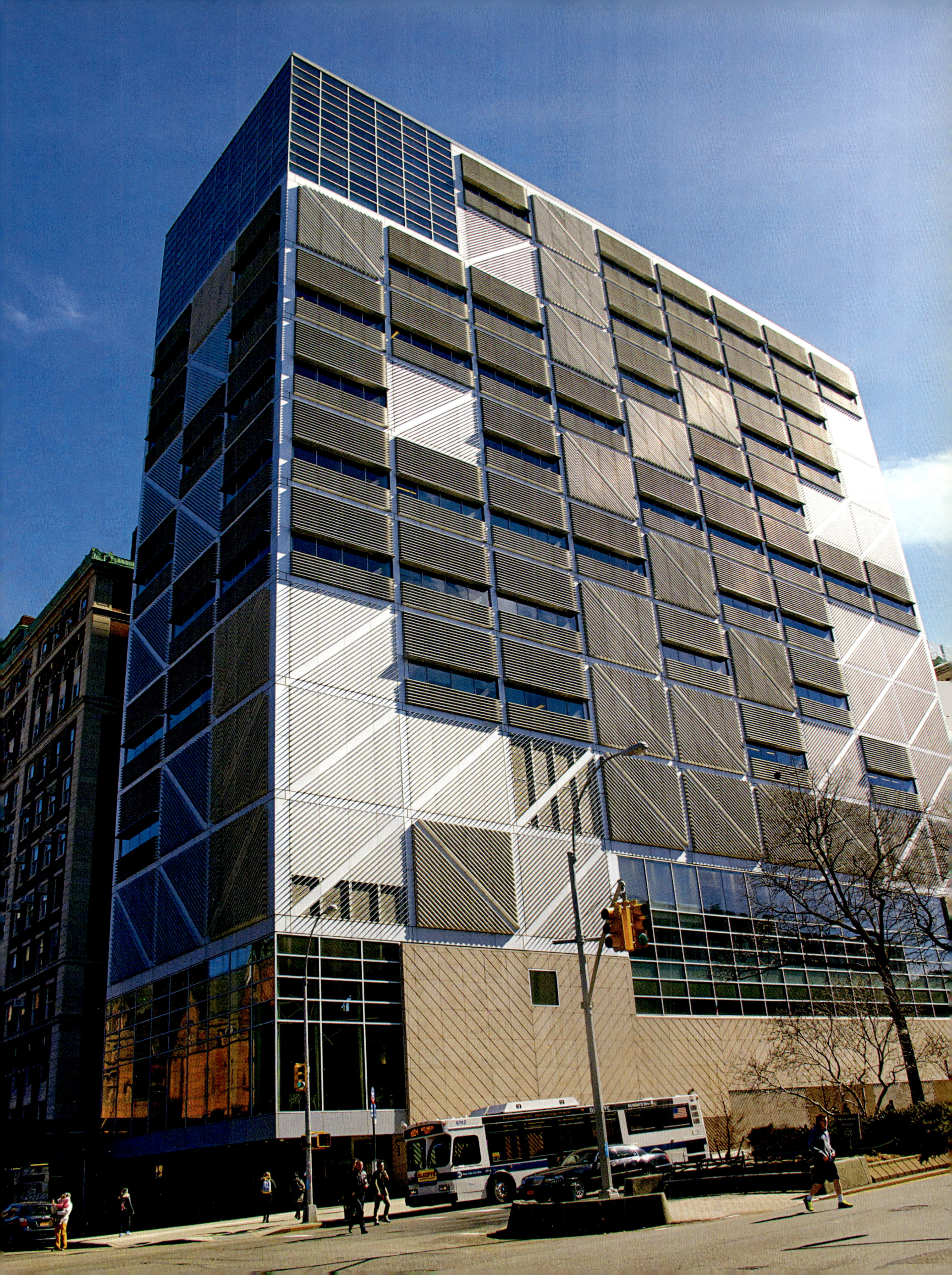

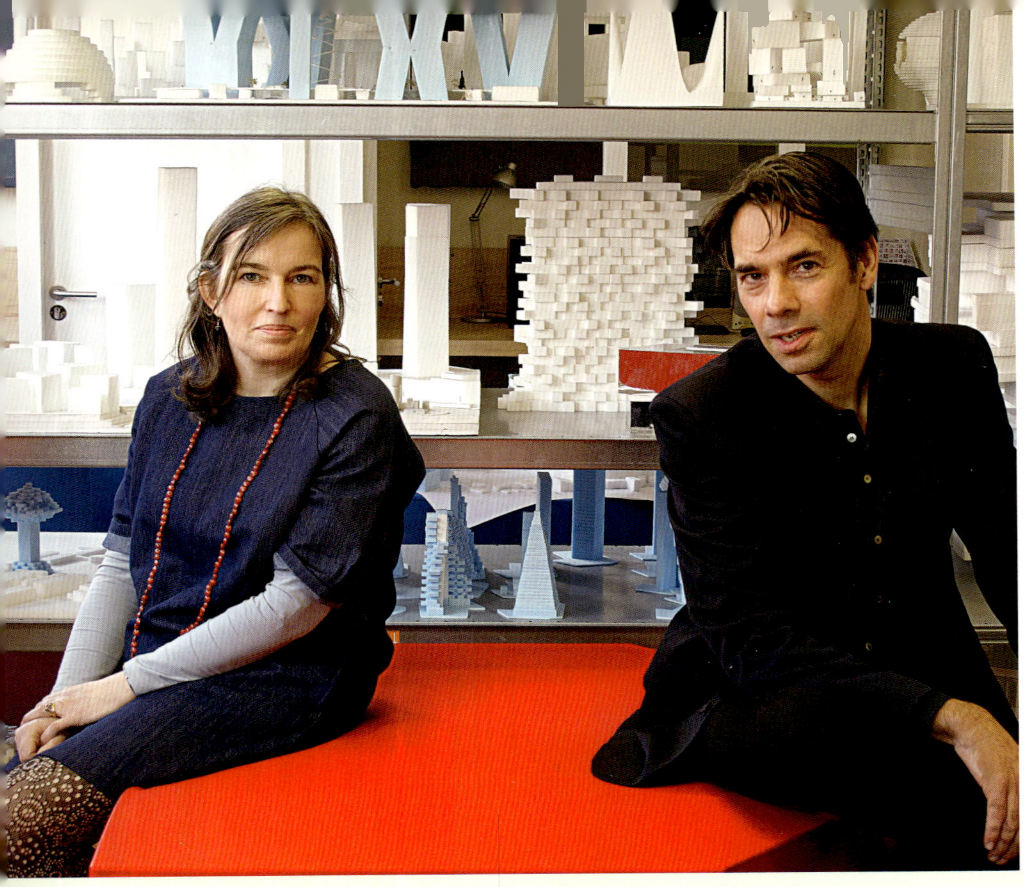

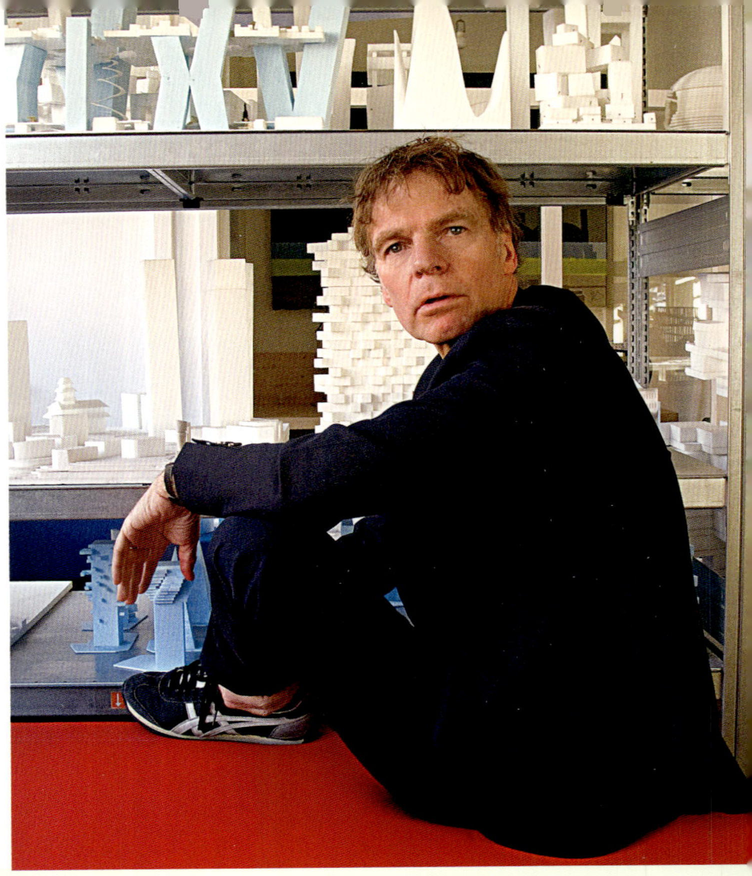

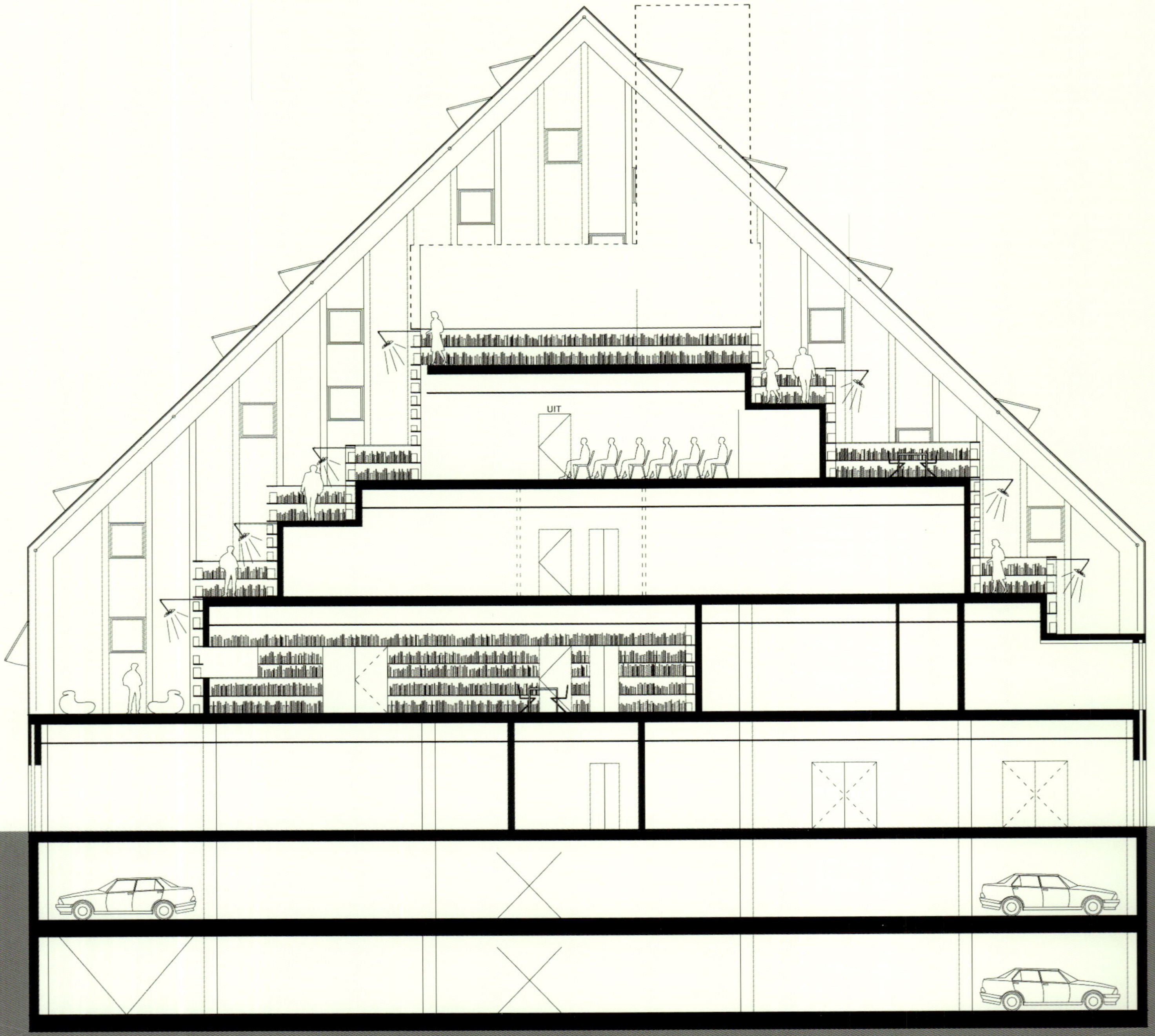

UIT

MVRDV

An acronym for its founding members, MVRDV was founded in 1993 in Rotterdam by Winy Maas, Jacob van Rijs, and Nathalie de Vries. By focusing on rational design, which takes into account statistical data gathered by the firm about the built world and the effect it has on the urban and natural environment, it aims to make an impact in decades to come. Along with producing over 600 projects, the firm also leads The Why Factory, a think tank run in conjunction with the Delft University of Technology that focuses on imagining what cities of the future will look like.

One possible prescription is using structures to advertise their contents, which is the case with the Spijkenisse Book Mountain, a public library located close to the Port of Rotterdam that was completed by the firm in 2012. Featuring 480 meters of bookshelves, the stacks are built in such a way that from a distance, they look like a rocky outgrowth. The construction is topped by a glass pyramid, which invites viewers from the outside to come in and read, while at the same time filling the space with natural light. The Book Mountain is connected to an adjacent "library quarter," which features forty-two housing spaces. With various references to Spijkenisse's agricultural past, including the peaked shape of the exterior structure and the recycled flowerpots used to make the bookshelves, the compound is reflective of MVRDV's vision of a more collective and community-driven future for mankind.

Top: Winy Maas, Nathalie de Vries,
and Jacob van Rijs of MVRDV.
Bottom: Rendering of the Spijkenisse
Book Mountain Library.

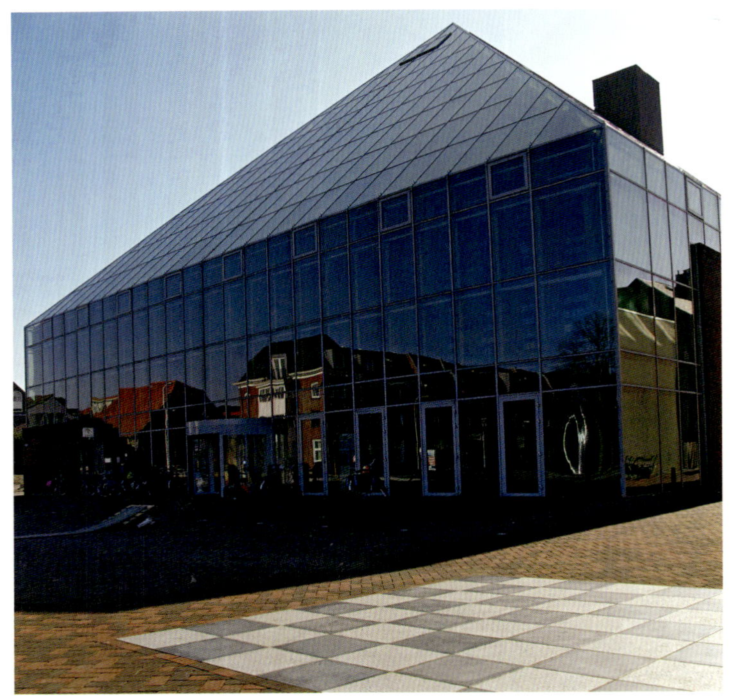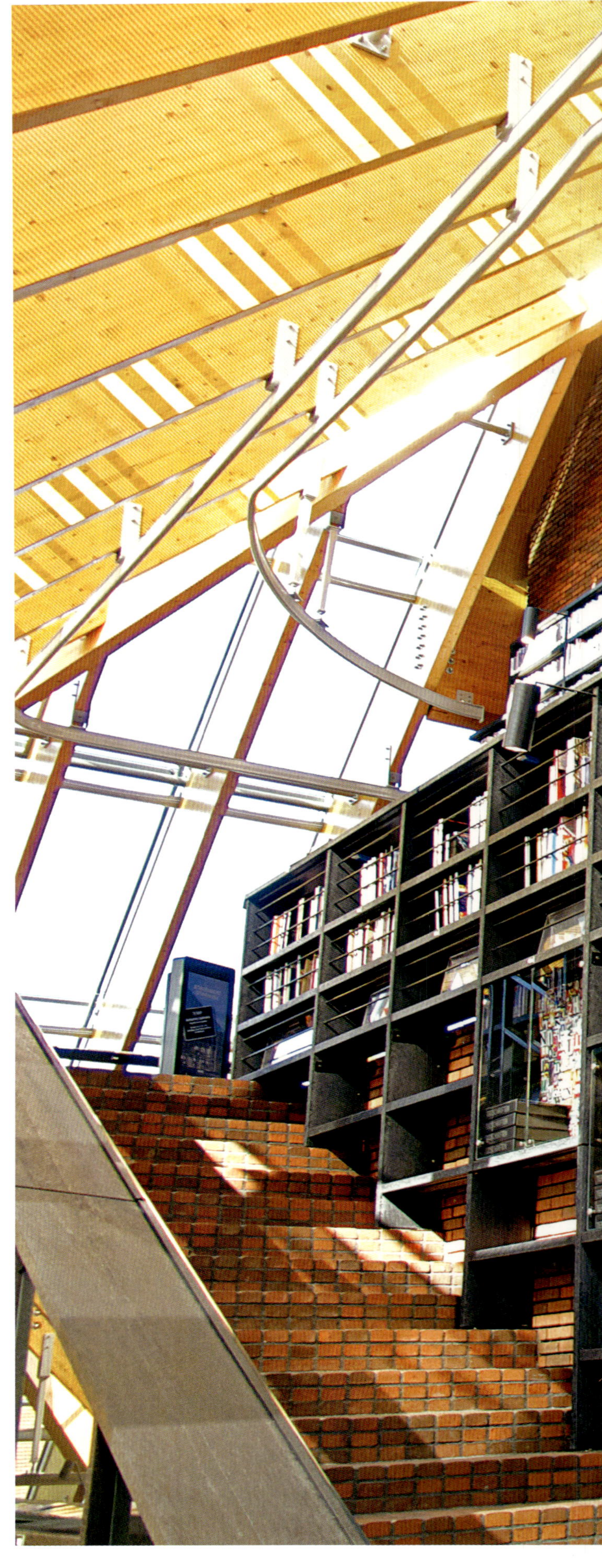

MVRDV. Spijkenisse Book Mountain Library,
Rotterdam, Netherlands, 2012.

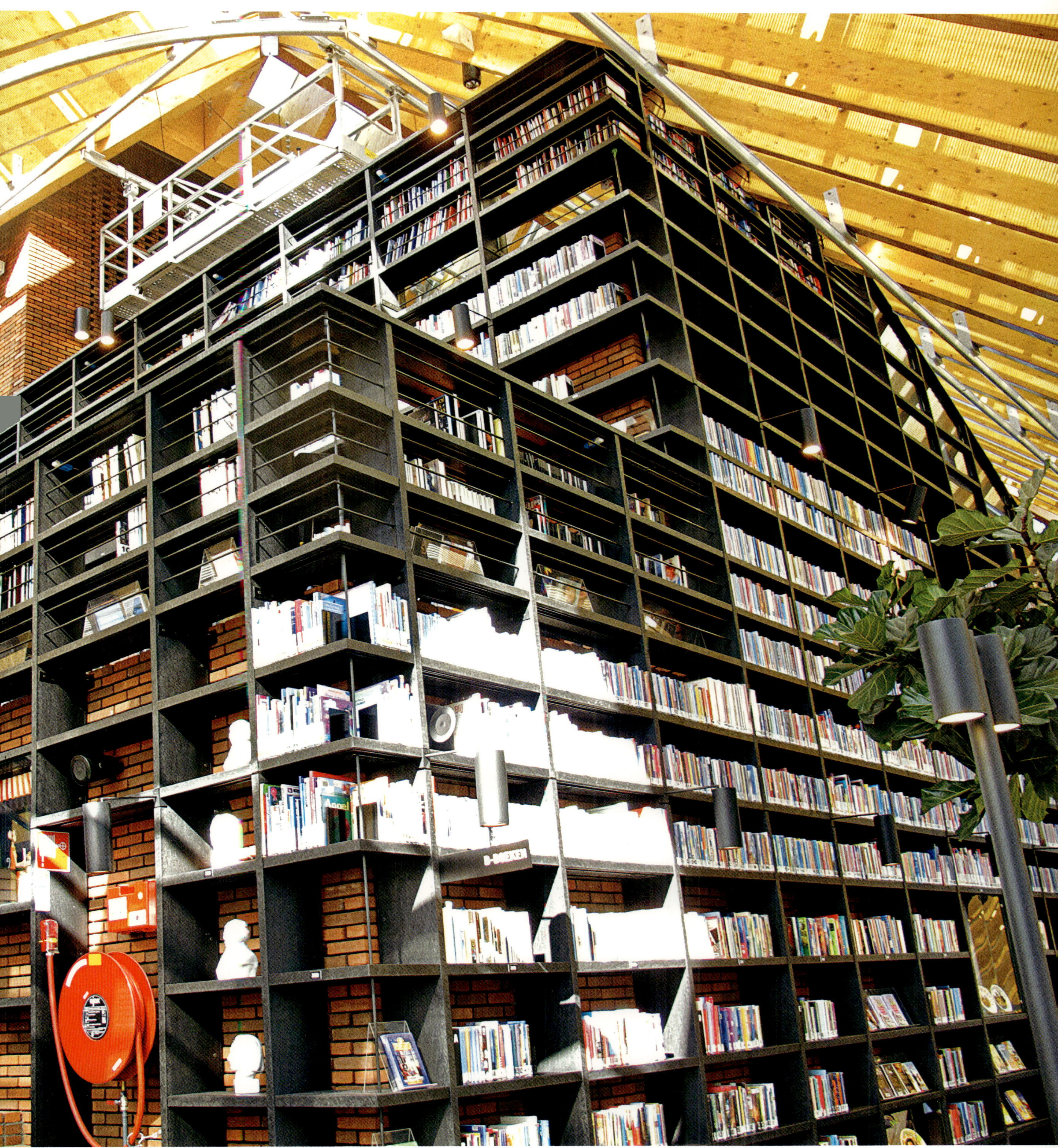

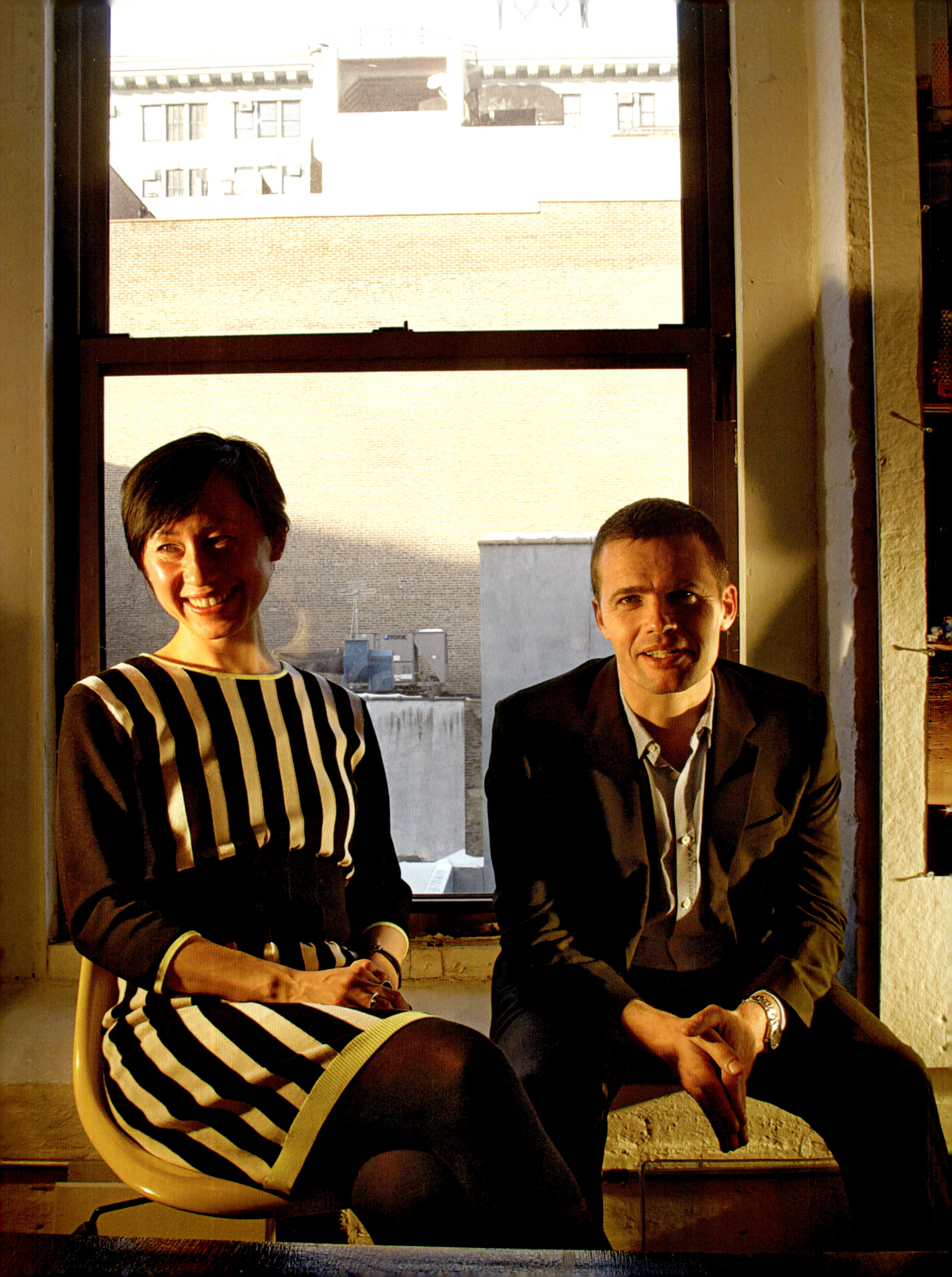

nARCHITECTS

In the dense urban landscape of New York City, light and air are precious commodities: difficult to find in old structures, and even more difficult to harness in new constructions, especially tightly zoned neighborhoods like the Lower East Side. In the Switch Building, a seven-story tower on Norfolk Street consisting of four floor-through apartments, a duplex penthouse, and a ground-floor-level art gallery, nArchitects managed to capture both light and air in abundance. Marked by curving bay windows on the facade that rise like flower petals greeting the sun, the apartments filter the street through to balconies in the back of each unit. The Switch Building, which is thus named because of the way the bay windows curve in different directions between different floors, promises residents subtle variations in light and shadow thanks to the pattern on its facade.

It is the first residential project completed by the firm, which is perhaps best known for the 30,000-square-foot bamboo installation constructed at MoMA PS1 in 2004 as the Young Architects Program winner. Founded in 1999 by Canadian-born architect Eric Bunge and Vietnamese-born Mimi Hoang, the young New York-based firm has recently received major commissions from the Department of Design and Construction in New York City, for whom they are designing a diesel pump that will improve traffic patterns, along with a new electrical transformer building. Ongoing work also includes the design of the Wyckoff House Museum in Brooklyn and the Pierscape at Chicago's Navy Pier. Most notably, nArchitects won a commission from New York City to design a micro-unit building in Manhattan—completion of the project is slated for 2015 and will bring even more visibility to the fledgling firm.

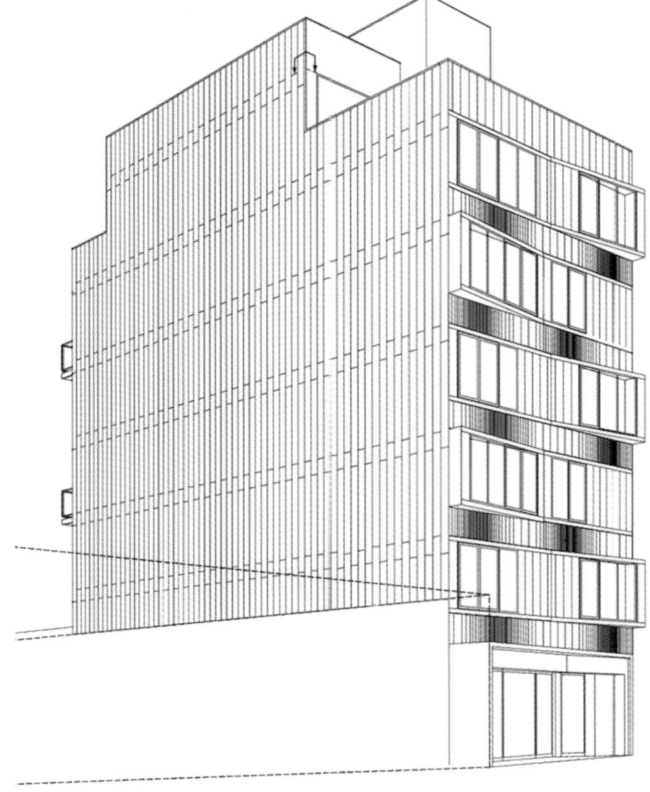

Rendering of the Switch Building.
Opposite: Mimi Hoang and Eric Bunge of nArchitects.

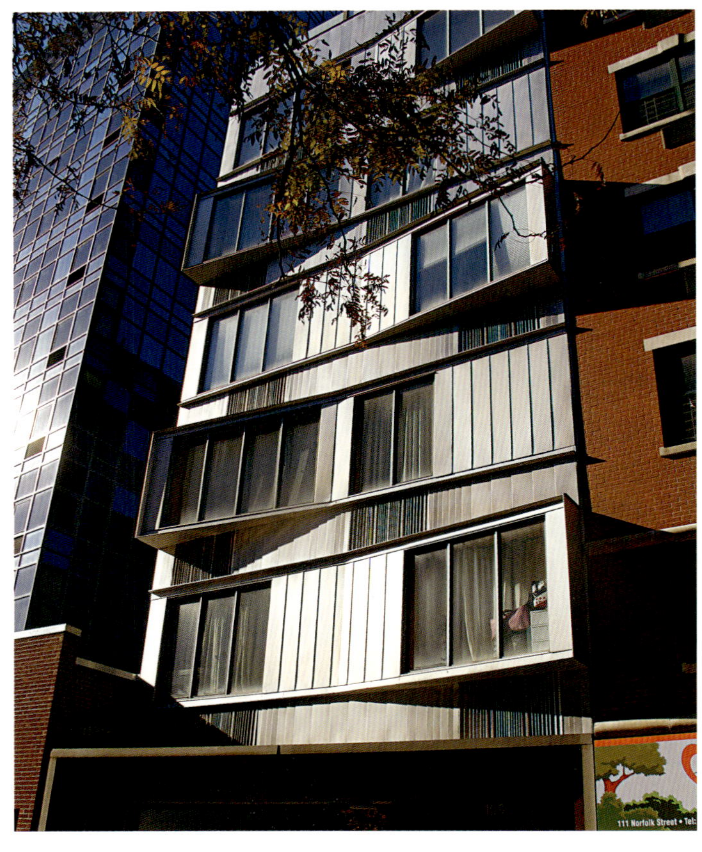

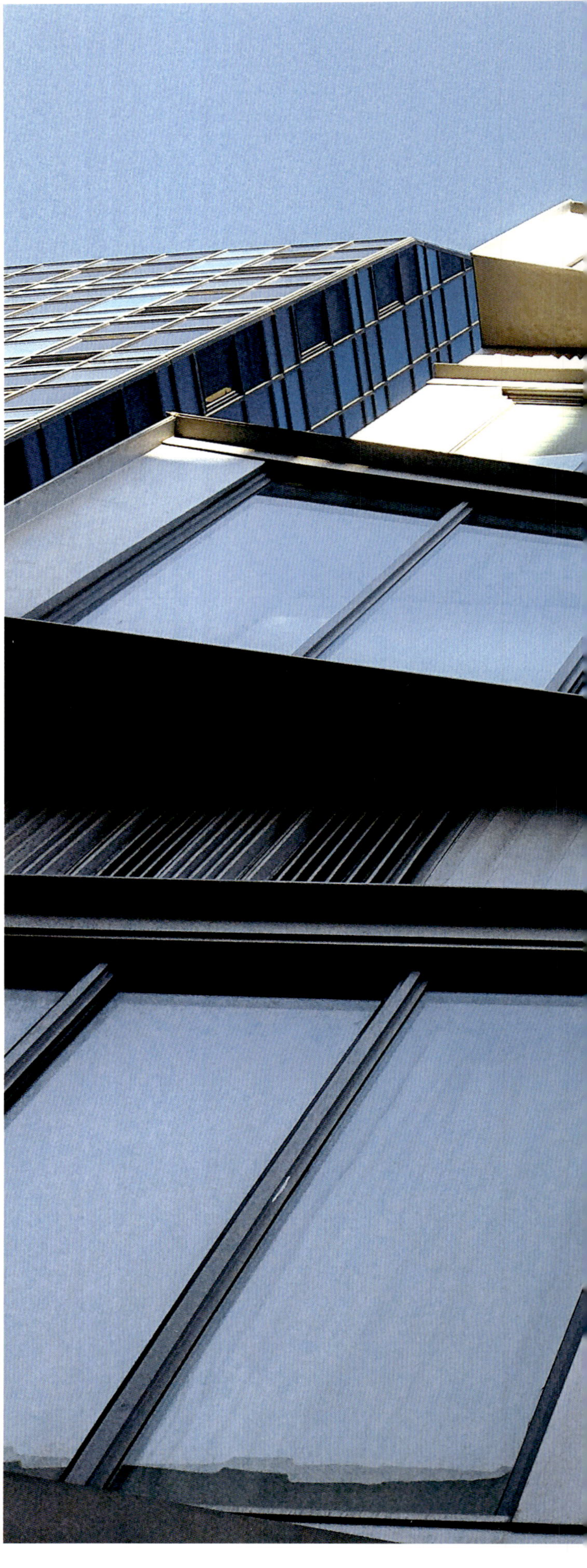

nArchitects, PLLC. Switch Building,
New York City, 2007.

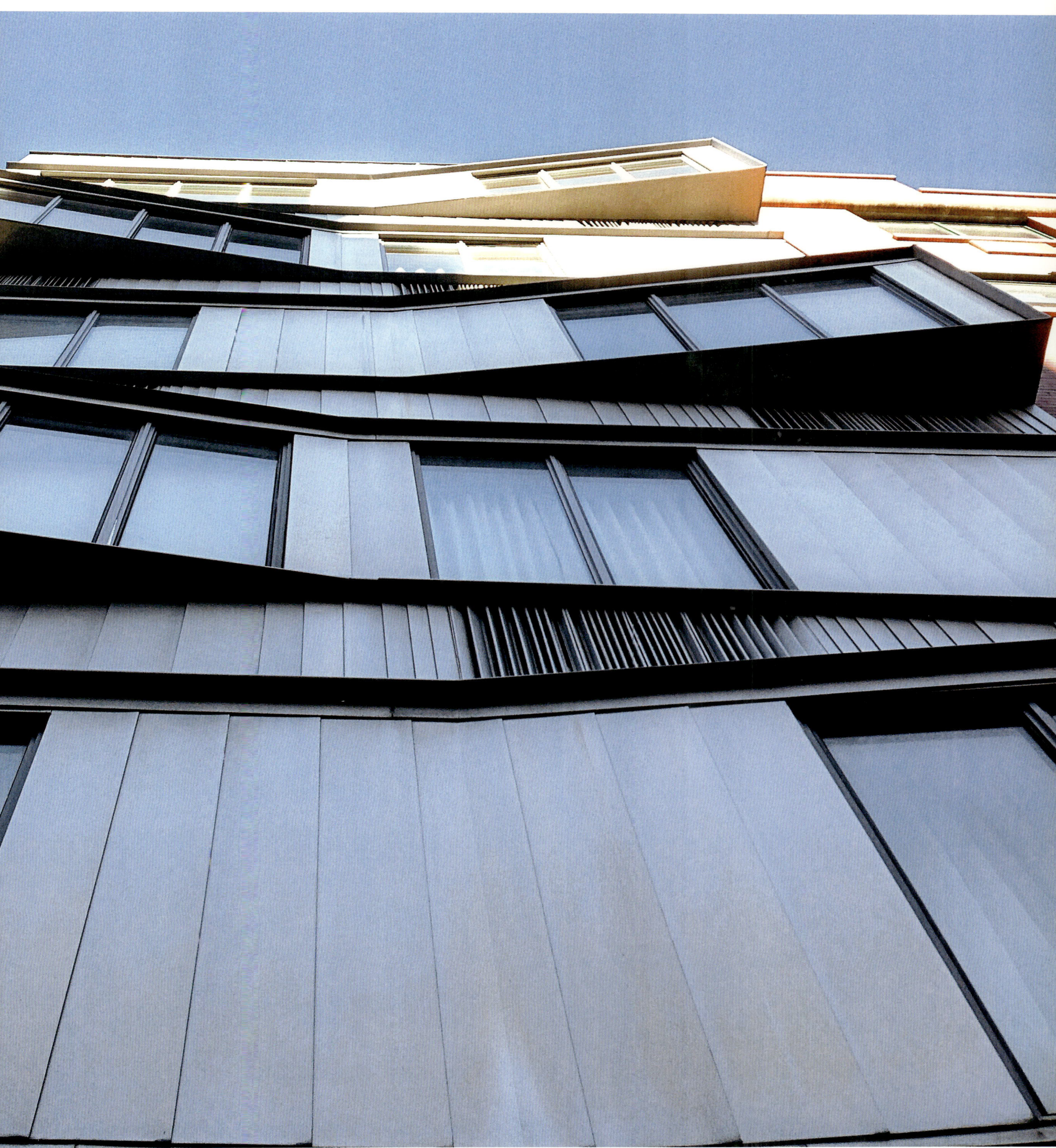

DOMINIQUE PERRAULT

One way to prevent an industrial building from becoming a blight on a natural landscape is to turn the building itself into a mirror that reflects said environment. Such was the thinking behind the Aplix Factory (1999), a building designed by Dominique Perrault Architecture. Clad in long sheets of woven steel, the exterior of the structure, which is located in the lush Le Cellier-sur-Loire in France, resembles a land art installation in the vein of Robert Smithson more than it does a functional building. It does function, however, as a factory that produces fascinating products for the French company that created hook and loop fasteners in the 1950s. Housing administrative offices, storage, a cafeteria, and production spaces, the monumental structure, though over three hundred meters long, reflects the environment so completely that it almost seems to disappear, a feat so magical that it won the first prize for the best industrial building at the World Architecture Awards in 2001.

Creating structures that become an integral part of the landscape is the mission of Dominique Perrault himself, a French architect best known for having won the competition to build the National French Library in 1989 at the age of thirty-six. Since completing the latter compound in 1996, Perrault has worked on a number of high-profile projects including the campus of Ewha University in Seoul (2008), the Olympic tennis center in Madrid (2009), and the Fukoku Tower in Osaka, Japan (2010). On a larger scale, he has also done extensive work as an urban planner, including developing the Garonne riverbanks in Bordeaux and Île de Nantes, and the Pudong business district in Shanghai, China.

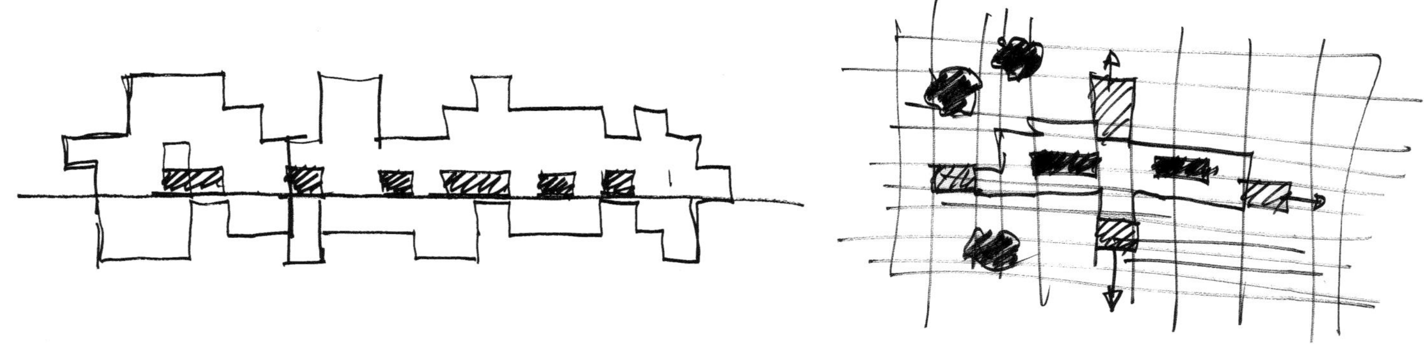

Sketches of the Aplix Factory.
Opposite: Dominique Perrault.

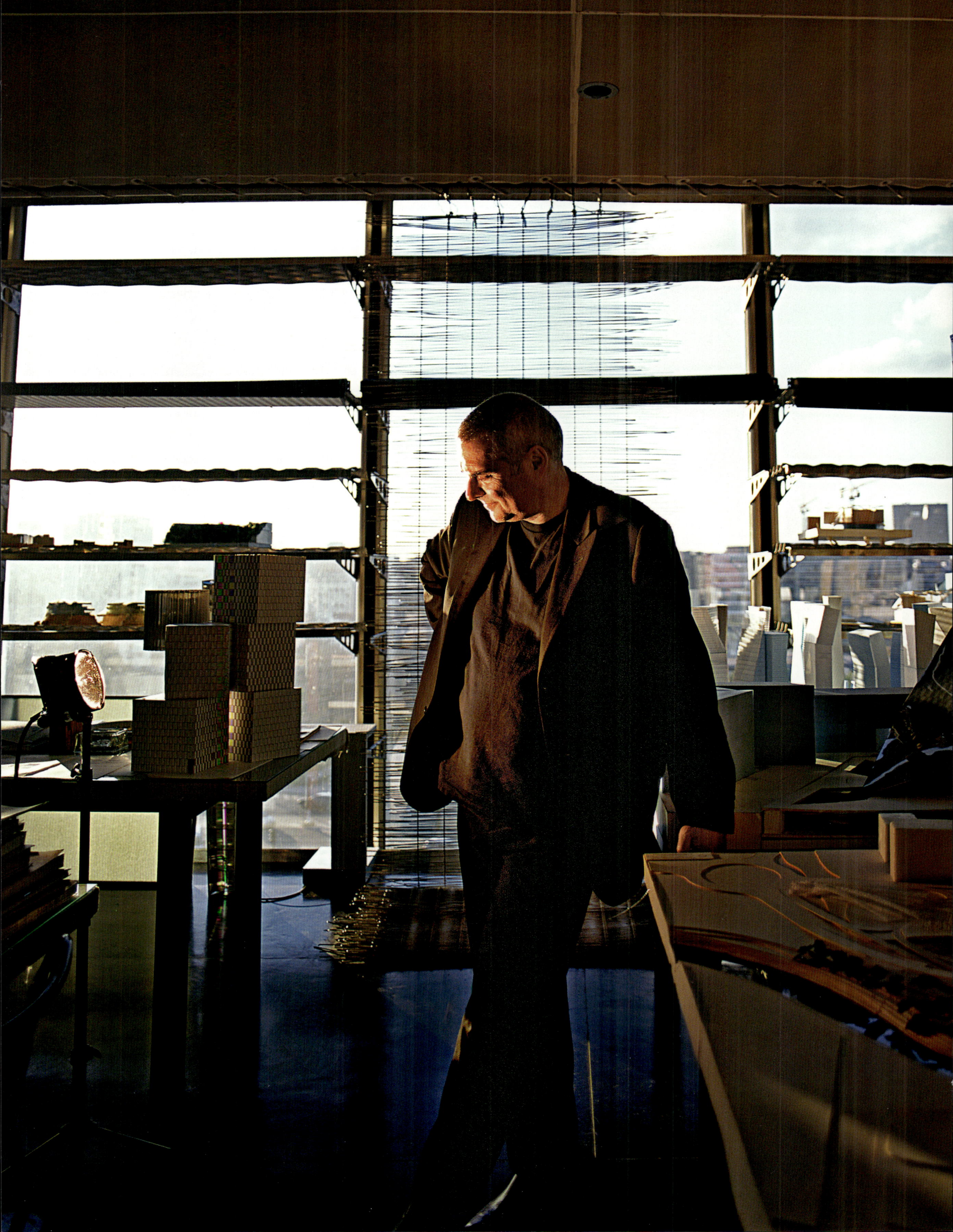

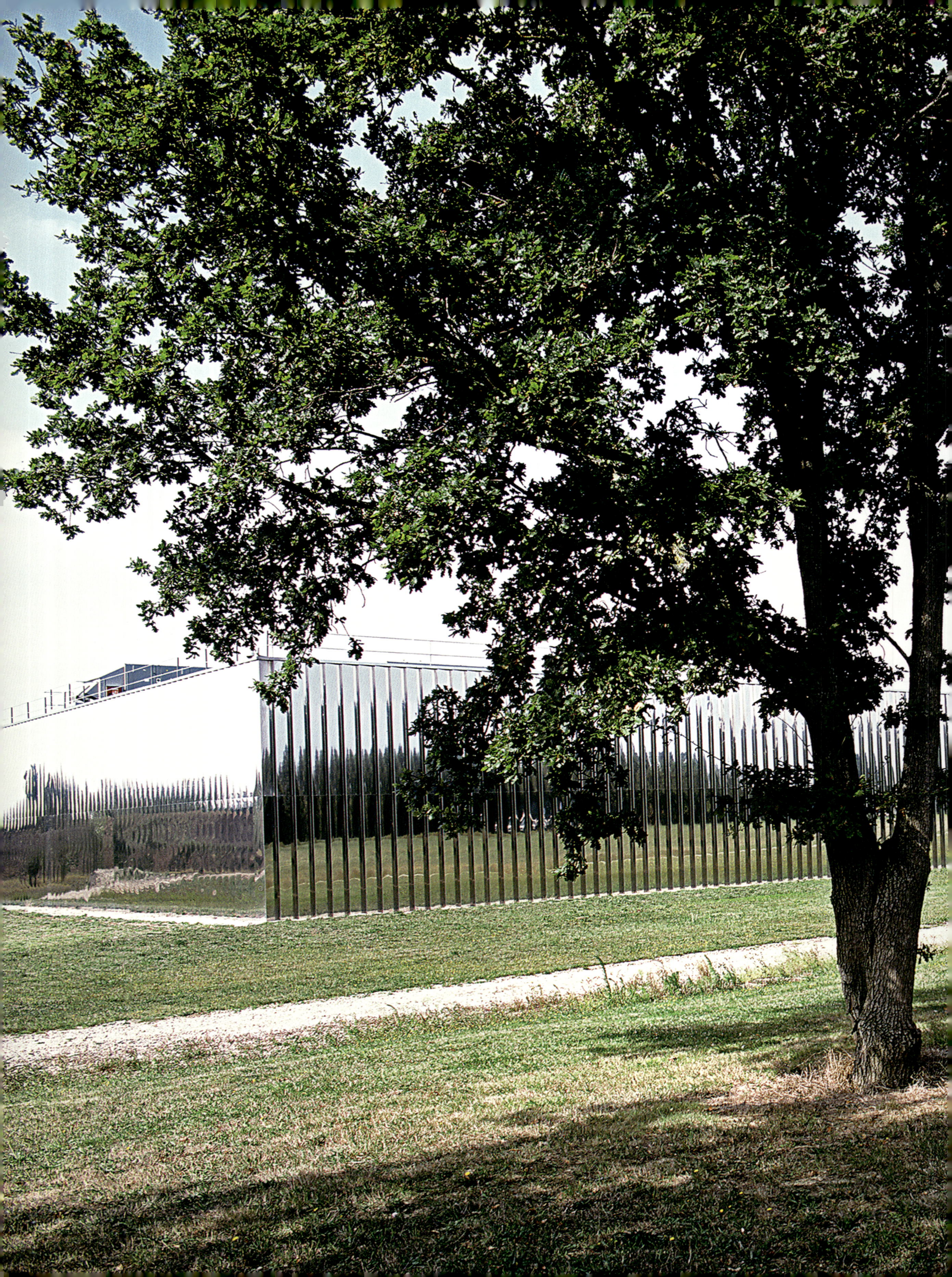

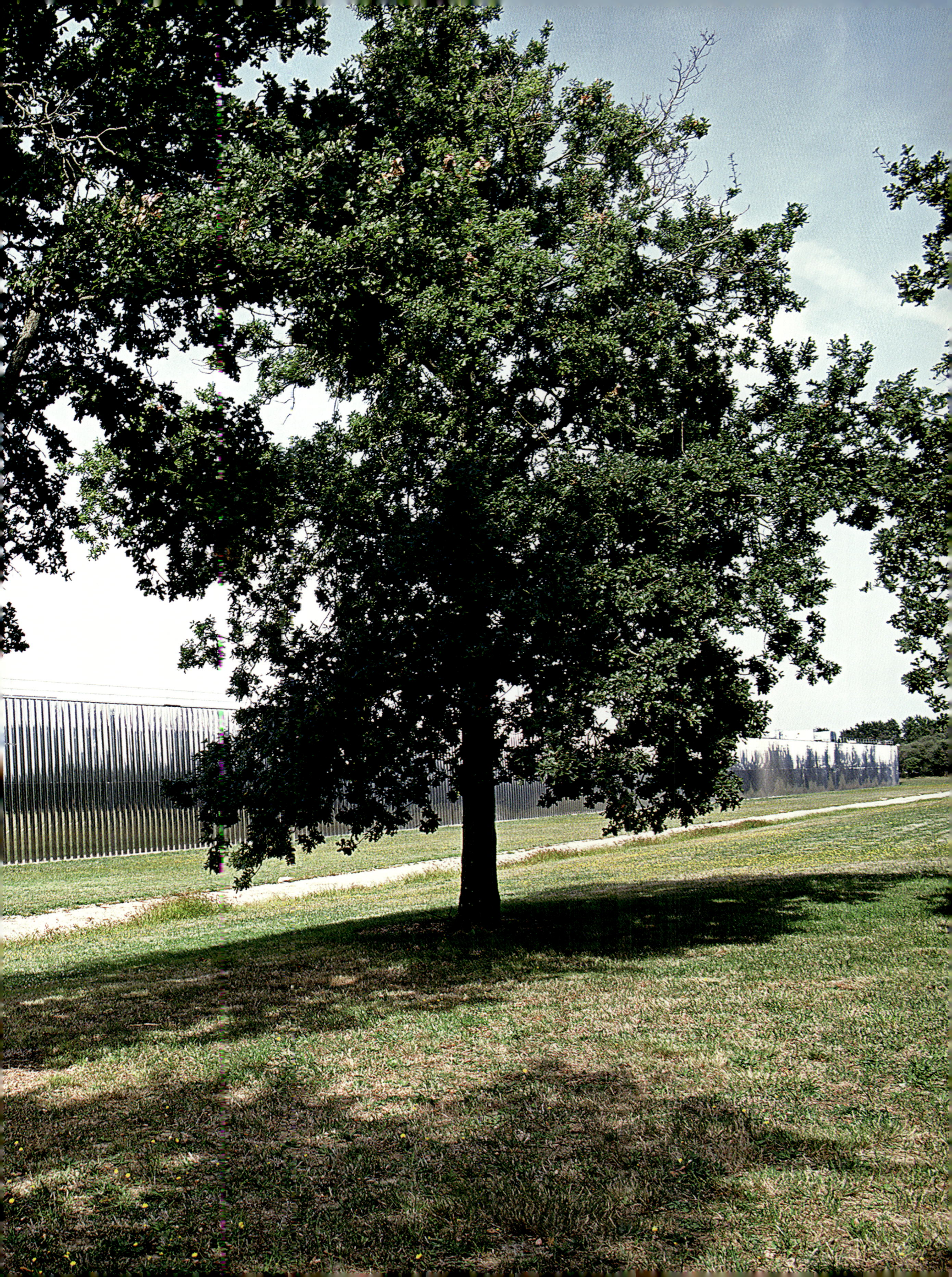

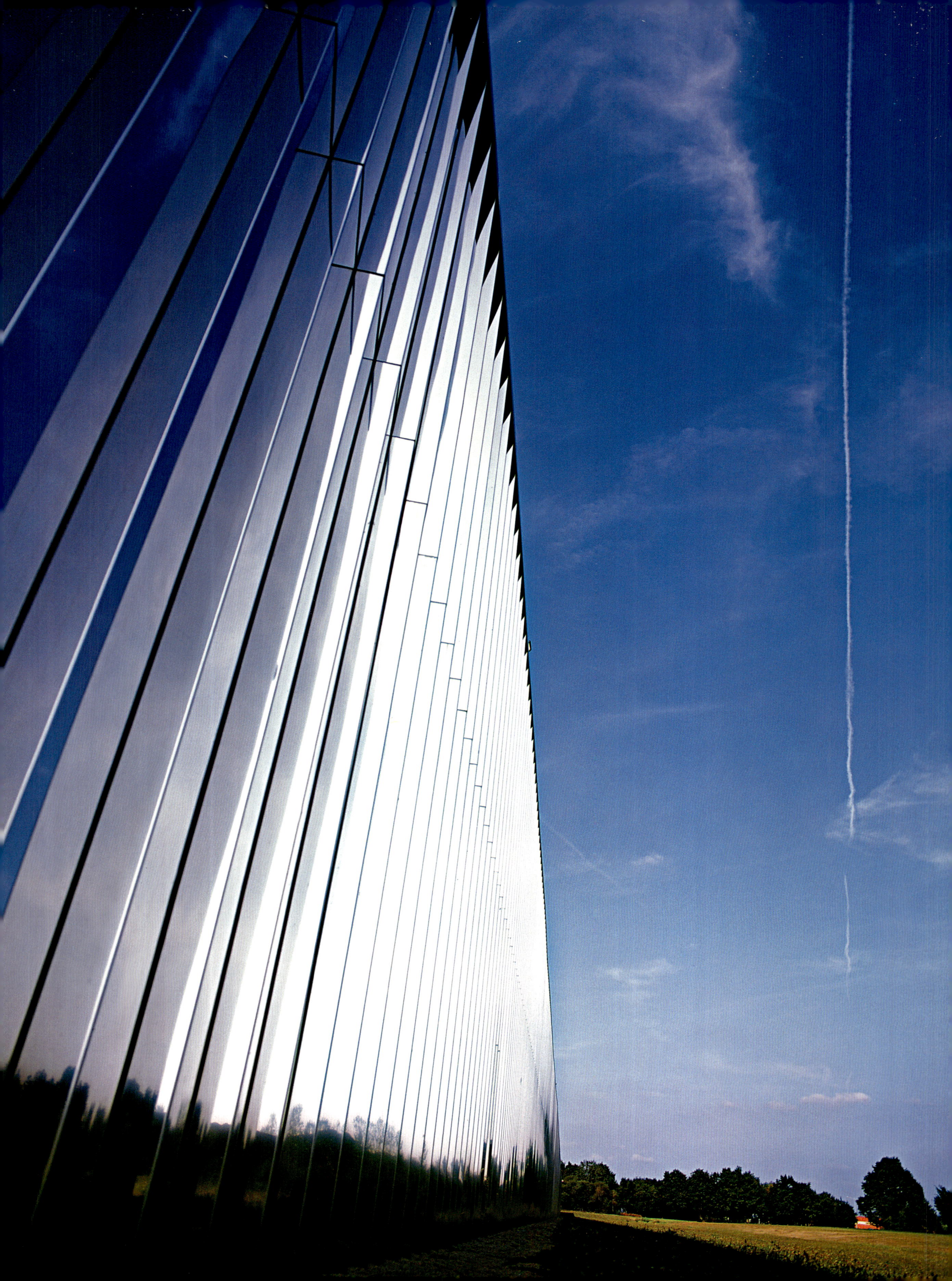

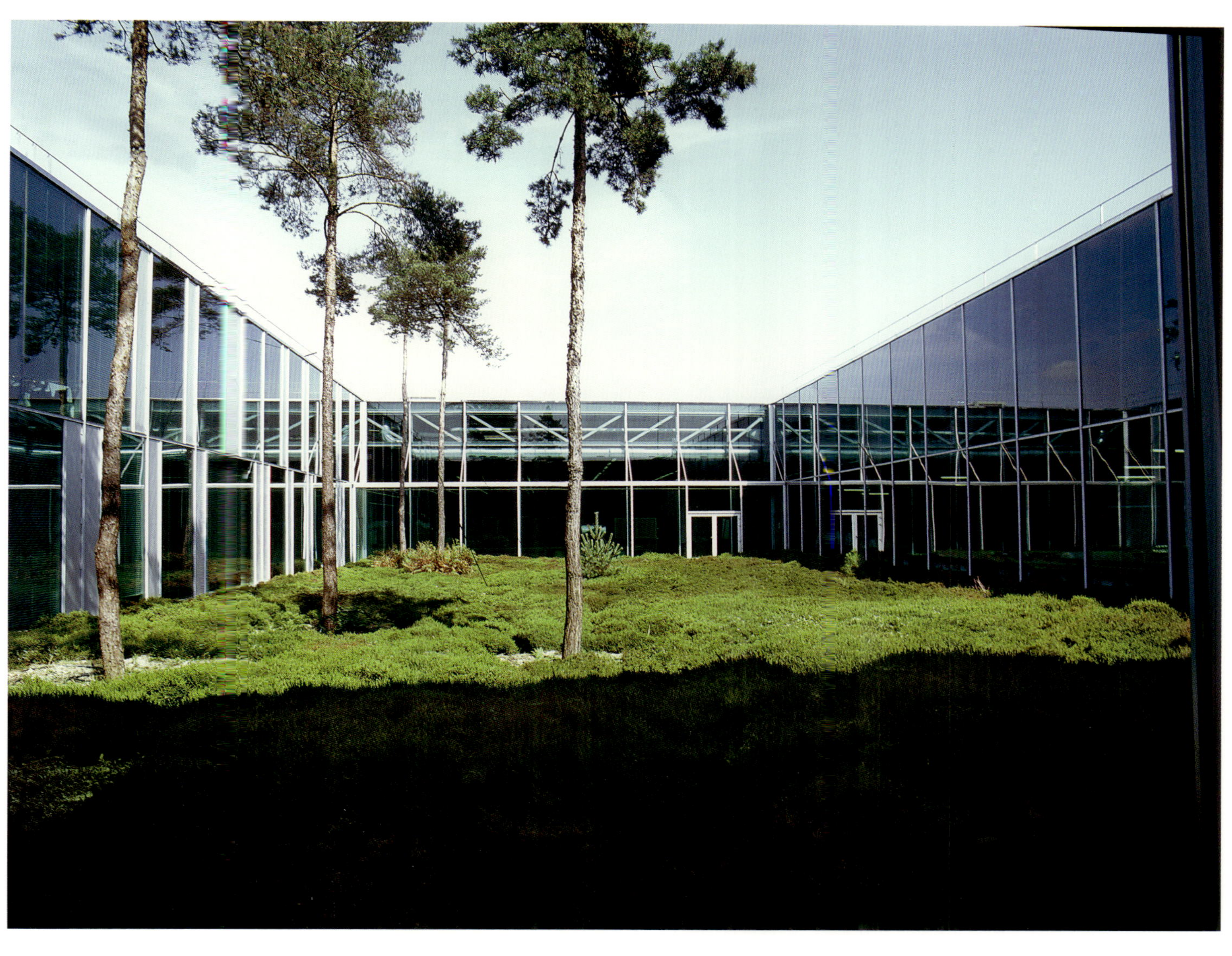

Above, opposite, and previous pages: Domin que Perrault Architecture. Aplix Factory, Nantes, France, 1999.

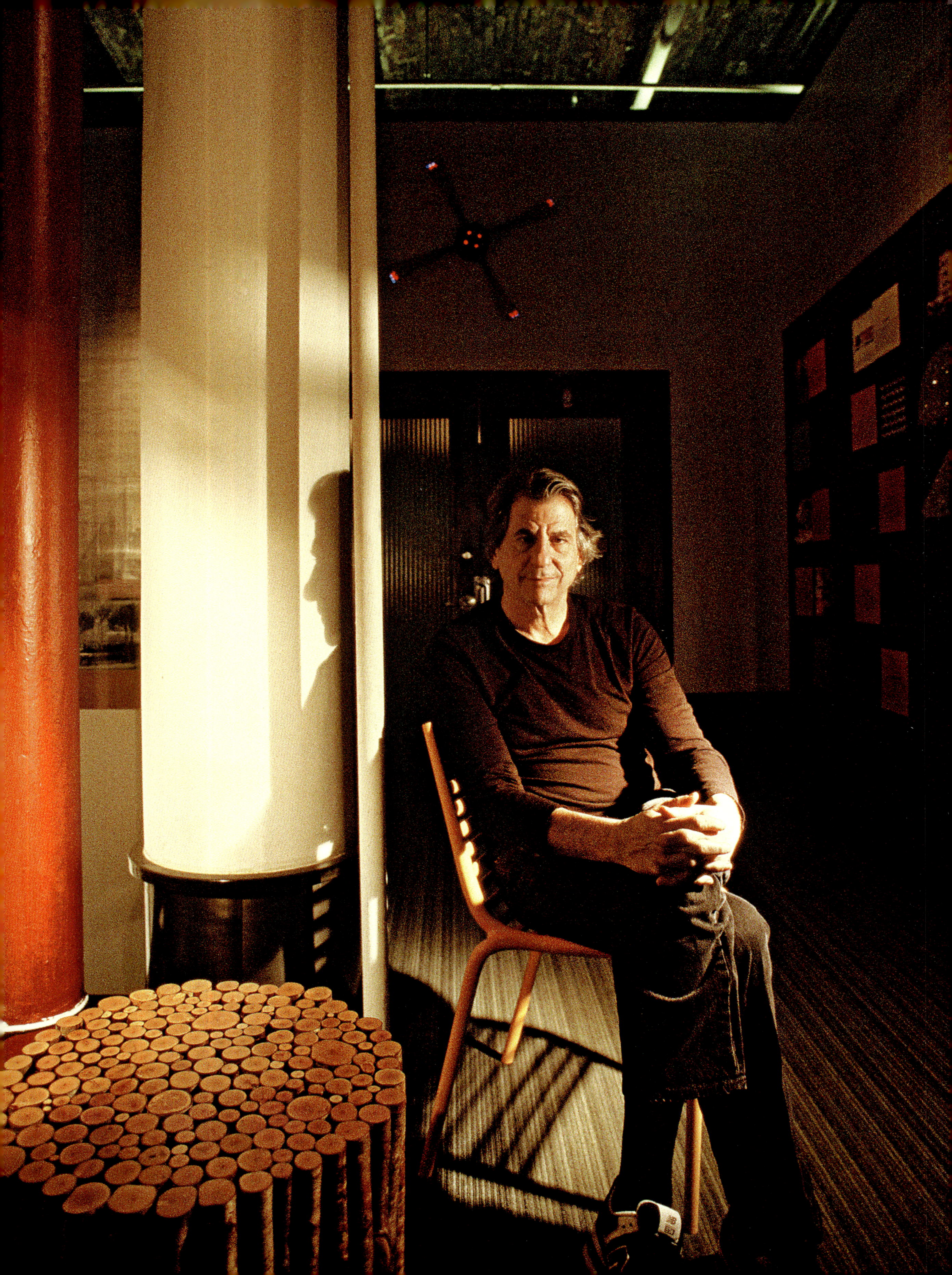

DAVID ROCKWELL

The Rockwell Group, founded in New York in 1984 by David Rockwell, is very much concerned with the theatrical possibilities of built environments. Known just as much for its architecture as it is for its special effects and set designs, which include the stage for the 82nd annual Academy Awards, the firm was the perfect fit to transform an underutilized office space and parking garage at Lincoln Center into the Elinor Bunin Munroe Film Center, an institution devoted to cinema history and programming in the twenty-first century. Consisting of two theaters, an amphitheater, and a café, the structure, commissioned by the Film Society of Lincoln Center, consists of a facade of windows that invites pedestrians to enter the building. Measuring 17,500 square feet, the building is fully equipped with state-of-the-art technology, opening up the possibility for numerous types of programming, including digital conferencing and multimedia storytelling. It is one of the many buildings recently renovated in conjunction with the $1.2 billion rejuvenation of the Lincoln Center campus, headed by the firm Diller Scofidio and Renfro.

Along with the film center, the Rockwell Group is responsible for designing sets for Broadway musicals such as *Hairspray* and *Kinky Boots*, as well as the recent construction of a portable theater for TED, a nonprofit organization that hosts speeches at various locations around the world. Other notable projects include the JetBlue terminal at John F. Kennedy Airport in New York, and the National Center for Civil and Human Rights, which opened in downtown Atlanta in summer 2014.

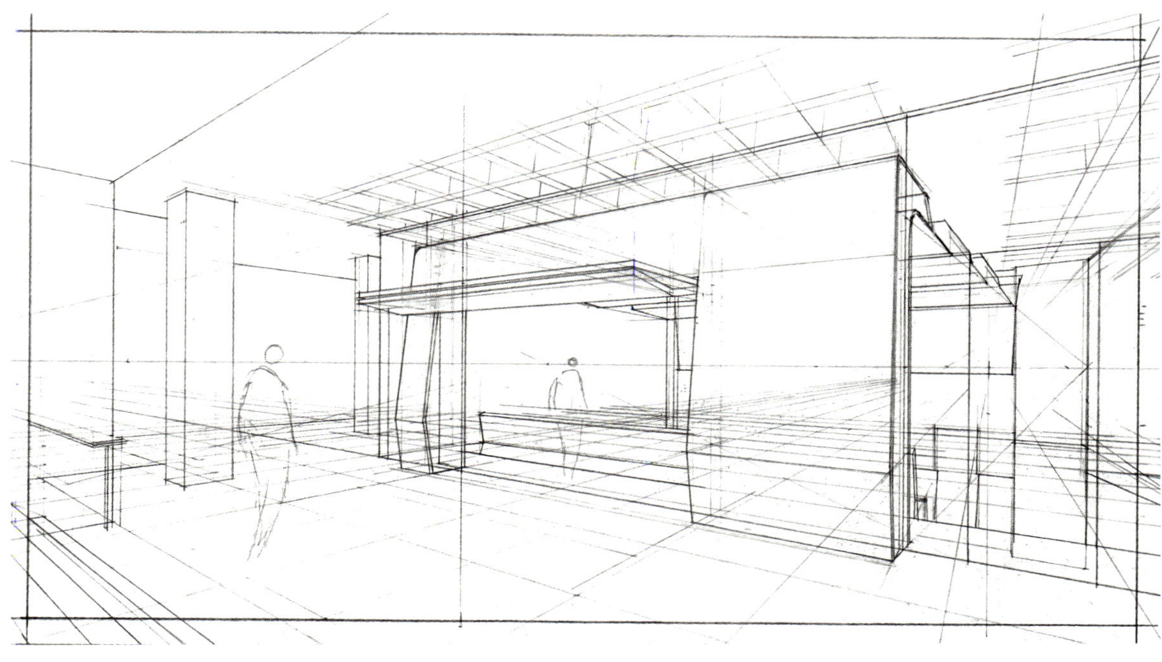

Sketch of the Elinor Bunin Munroe Film Center.
Opposite: David Rockwell.
Following pages: Rockwell Group. Elinor Bunin Munroe Film Center, New York City, 2011.

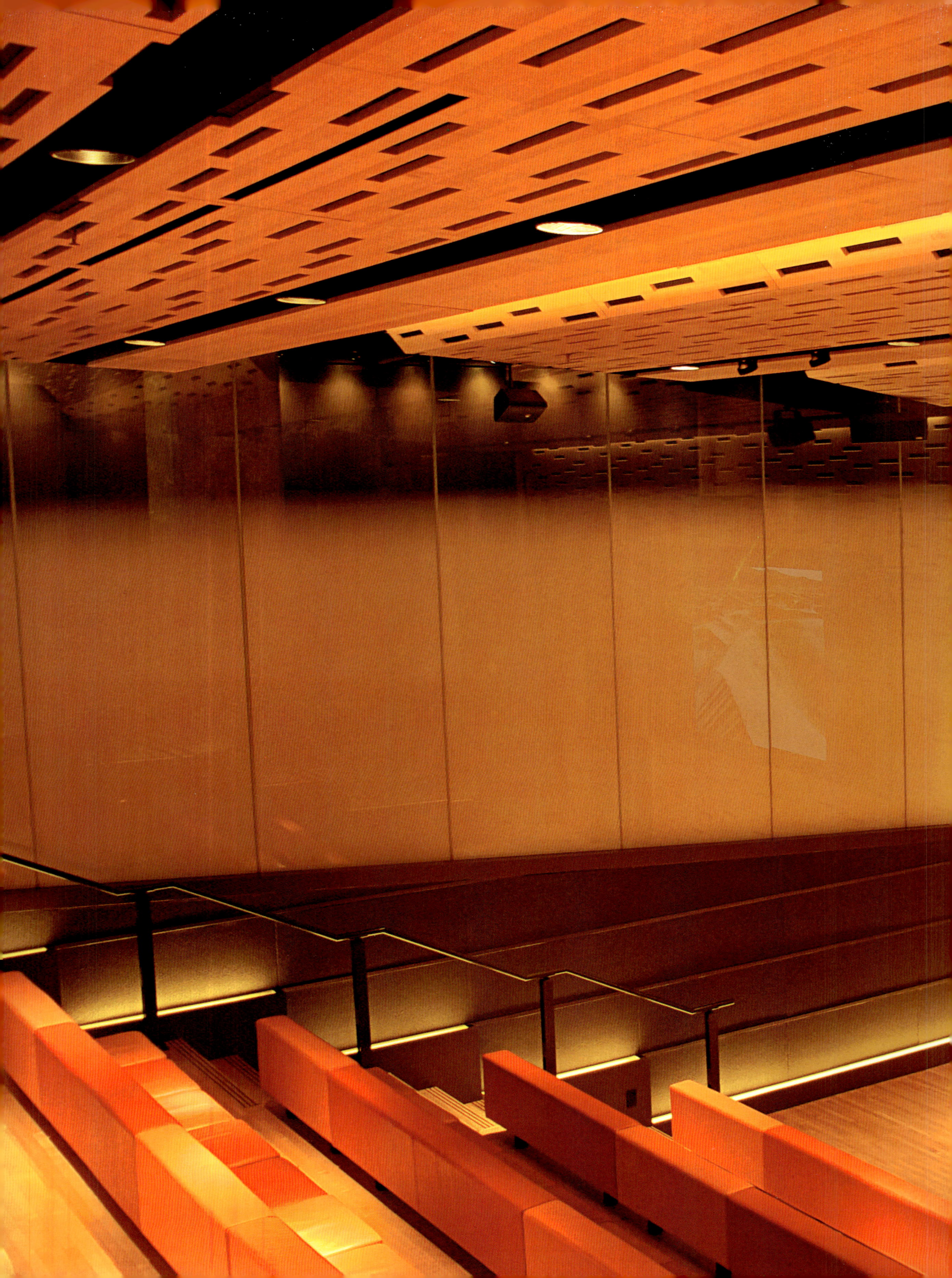

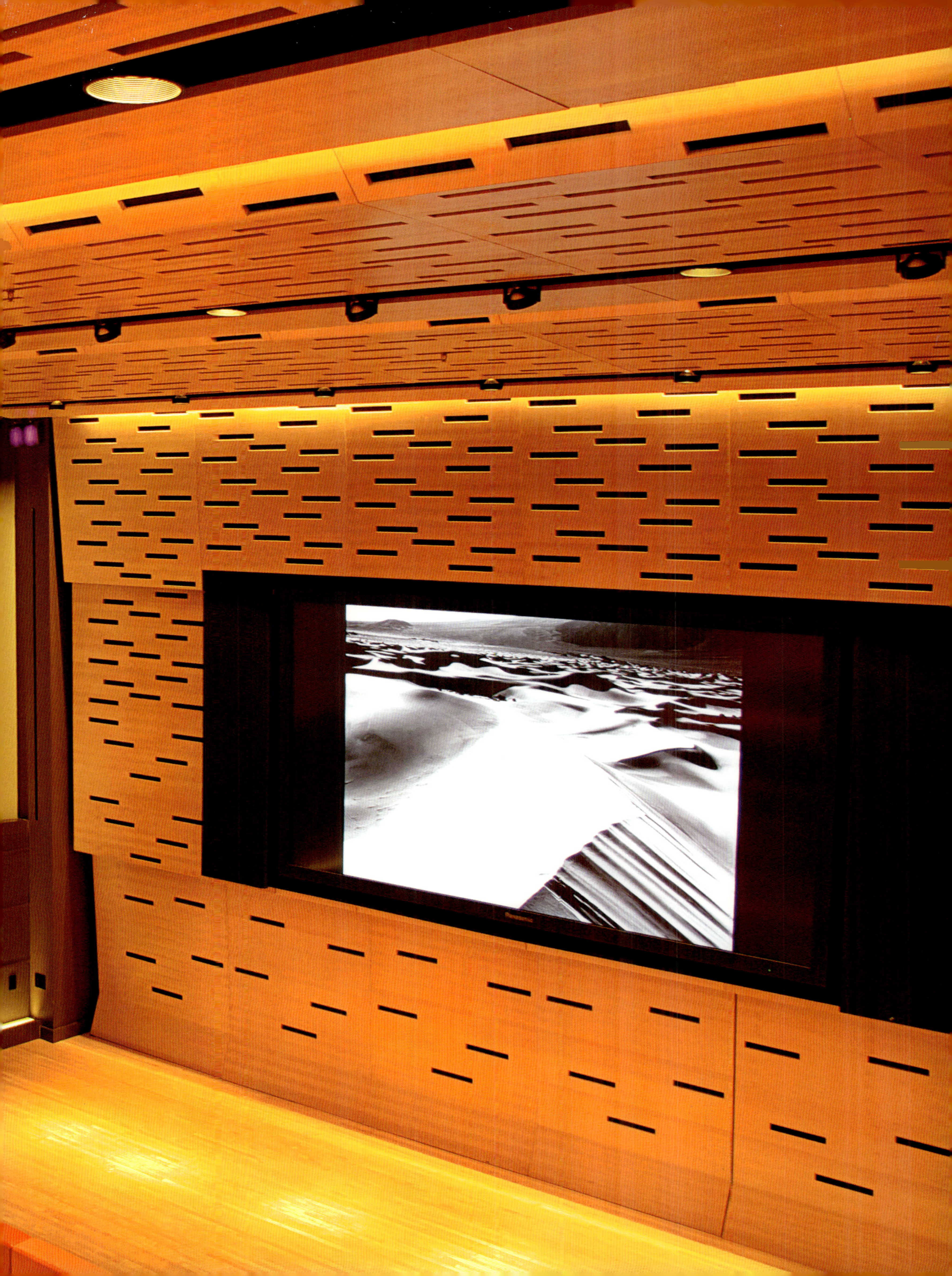

FERNANDO ROMERO

Built to house a collection of seventy thousand objects from the fifteenth to the mid-twentieth century accumulated by Mexican billionaire Carlos Slim, the Soumaya Museum is named after its founder's late wife. It is also designed by his son-in-law, Fernando Romero, a young architect who apprenticed for Rem Koolhaas and Jean Nouvel before founding his own firm, Fernando Romero Enterprise (FR-EE) in Mexico City in 2000. His latest construction for his father-in-law—for whom he is also designing an entire ten-acre business campus around the museum that locals have taken to calling "Ciudad Slim," or "Slim City"—is located in the Plaza Carso in Polanco, Mexico City, right across from the Museo Jumex.

Although the collection at the Soumaya Museum is not contemporary, the building, a curved pedestal-shaped construction covered with 16,000 hexagonal tiles of mirrored steel, has a high-tech sheen that marks it firmly as a product of the twenty-first century. Designed using computer programs and inspired by native colonial ceramic tiled facades, the outer skin, which looks like the neck of an alien lizard, conceals an interior promenade that winds up the museum's six levels to a top gallery flooded with light from skylights on the roof. The interior recalls Frank Lloyd Wright's Guggenheim Museum in New York, but the exterior, which utilizes twenty-eight uniquely curved steel columns to create its sculptural form, is entirely singular.

The Soumaya Museum brought a rush of international attention to Romero, who has proven that his value lies far beyond nepotism. Along with the Soumaya Museum, he recently completed the G20 Convention Center (2012) in Los Cabos, Mexico, as well as a teahouse in Jinhua (2006), a small city in China.

Fernando Romero.

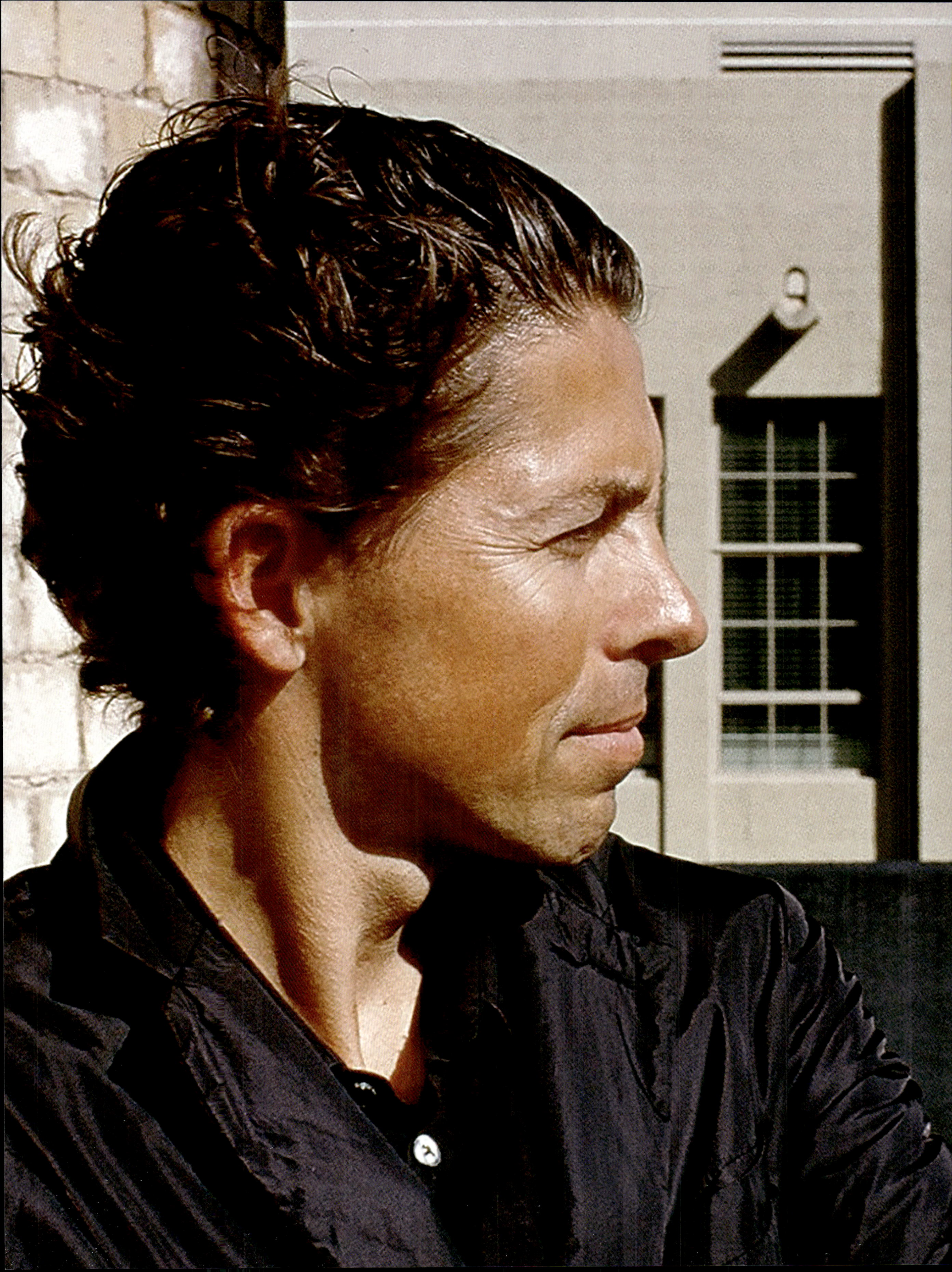

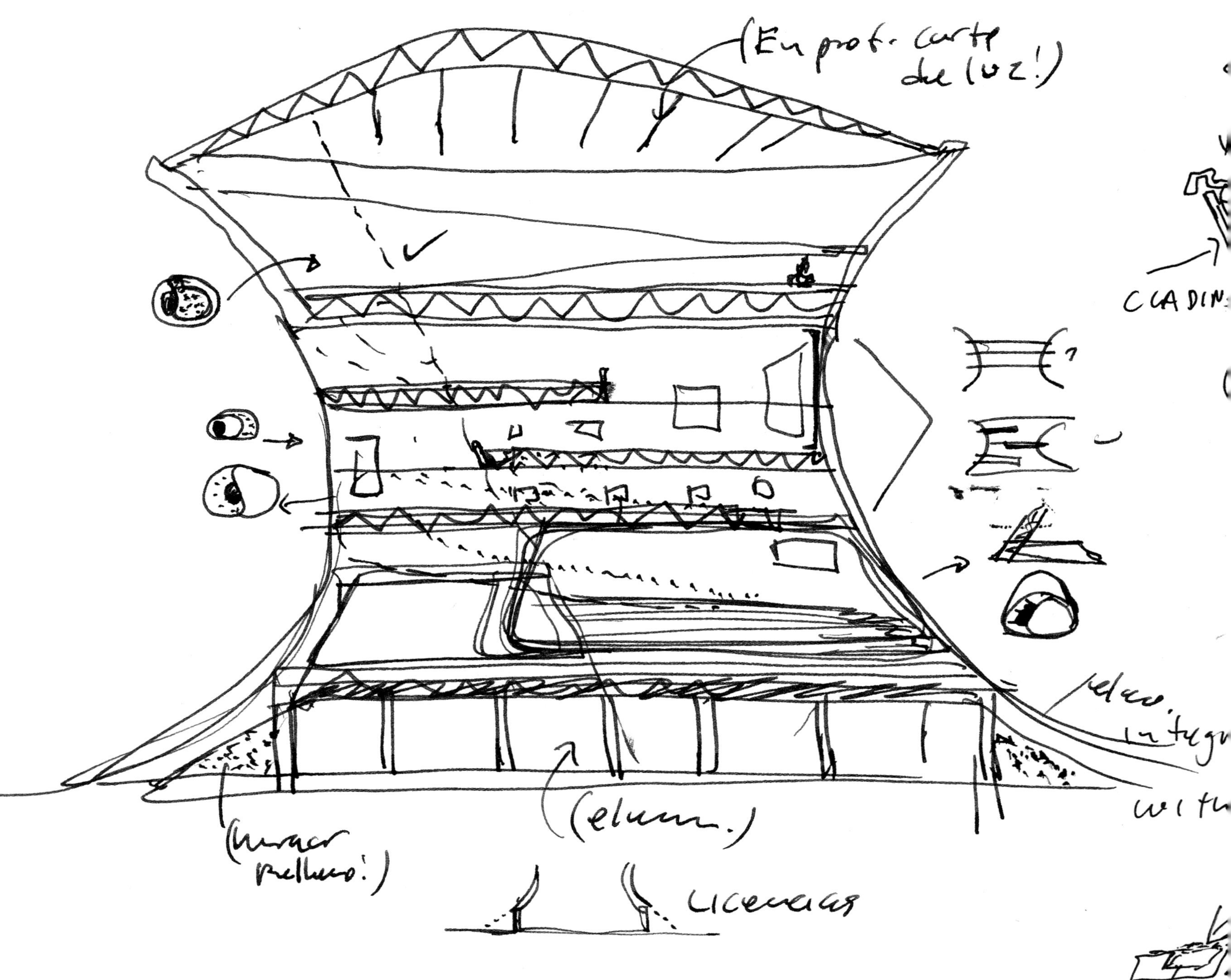

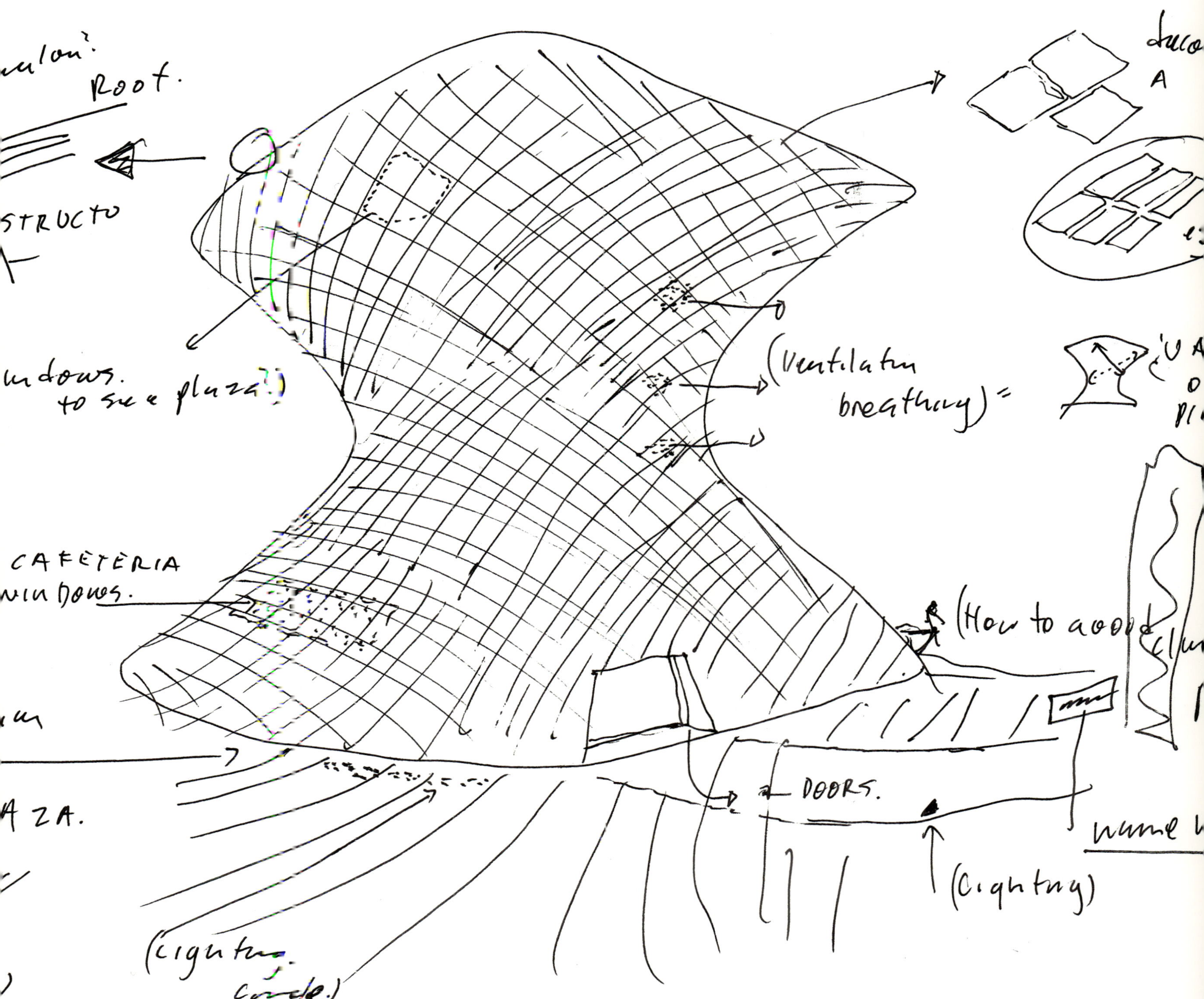
Roof.
STRUCTO
ndows.
to see a plaza)
CAFETERIA
windows.
ZA.
(Lighting.
circle.)
(Ventilation
breathing) =
(How to avoid
DOORS.
name
(Lighting)
A

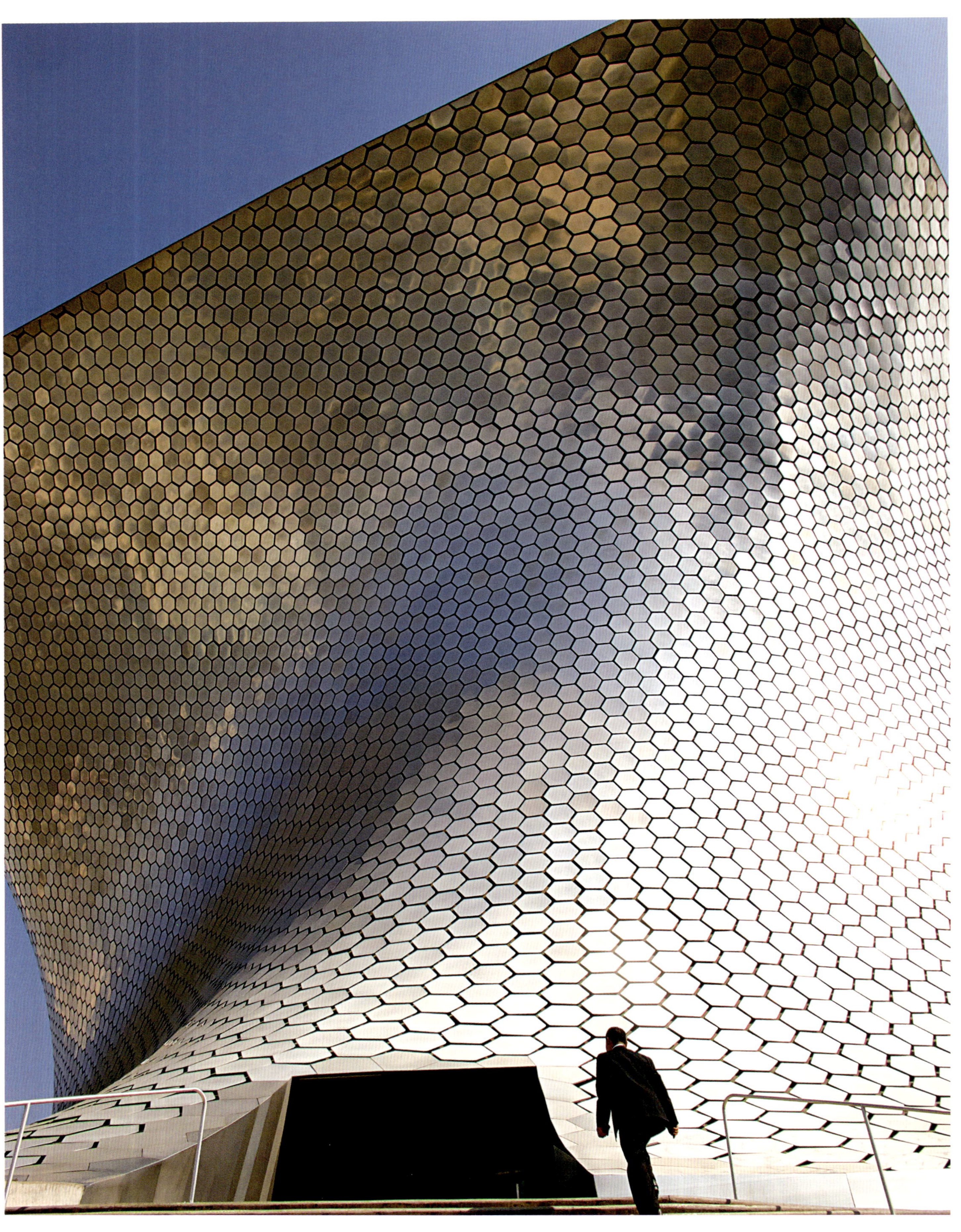

Fernando Romero Enterprise. Museo Soumaya,
Mexico City, Mexico, 2011.

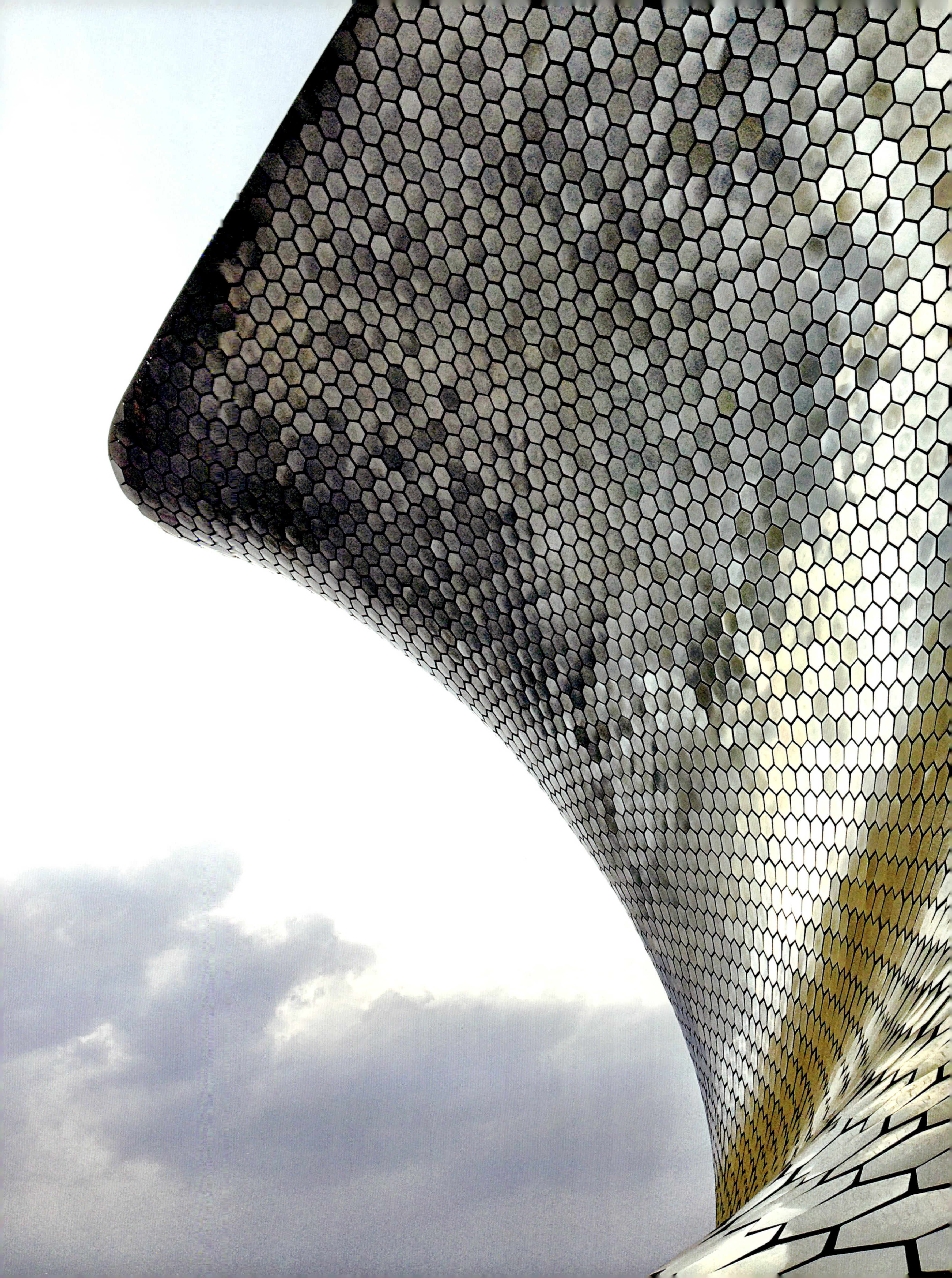

MOSHE SAFDIE

Mirroring the function of the think tank it was constructed for, the United States Institute of Peace, completed by Safdie Architects in 2011, has a roof that resembles the wings of a dove. Organized around two large atria—one that faces the Potomac River, and the other, the Lincoln Memorial—the structure, which is located on the National Mall, includes administrative offices, a library, a conference hall, and an educational center. The glass veils that protect the atria from the external world make the interior structure transparent—at night, the building glows from within. More than serving as a metaphor for the Congressionally-funded Institute's mission, which is to find nonviolent solutions for managing international violence, it has practical applications for the center's constant influx of international visitors—receptions for world leaders are frequently held in the expansive double atria. Its open facade, which invites ordinary people to peer inside, accomplishes one of Safdie Architects' main philosophies, which is to humanize the mega-scale of architecture—and in doing so, promotes an ideological mission of peaceful compromise.

Founded in 1967 by Moshe Safdie, who was born in Israel in 1938 and raised in Canada, the firm's first project was Habitat 67 at the World's Fair, one of the most iconic building projects of the twentieth century. Safdie has since worked on a number of high-profile projects, which include the Yitzhak Rabin Center (2010) in Tel Aviv, Israel; the Crystal Bridges Museum of American Art (2011) in Bentonville, Arkansas; and the Skirball Cultural Center (1996) in Los Angeles, California.

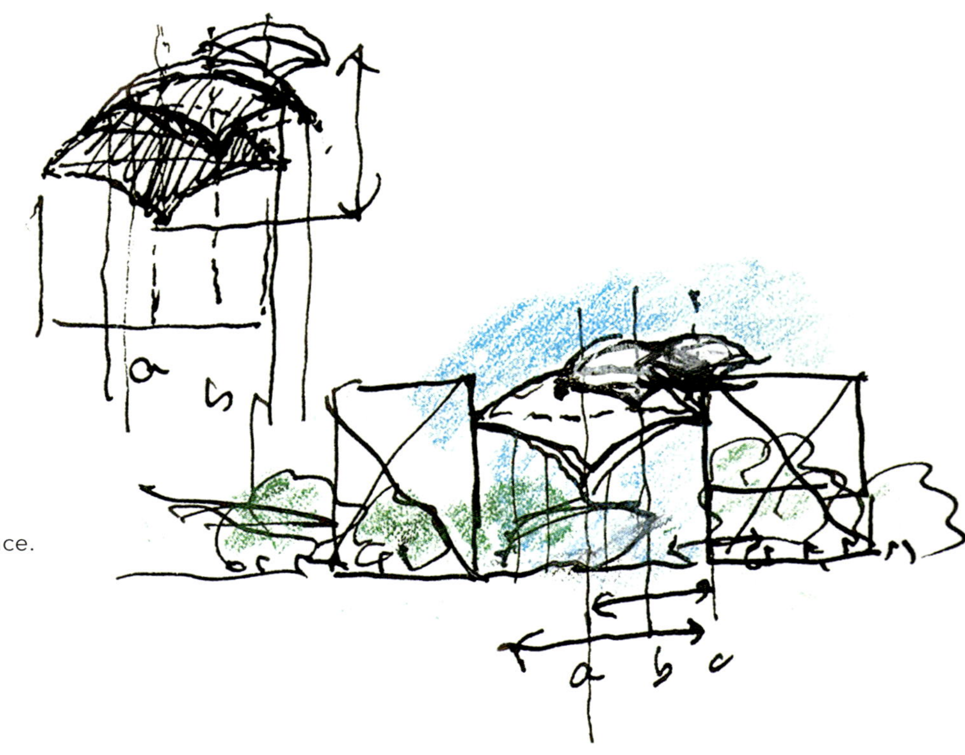

Sketches of the United States Institute of Peace.
Opposite: Moshe Safdie.

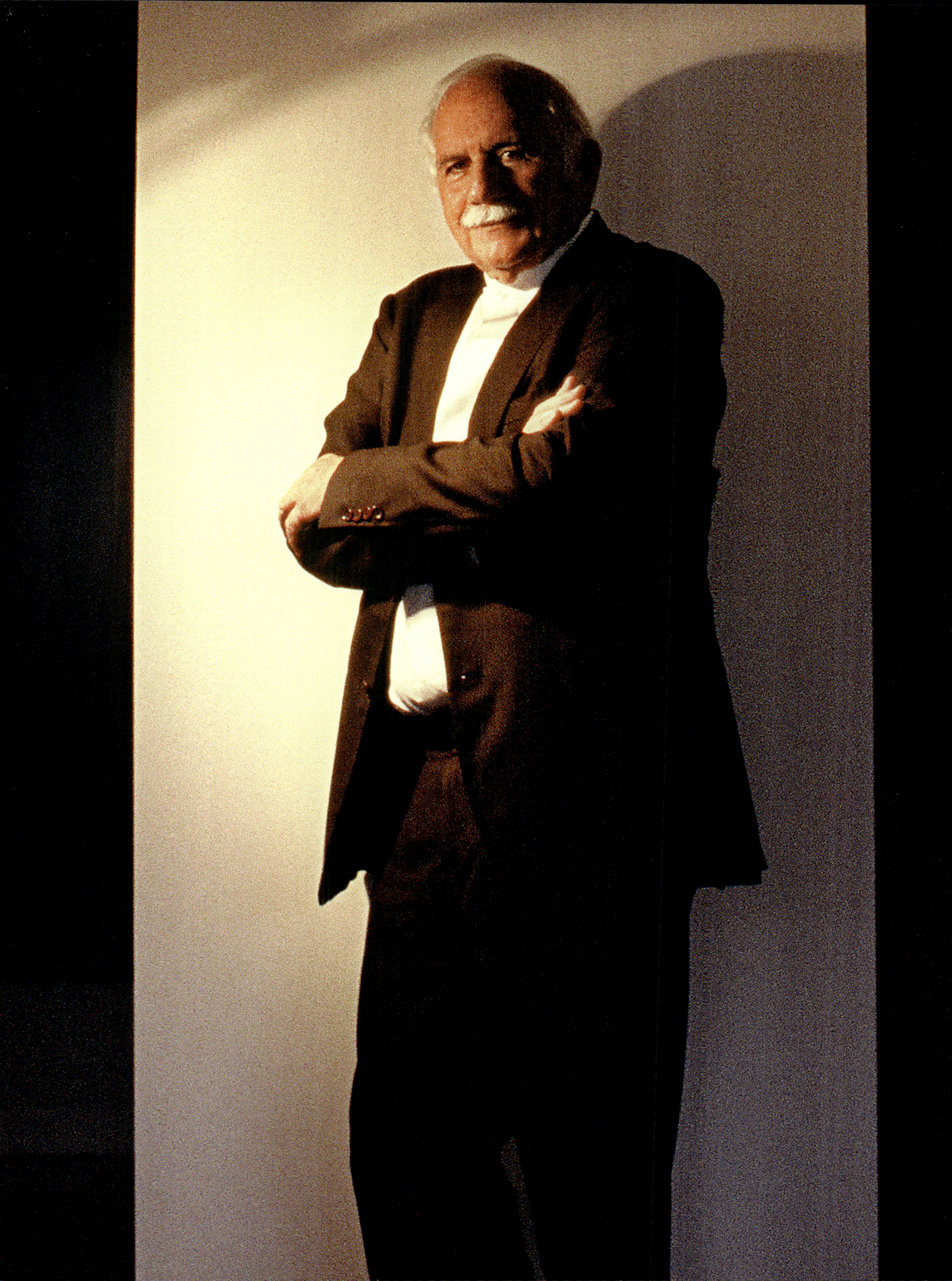

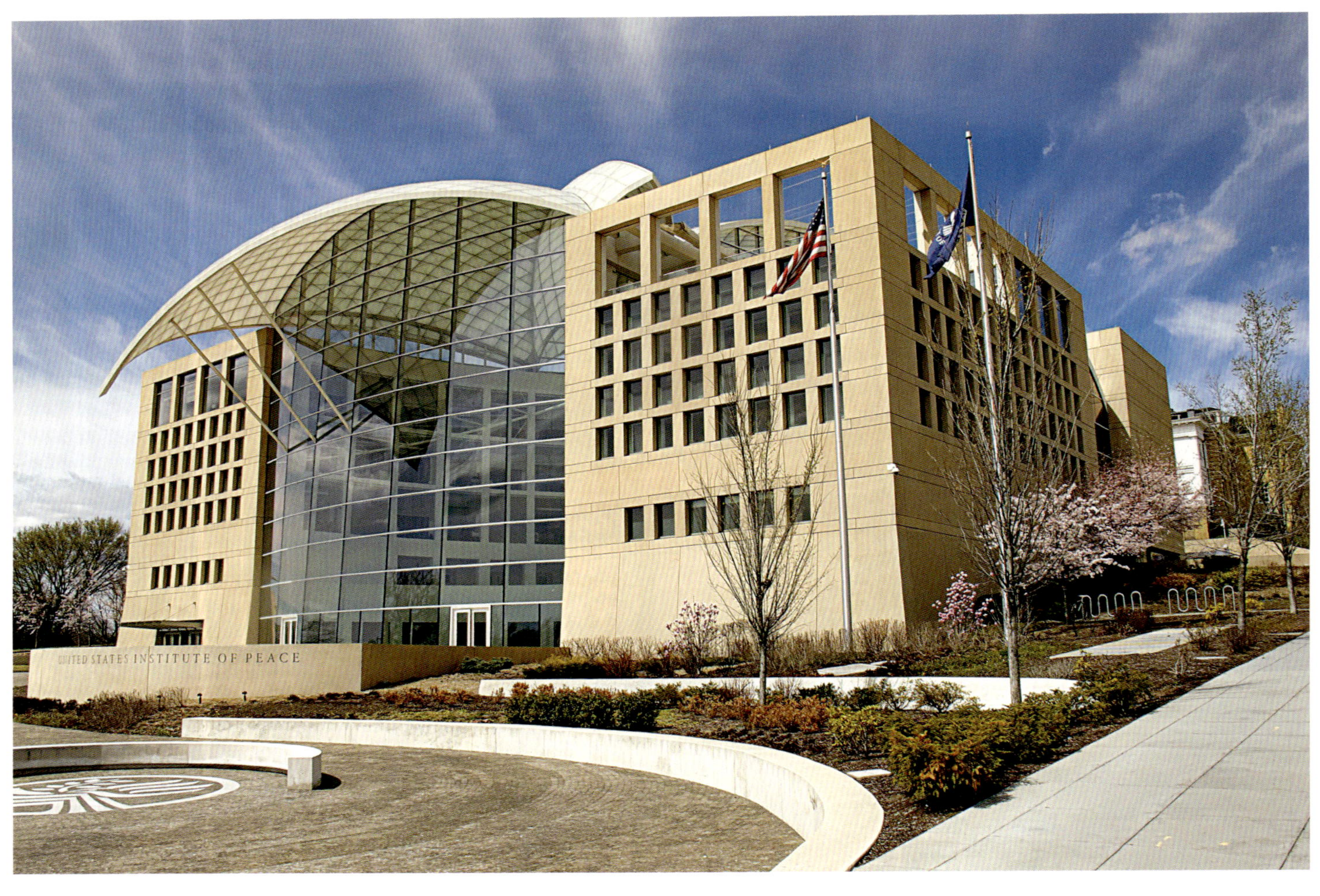

Safdie Architects. United States Institute of Peace, Washington, D.C., 2011.

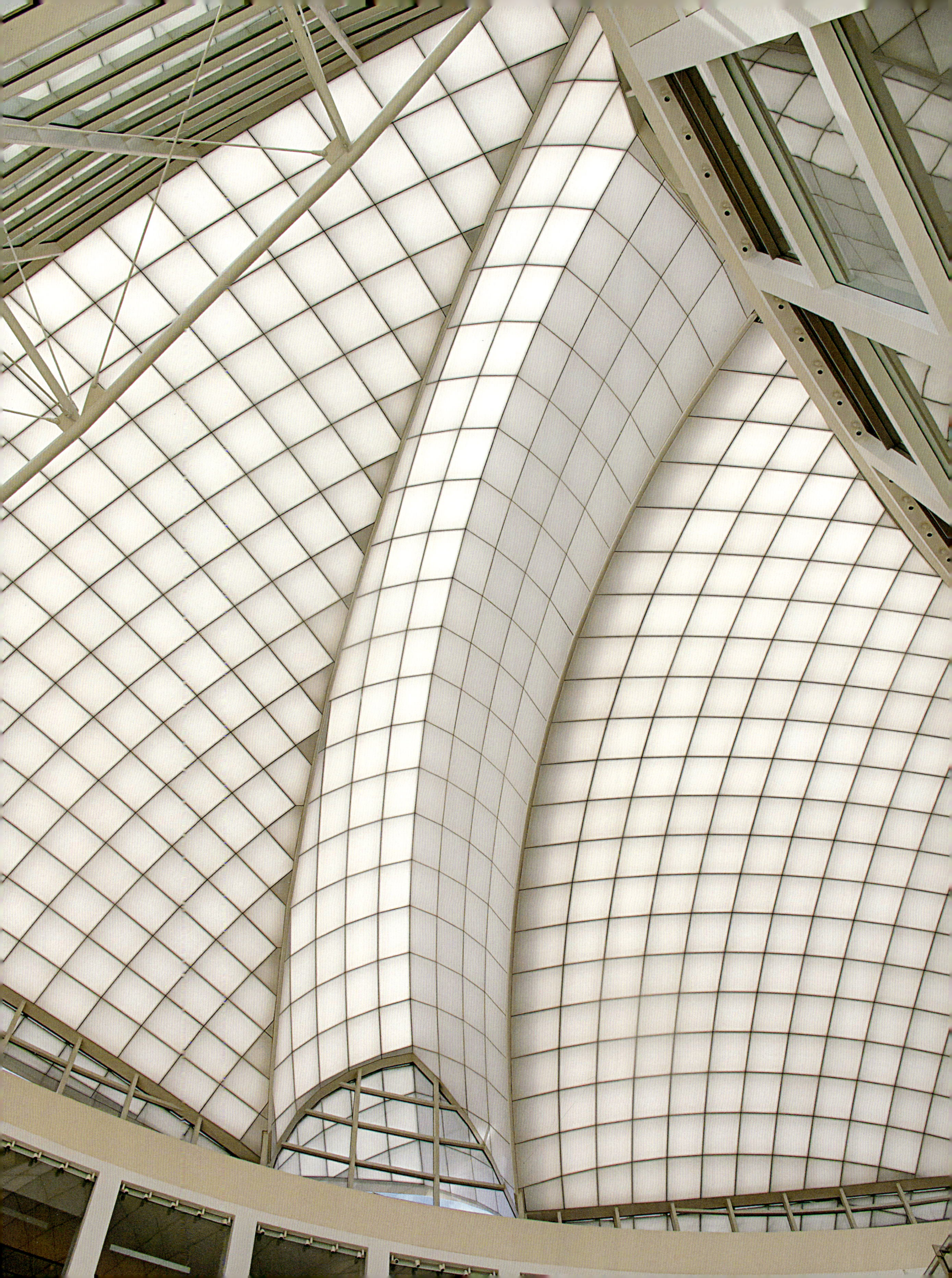

ANNABELLE SELLDORF

For 200 Eleventh Avenue, a nineteen-story residential building with sixteen duplex apartments, New York-based architect Annabelle Selldorf designed a unique building without entirely bucking tradition. Located in the Chelsea district of Manhattan—once home to many industrial warehouses, and now best known for art galleries—the building, which has unobstructed views of the Hudson River, manages to reference both old New York and current trends in architecture. Its three-story base is covered in terracotta, a material frequently used for architectural ornament on nineteenth-century structures in New York—and above the base, the tower is constructed of a stainless steel rainscreen, a technologically advanced construction that deflects water from the lattice of windows on the facade. To add to the high-tech allure of the structure, fourteen of the apartments are equipped with elevated car garages—those lucky enough to afford a unit can literally drive to the front door of their apartment, even if that apartment is high in the sky.

Lucky is a universally safe word to use to describe those who live in a building designed by Selldorf. Founded in Union Square in 1988, her firm specializes in creating housing for New Yorkers that is both innovative and respectful to the existing environment—rare for a starchitect building in a metropolis in the twenty-first century. Along with 200 Eleventh Avenue, she has designed 10 Bond Street, an eleven-unit building just north of SoHo, as well as a number of gallery spaces, including renovated homes for mega-galleries David Zwirner and Hauser & Wirth in Chelsea.

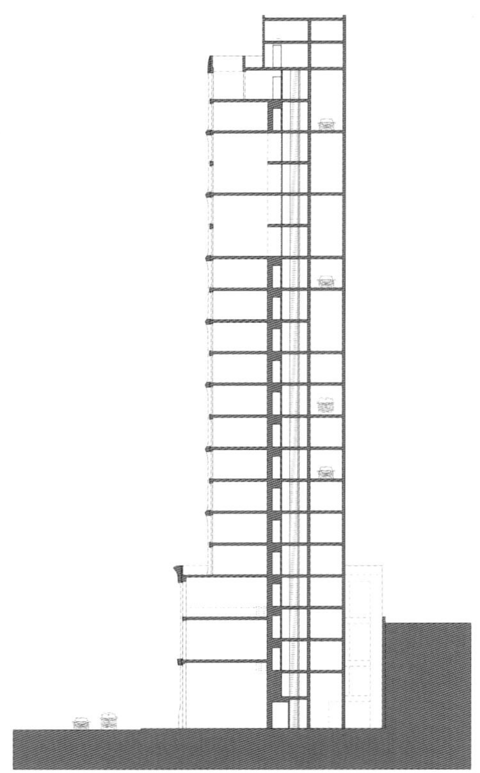

Rendering of 200 Eleventh Avenue.
Opposite: Annabelle Selldorf.

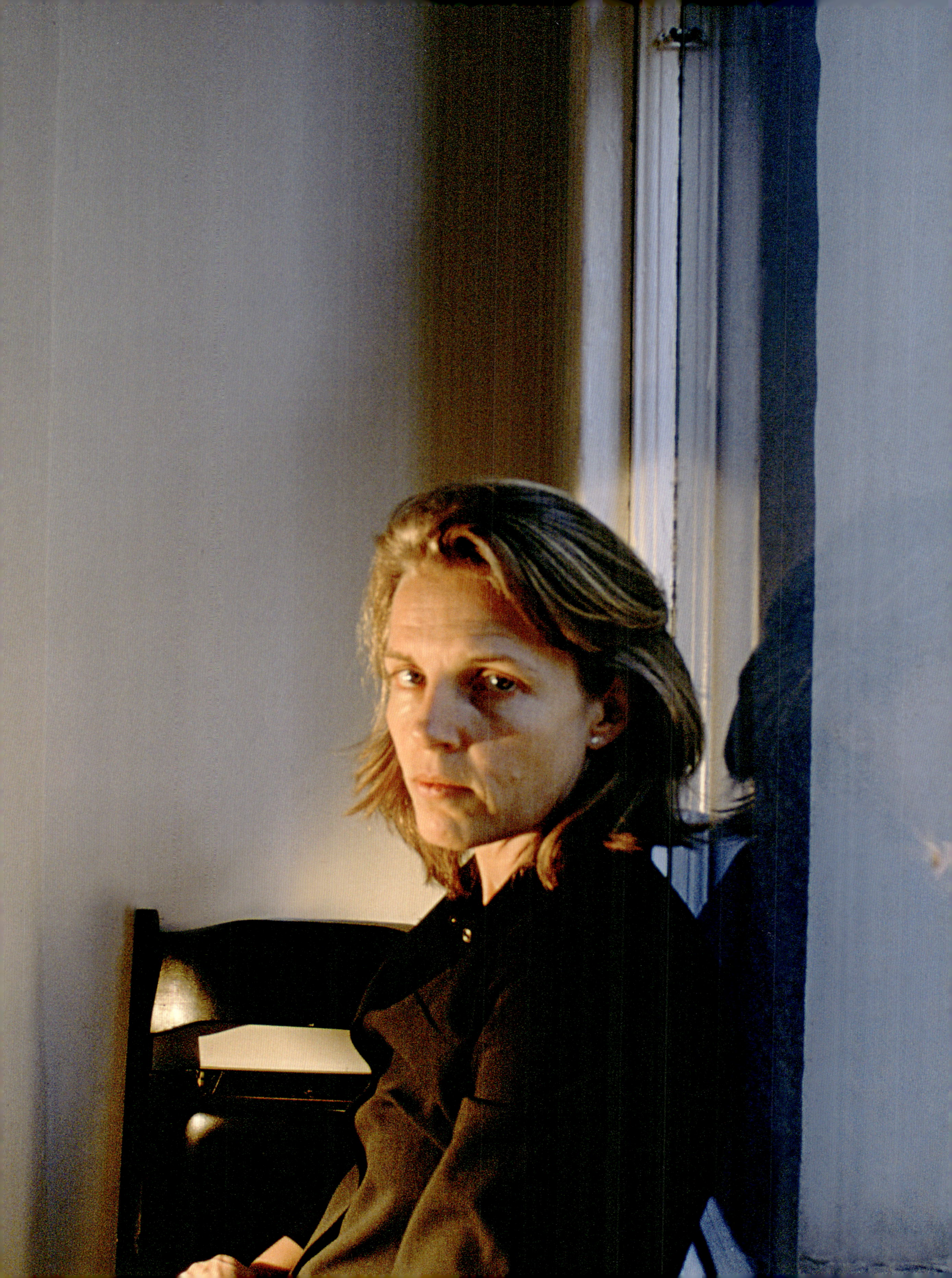

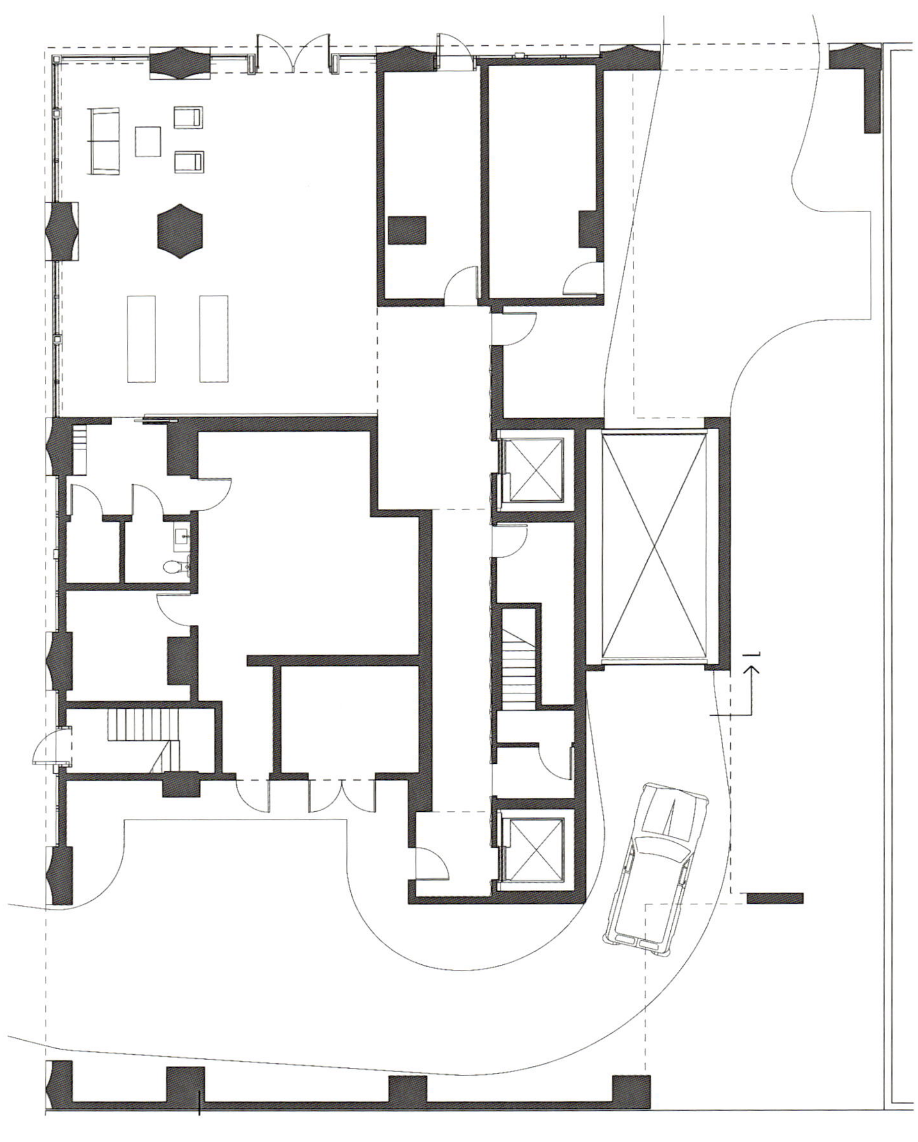

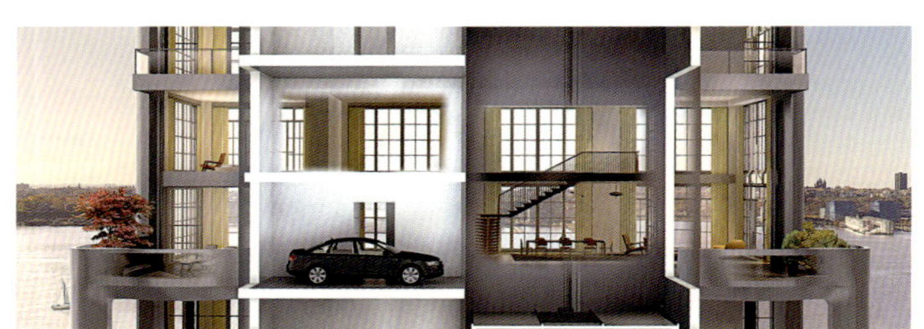

Rendering and plan of 200 Eleventh Avenue.
Opposite: Selldorf Architects. 200 Eleventh Avenue,
New York City, 2010.
Following pages: Interior of 200 Eleventh Avenue.

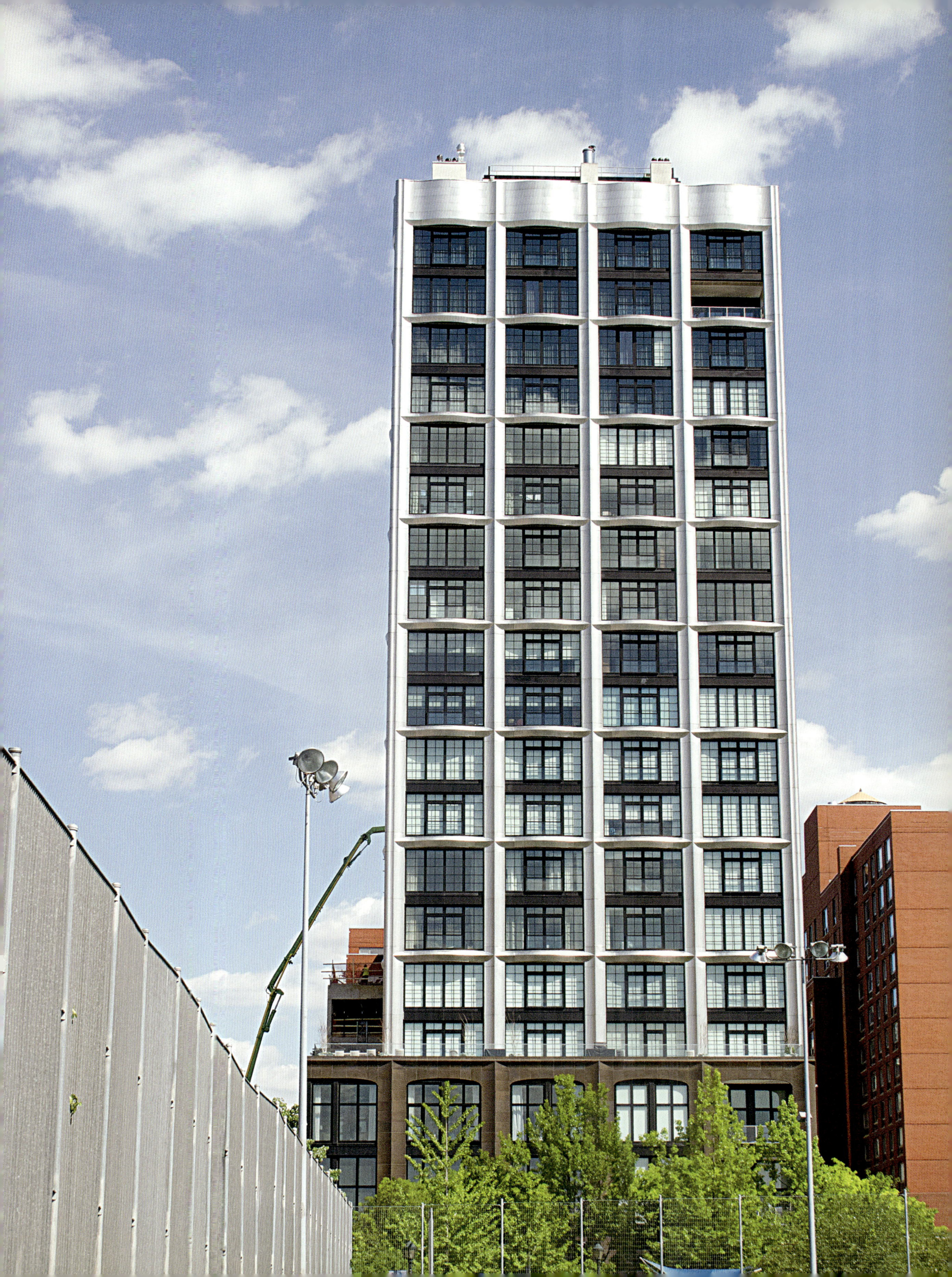

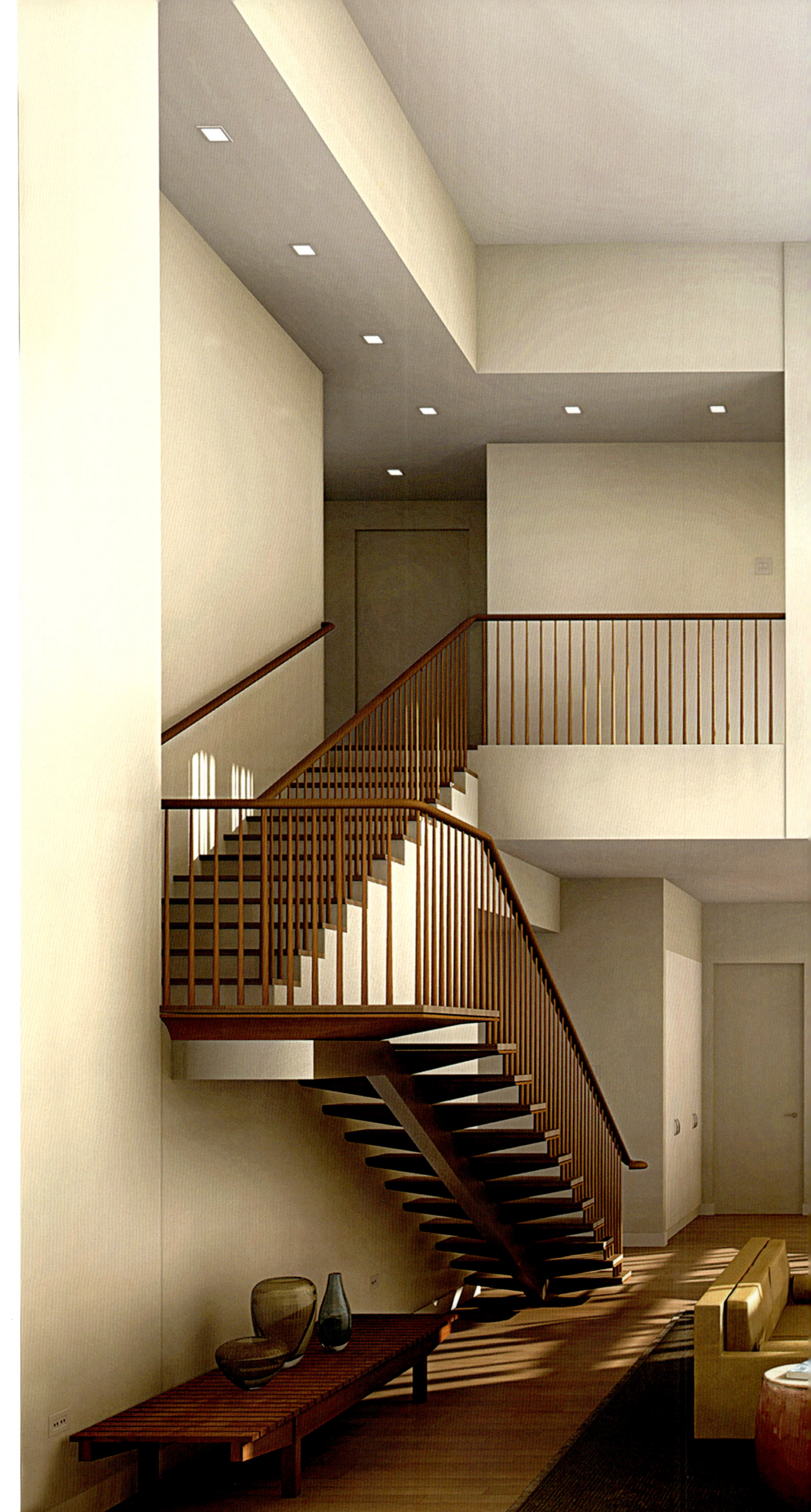

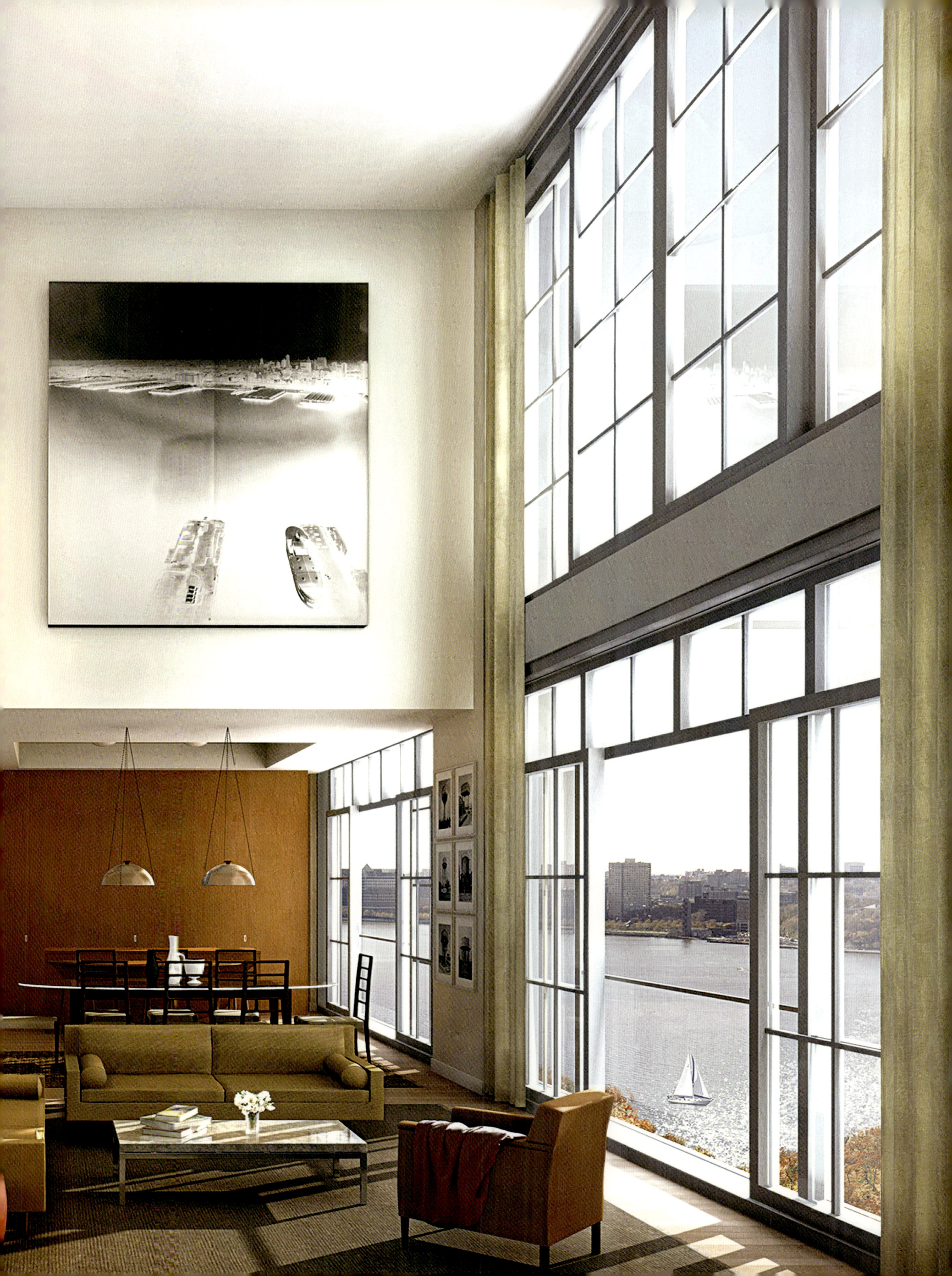

ÁLVARO SIZA

Located on a pier in Rotterdam right near the Erasmus Bridge, in an area known as "Manhattan on the Maas" for its cluster of towering skyscrapers, the New Orleans tower, designed by award-winning Portuguese architect Álvaro Siza, is the tallest residential building in the Netherlands. Standing forty-three stories high and accommodating 238 luxury apartments, the building is a clean monolith constructed from beige marble imported from China. The tower's name is fitting because it is attached to a jazz theater, the LantarenVenster.

For its design, Siza—who was born in 1933 in Portugal and has been awarded a Pritzker Prize in 1992 and a Golden Lion from the Venice Biennale in 2012, to name just two awards—looked to the early skyscrapers in Chicago and New York City—most specifically those from the nineteenth century. In doing so, he established an architectural language used to argue that Rotterdam, a port city established in 1270, is just as powerful as Amsterdam, the city in the Netherlands that attracts the most tourists.

Aesthetically, the New Orleans tower is consistent with the minimal, monochrome style that characterizes Siza's earlier work, which was first brought to international attention in 1966 by the Leça Swimming Pool complex: a series of infinity pools overlooking the ocean in northern Portugal. Recent constructions include the Iberê Camargo Foundation (2008), a museum dedicated to a single painter in Porto Alegre and marked by suspended bands of bleached concrete; and the Mimesis Museum (2009), a sinuous white building in the new town of Paju Book City in South Korea.

Álvaro Siza.

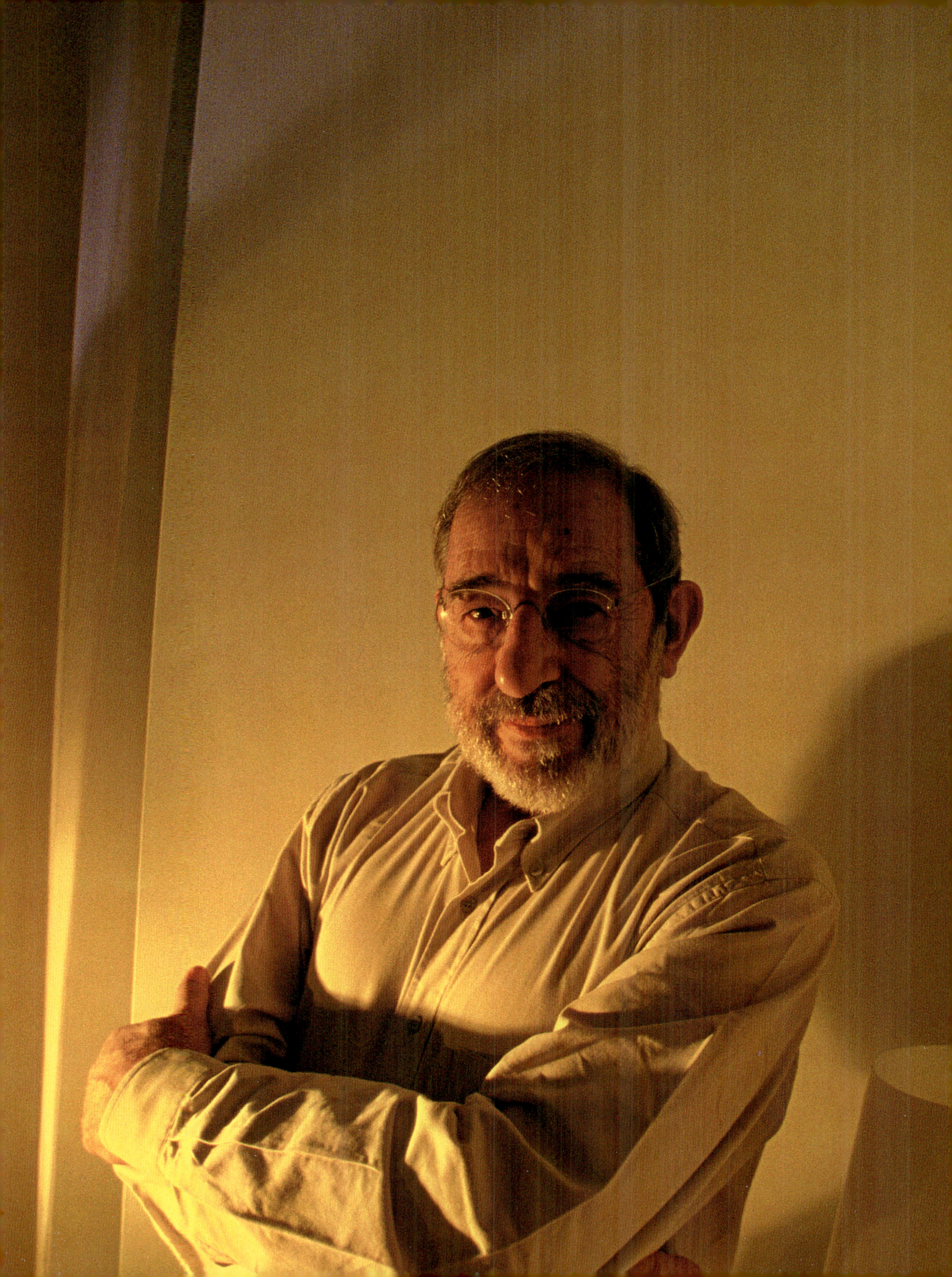

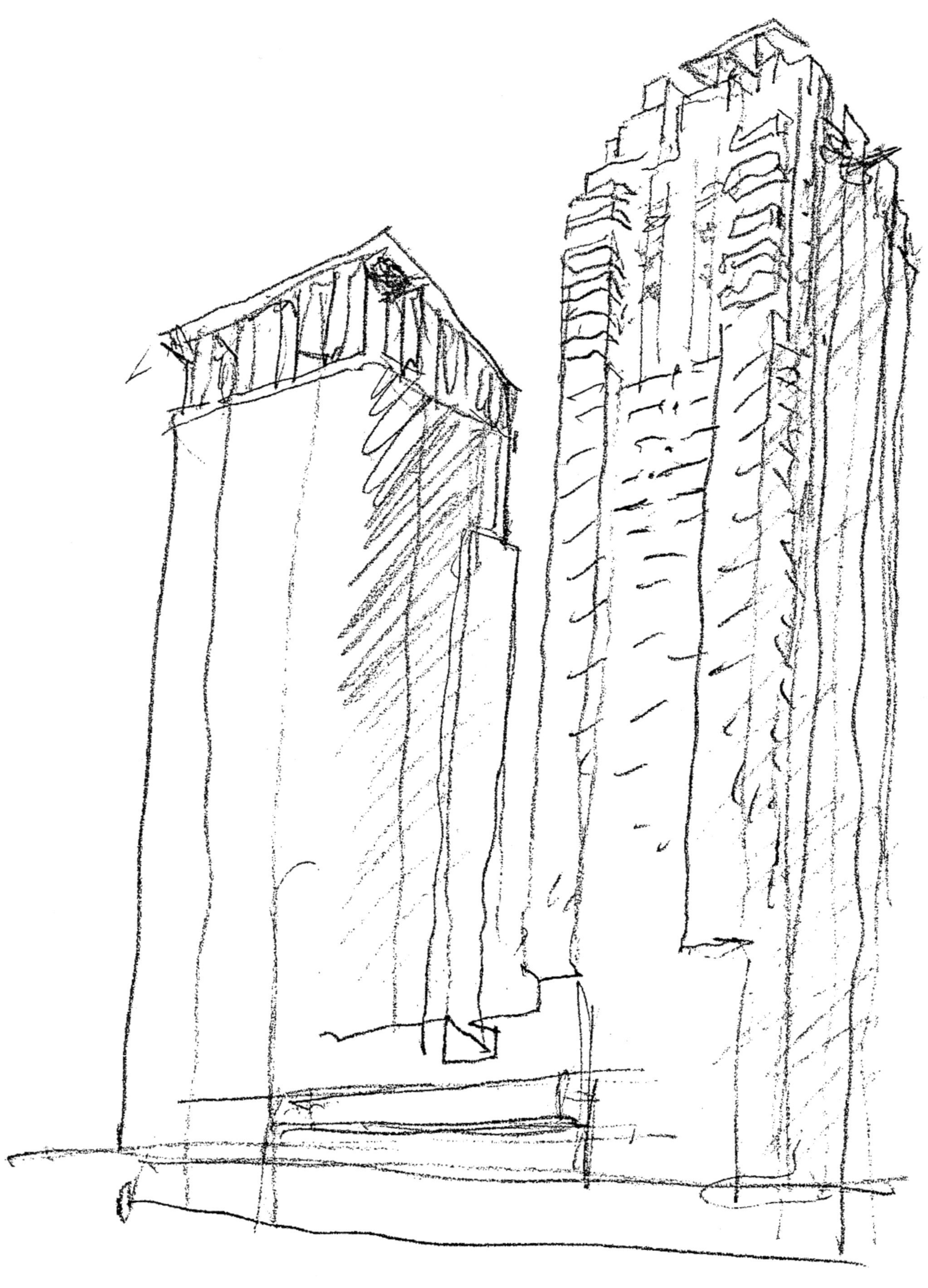

Sketch of the New Orleans Tower.
Opposite: Álvaro Siza. New Orleans Tower, Rotterdam, Netherlands, 2010.

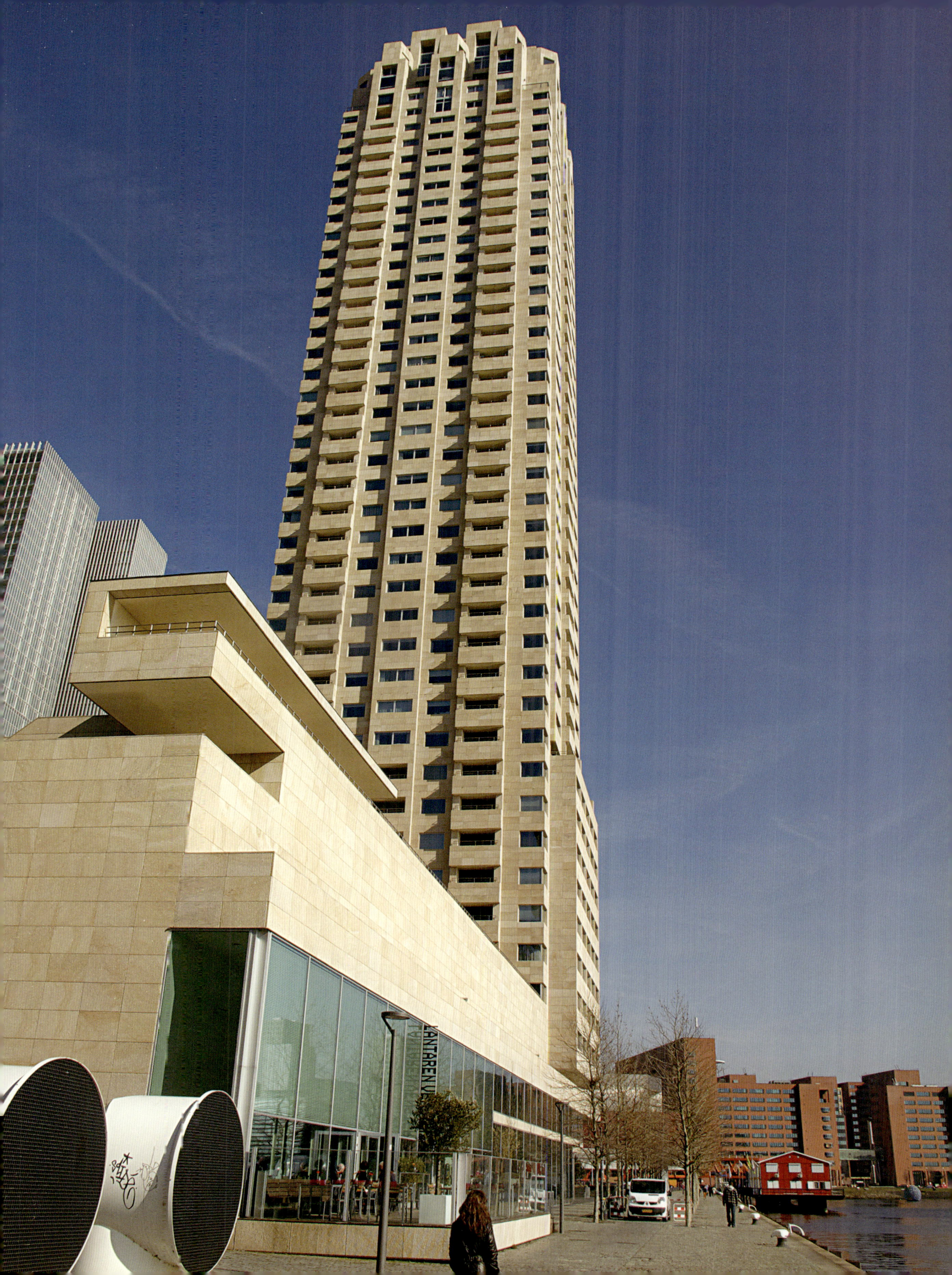

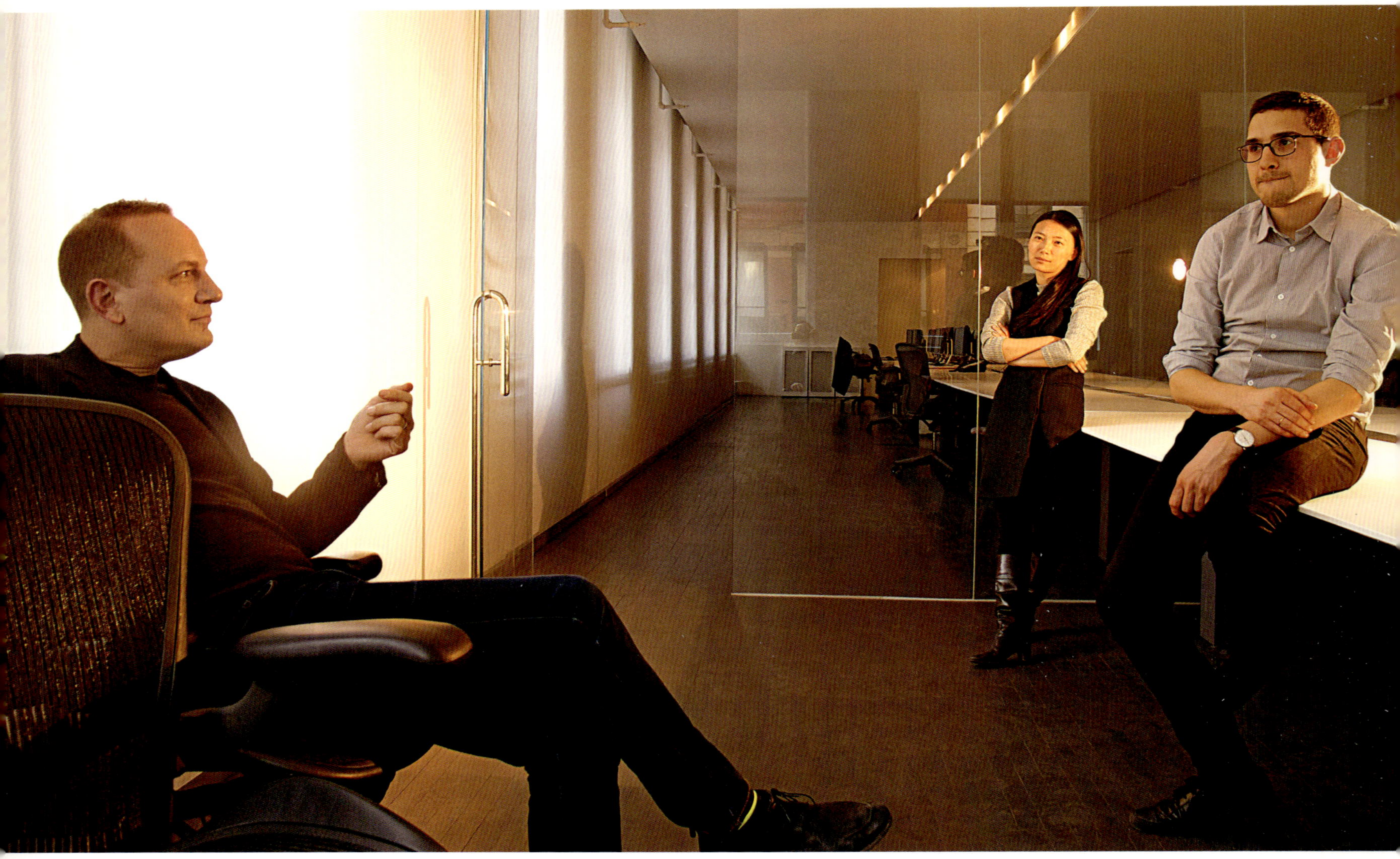

Florian Idenberg,
Jing Liu, and Ilias
Papageorgiou of SO-IL.
Opposite: Plan of the
Logan Offices.

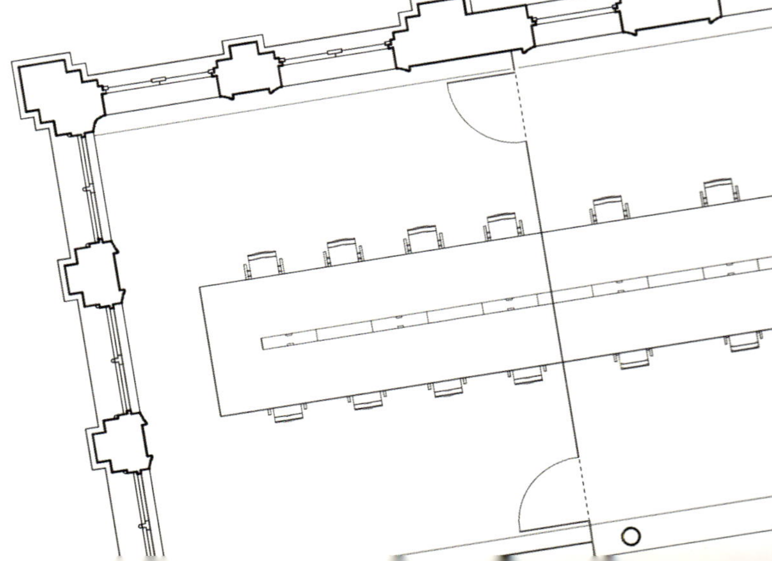

SO-IL

Solid Objectives–Idenburg Liu (SO-IL), a Brooklyn-based firm founded in 2008 by Florian Idenburg and Jing Liu, describes itself as an "idea-based" design office rather than an architecture studio. "Idea-based" could aptly be used to describe many of their projects, which require activation by human presence in order to function in the physical world. One such space is the Logan Offices, which house a creative studio for a production company whose staff consists largely of consultants hired on a per-project basis. Rather than creating permanent offices for impermanent employees, SO-IL converted the firm's 6,500-square-meter loft in the historic SoHo district in New York City into two identical rectilinear spaces. In the center of each of these spaces runs a single sixty-five-foot white worktable, upon which freelancers can plug in their equipment— the spaces are divided by a translucent fabric wall, which creates a dreamlike, shadowy state in the shared environment. The end section of each table is divided by a series of glass walls, allowing for privacy when necessary. Without workers, it's a cold space. When employees arrive, they fill it with purpose.

The conceptual nature of SO-IL's work means that they are frequently hired to work on unconventional projects, such as the temporary tent the firm built for the Frieze Art Fair on Randall's Island in New York in 2012, or the metal canopy for the fifth China International Architectural Biennial 2013, which SO-IL named "Spiky." Heralded with much critical acclaim, including the AIA Young Practices Award and the Emerging Voices award by the Architectural League of New York, the firm's recent and upcoming large-scale projects include student housing in Athens, Greece, and a campus museum at the University of California at Davis.

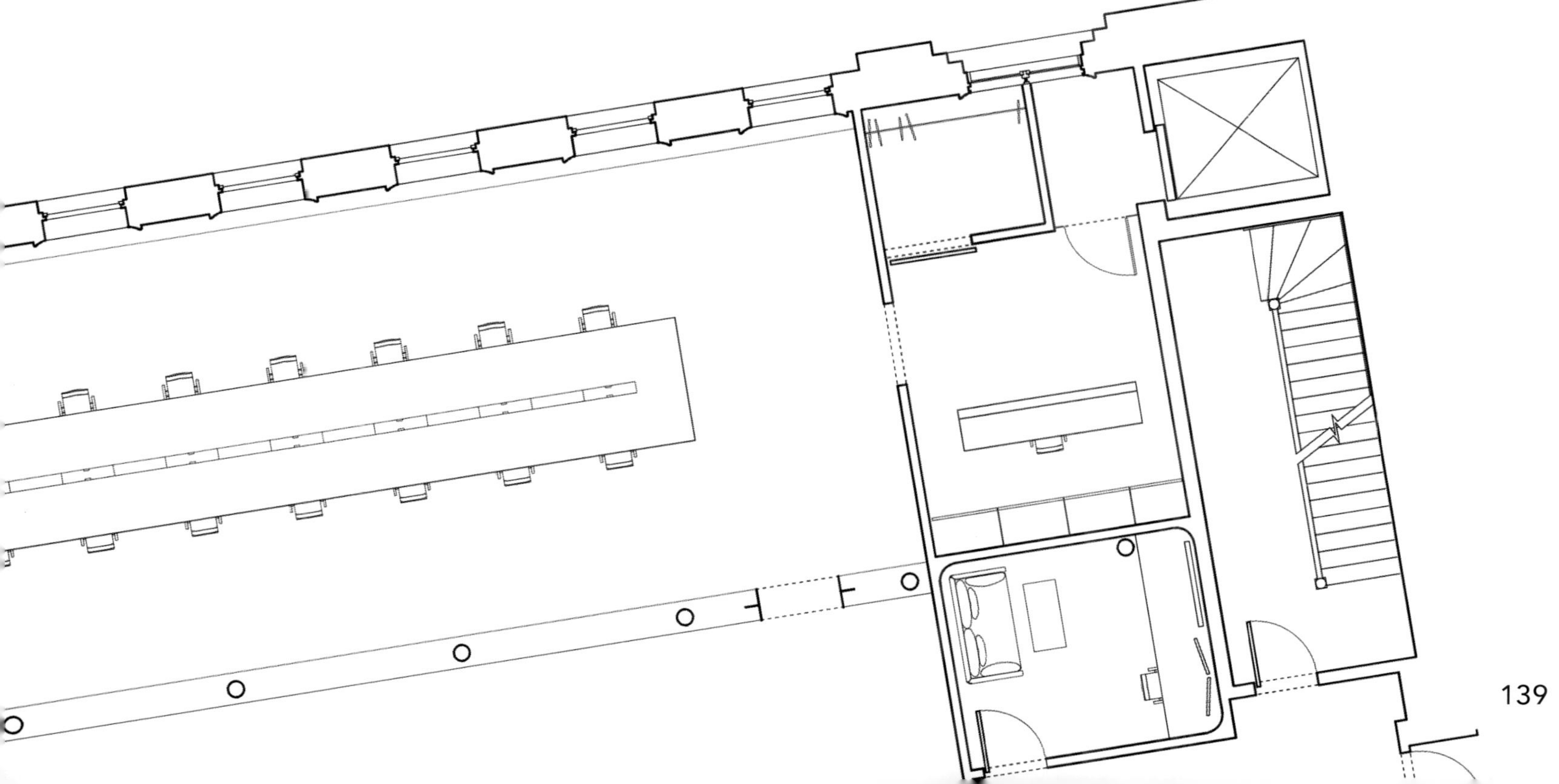

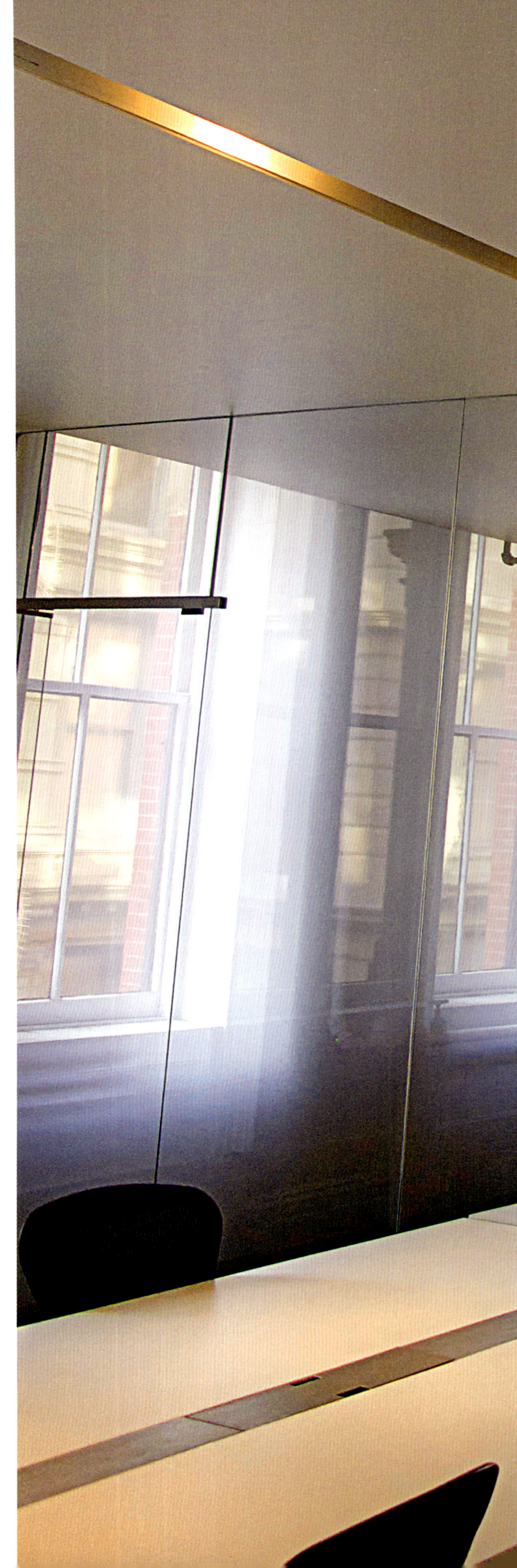

SO-IL. Logan Offices, New York City, 2012.

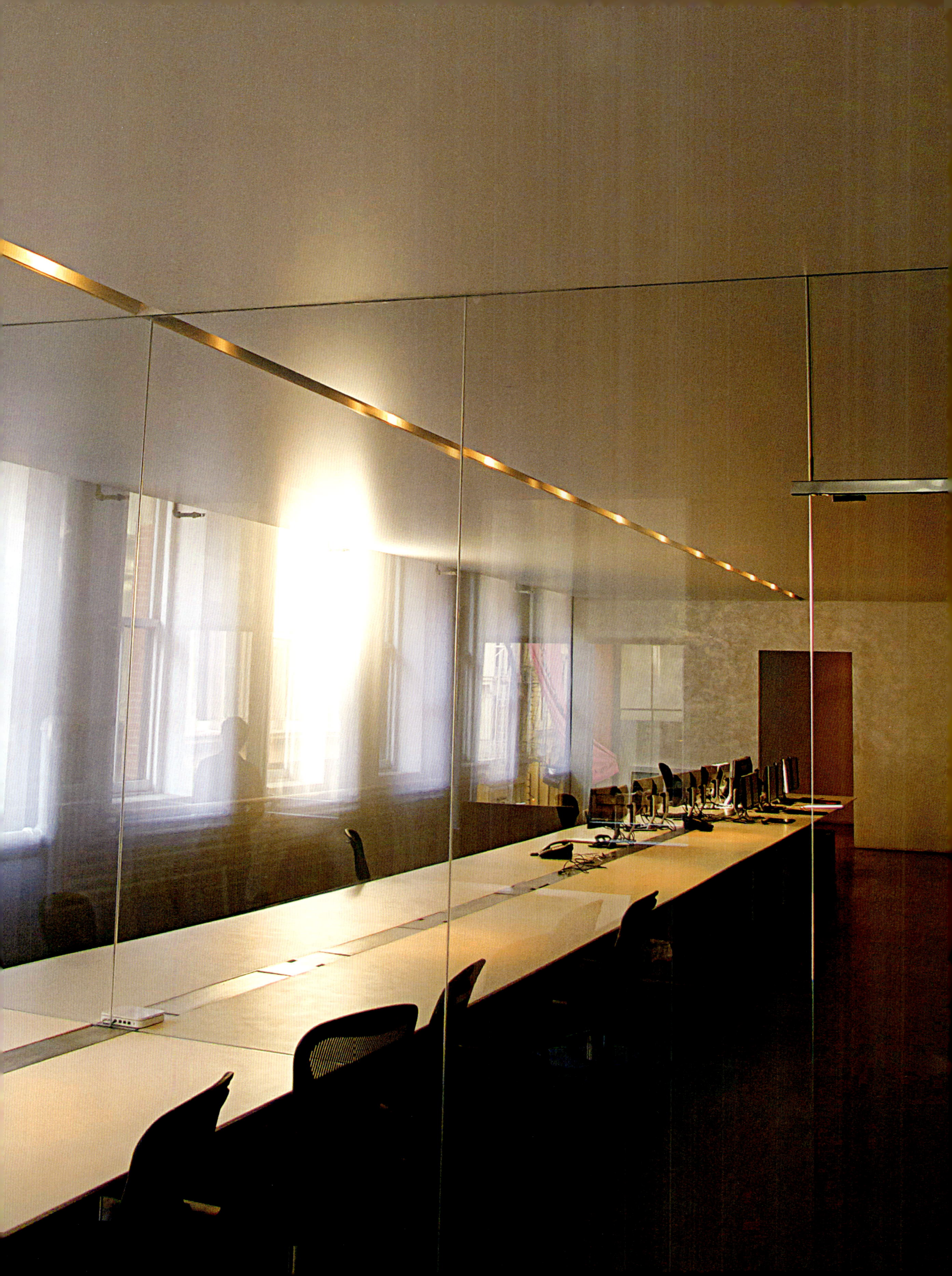

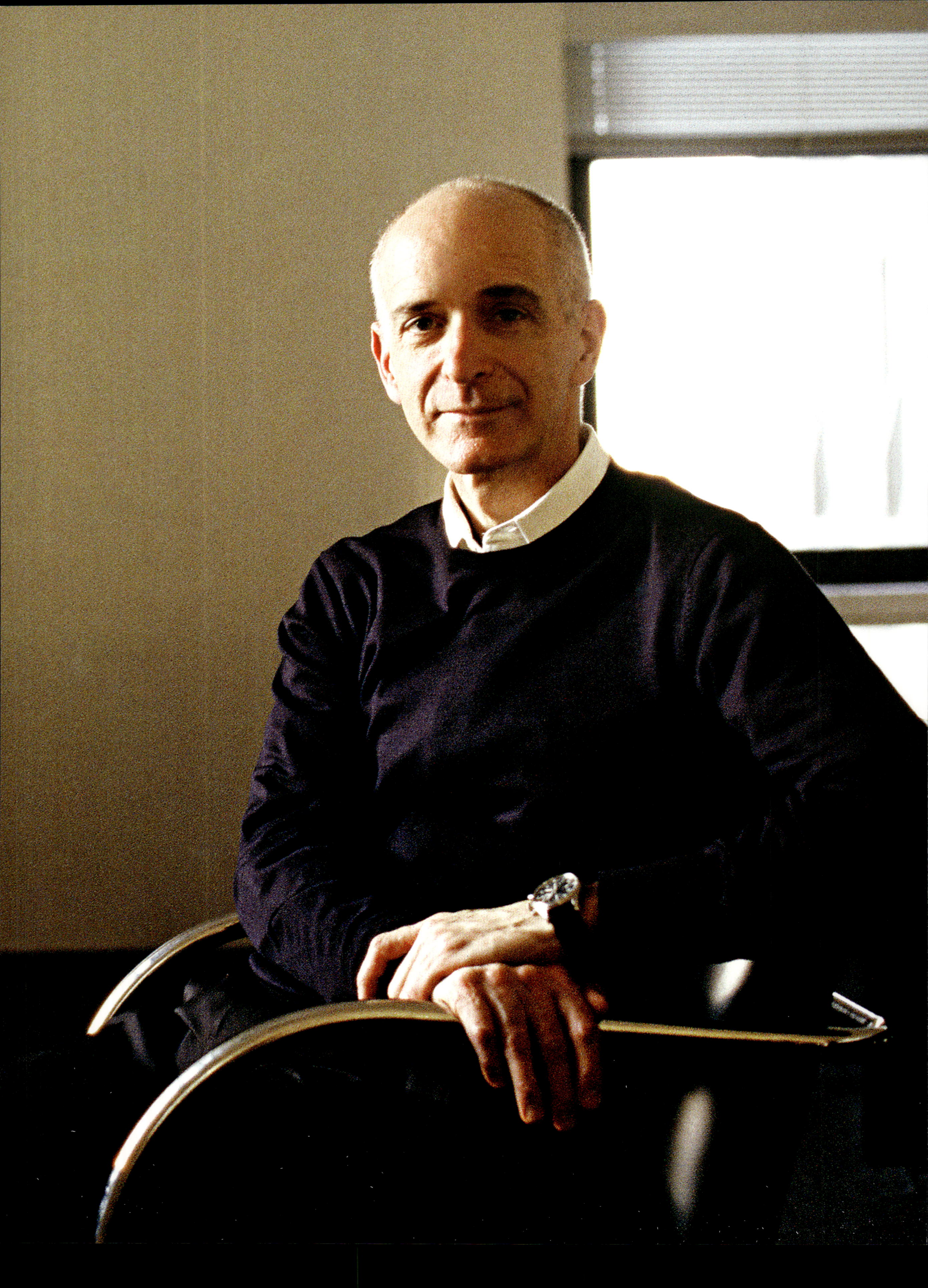

SOM—ROGER DUFFY

Housing an entire university in a single building is no small feat. But that's exactly what Roger Duffy, a design partner at Skidmore, Owings & Merrill (SOM), did for the University Center at the New School in New York. Consisting of 200,000 square feet of academic space on the first seven stories of the building, which includes fashion and drawing studios, classrooms, science labs, an auditorium, and a library, the structure also houses a six-hundred-bed dormitory on the top nine floors. Social interactions are encouraged throughout, with open staircases defining both the interior space and the exterior—on the latter, the path of the staircase is marked by glass windows that puncture the aged brass facade. The building embodies a popular trend in university architecture today—one that encourages social interaction rather than hermetic study.

As a partner at SOM, Duffy has worked on a number of high-profile projects, including the cafeteria at Condé Nast (2006), which encourages individual workers to come out of their cubicles and interact with colleagues, and the Integrated Terminal Building at Mumbai's Chhatrapati Shivaji International Airport. For the Greenwich Academy Upper School in Connecticut, Duffy collaborated with light artist James Turrell to create color-coded wings for each of the school's four disciplines—science, math, arts, and humanities. Color is one of many tools with which Duffy shapes his unique environments.

Roger Duffy of SOM.

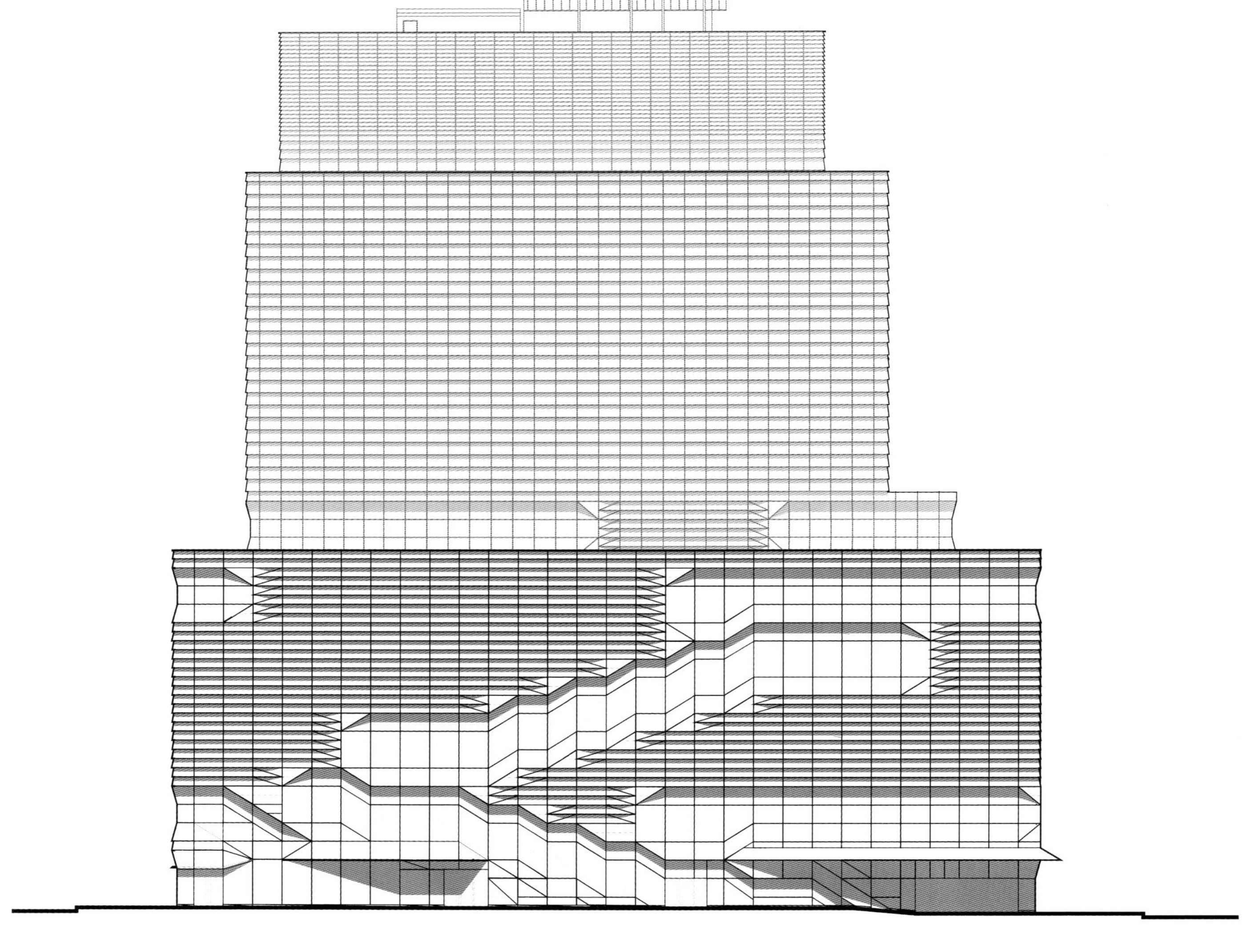

Rendering of the New School University Center.
Opposite: Skidmore, Owings & Merrill/Roger Duffy. New School University
Center, New York City, 2014.

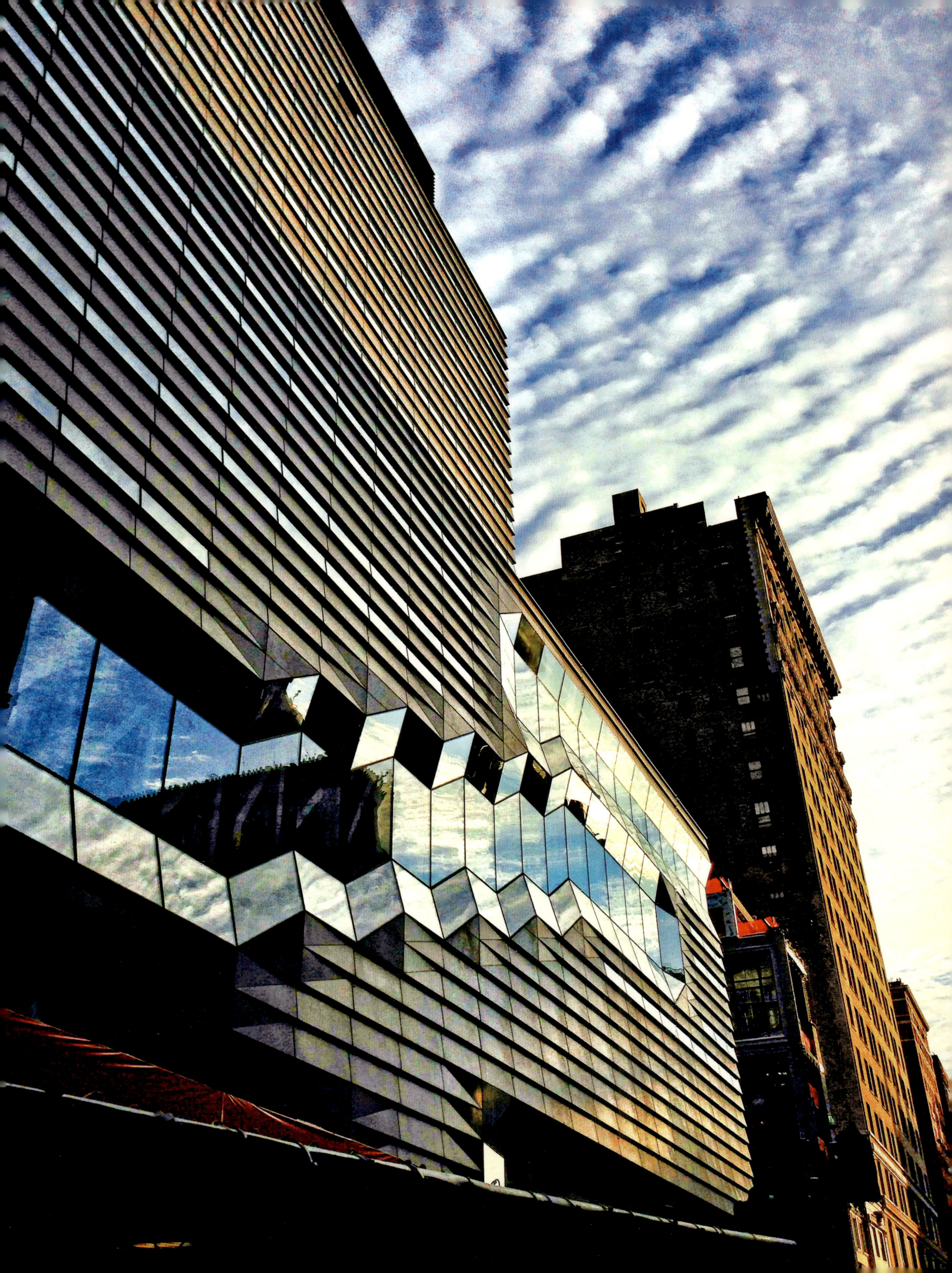

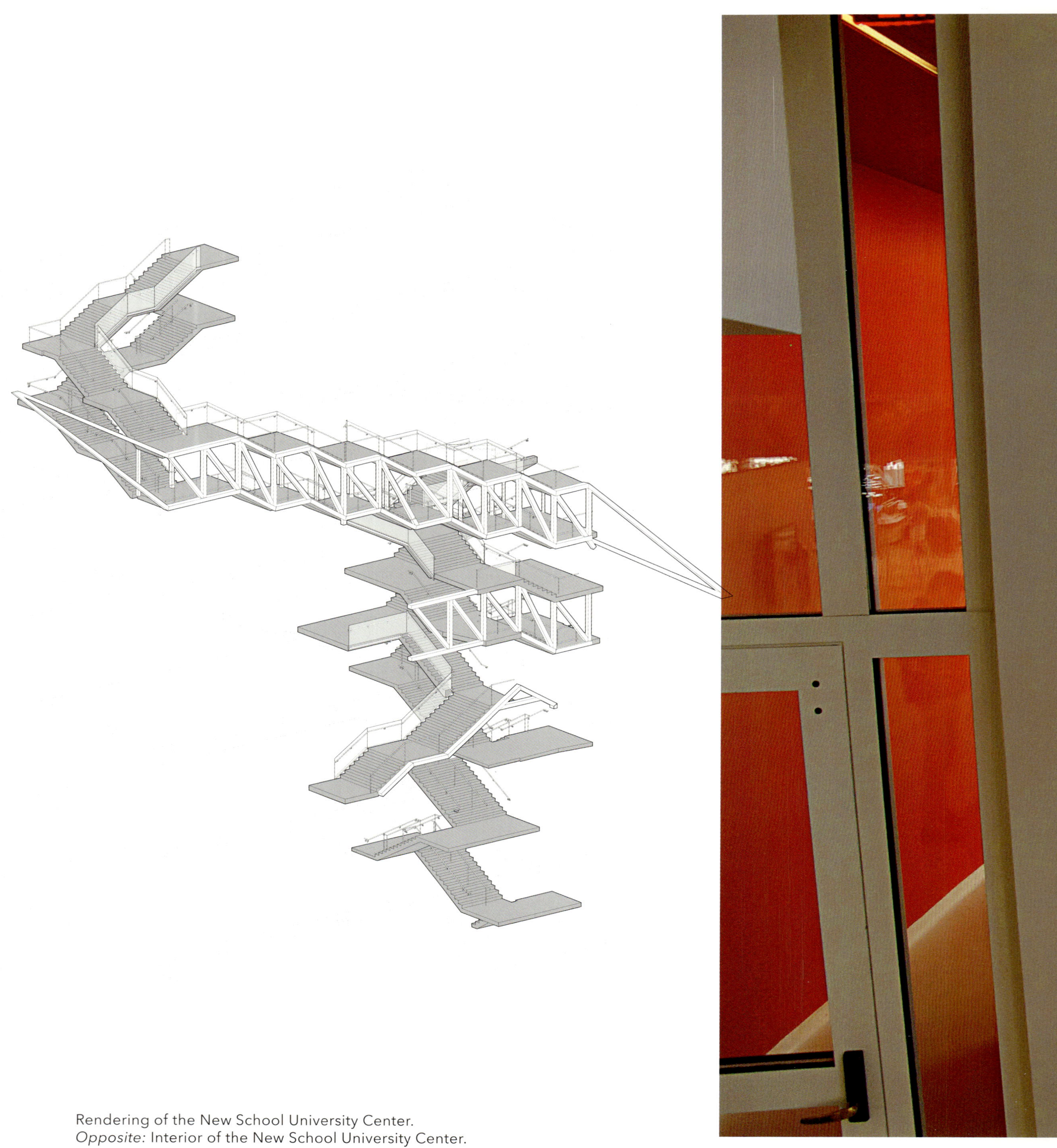

Rendering of the New School University Center.
Opposite: Interior of the New School University Center.

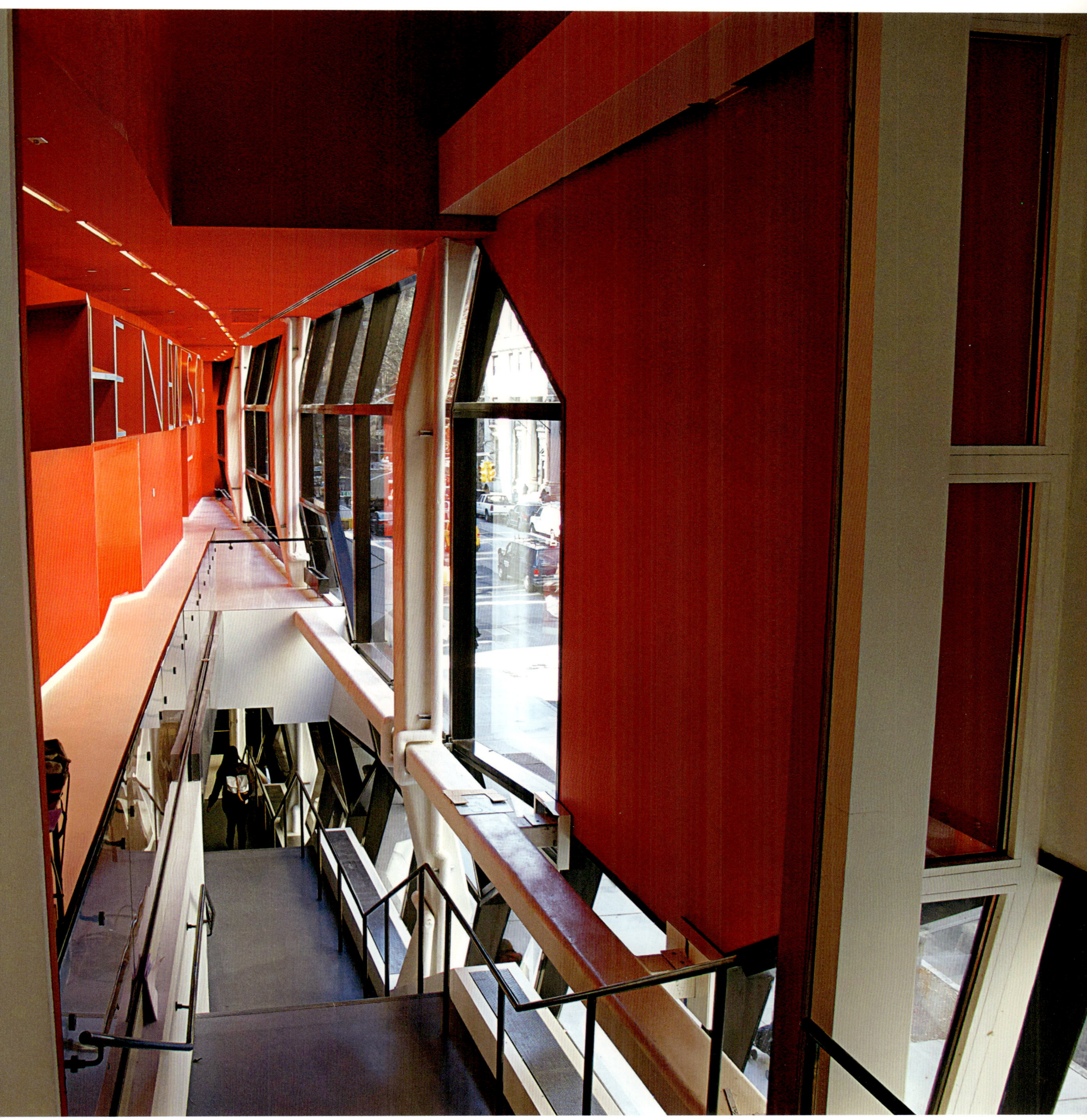

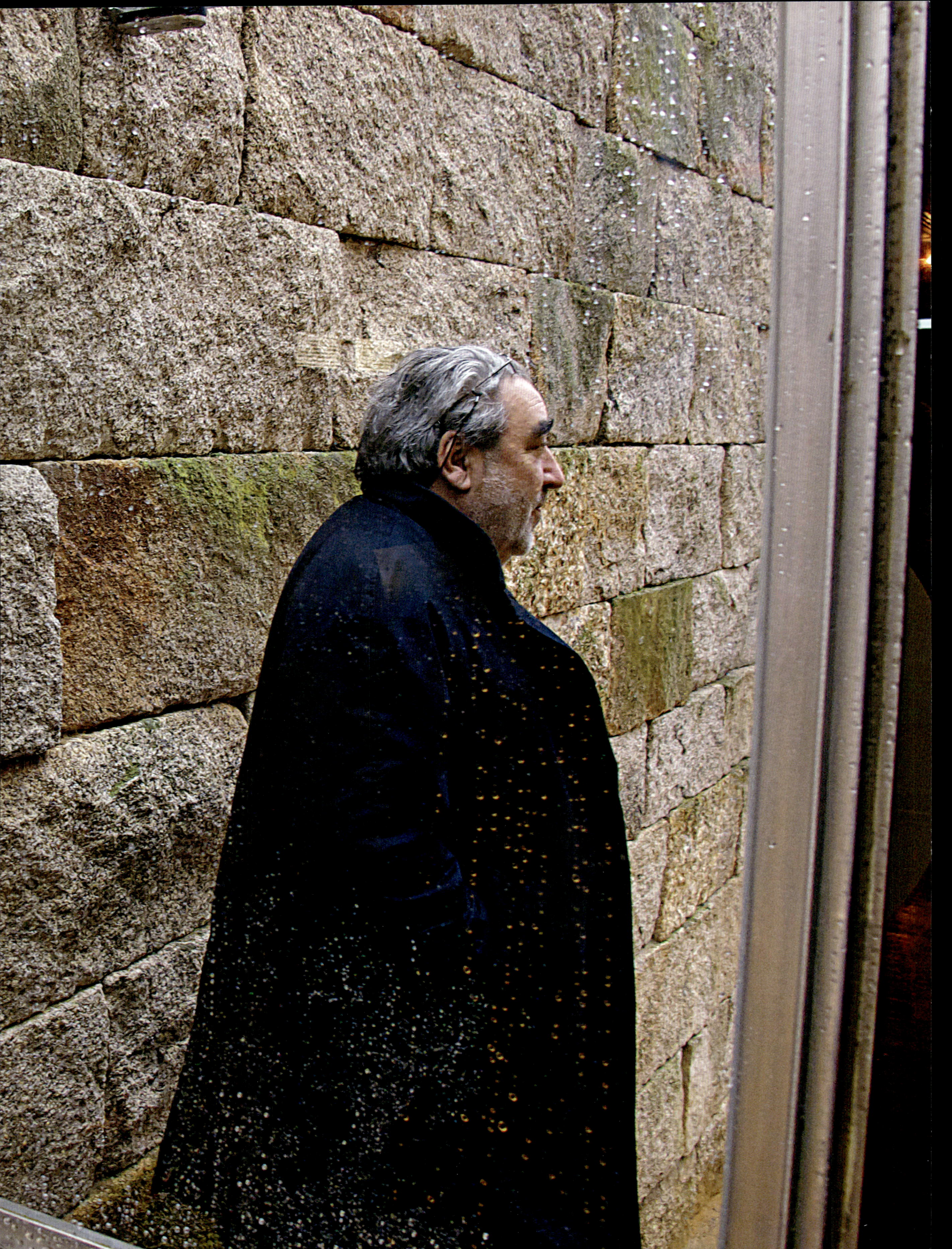

EDUARDO SOUTO DE MOURA

A protégé of Álvaro Siza, Eduardo Souto de Moura was the second Portuguese architect after his mentor to receive the Pritzker Prize, an honor he was awarded in 2011. Born in Porto in 1952, Souto de Moura credits his meeting Donald Judd in Zurich for his chosen profession—before switching to architecture, he studied sculpture at the School of Fine Arts at the university in his hometown. The minimal language of artists like Judd, and fellow architects such as Mies van der Rohe, have very much informed his work—in his opinion, it is better to be good than to be original, which is why he embraces rather than rejects comparison.

Where Souto de Moura sets himself apart is in his choice of materials, which range among brick, concrete, granite, marble, steel, and wood. Materials are used to breathtaking effect in structures such as the Paula Rego Museum, a compound of pyramids made from red concrete, as well as a state inn near Amares, Portugal, which Souto de Moura constructed within the ancient walls of a twelfth-century convent.

The majority of his built work resides in his native country, where structures such as a commercial building in Boavista, a neighborhood in Porto, make for a unique urban landscape. Consisting of a series of glass and concrete boxes resting on top of a rectangular platform, the building reads like sculpture despite its practical application. It embodies the true essence of Souto de Moura's genius—his ability to create sculptural architecture that can be used as well as admired.

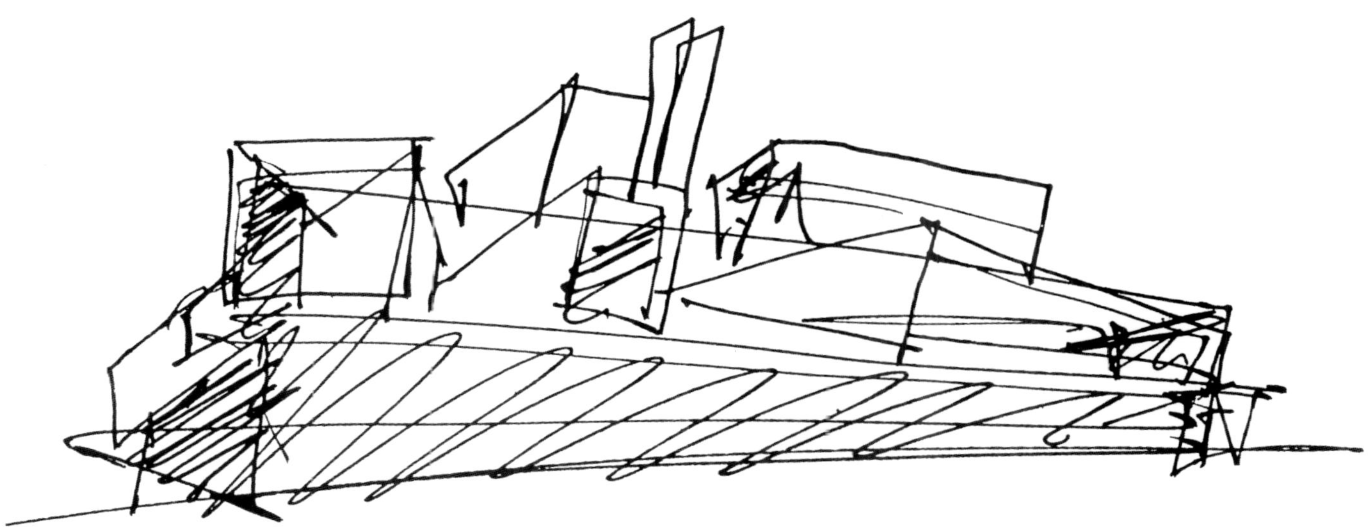

Sketch of Commercial Building in Boavista.
Opposite: Eduardo Souto de Moura.
Following pages: Eduardo Souto de Moura. Commercial Building, Boavista, Porto, Portugal, 2008.

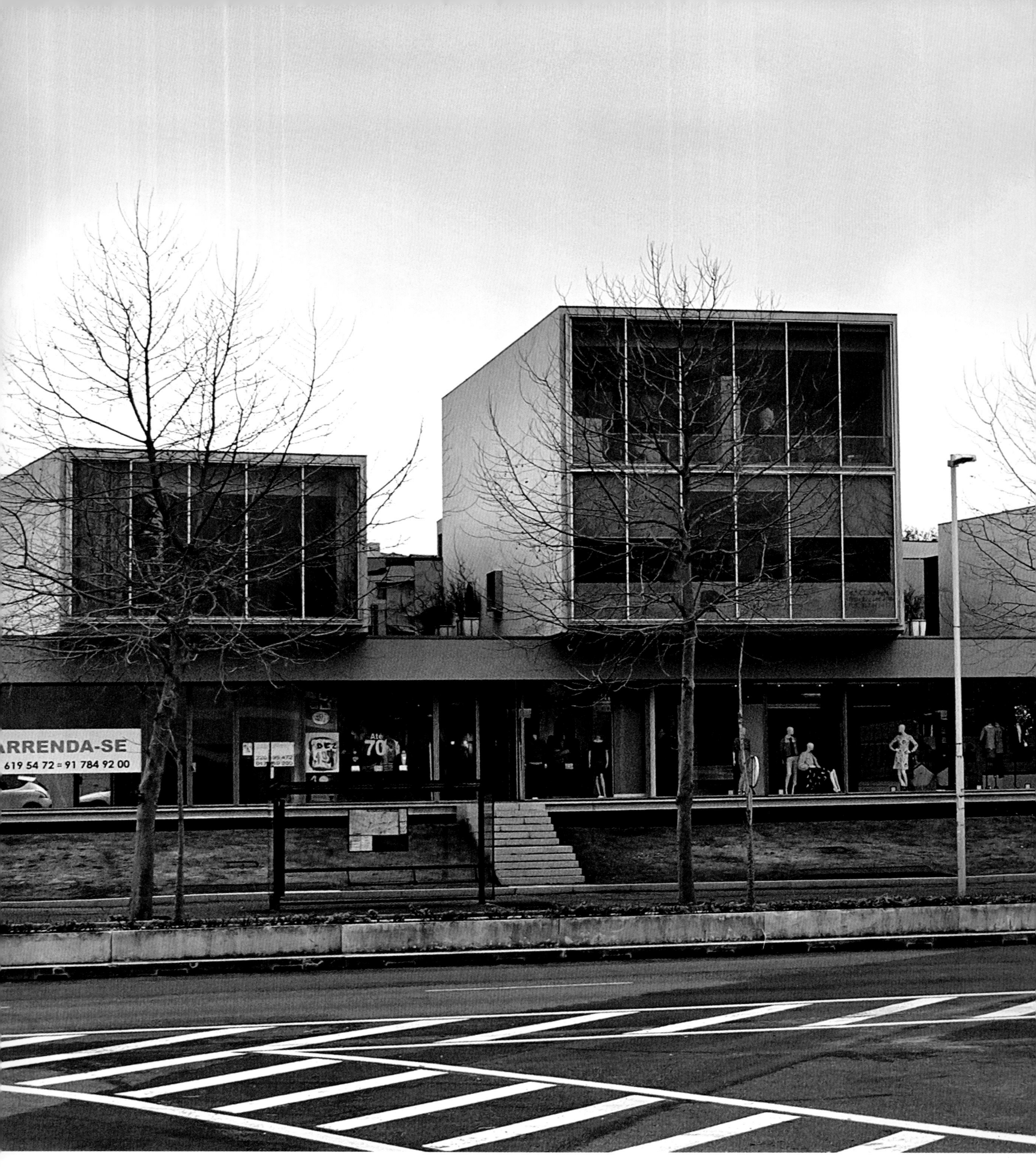
ARRENDA-SE
619 54 72 = 91 784 92 00

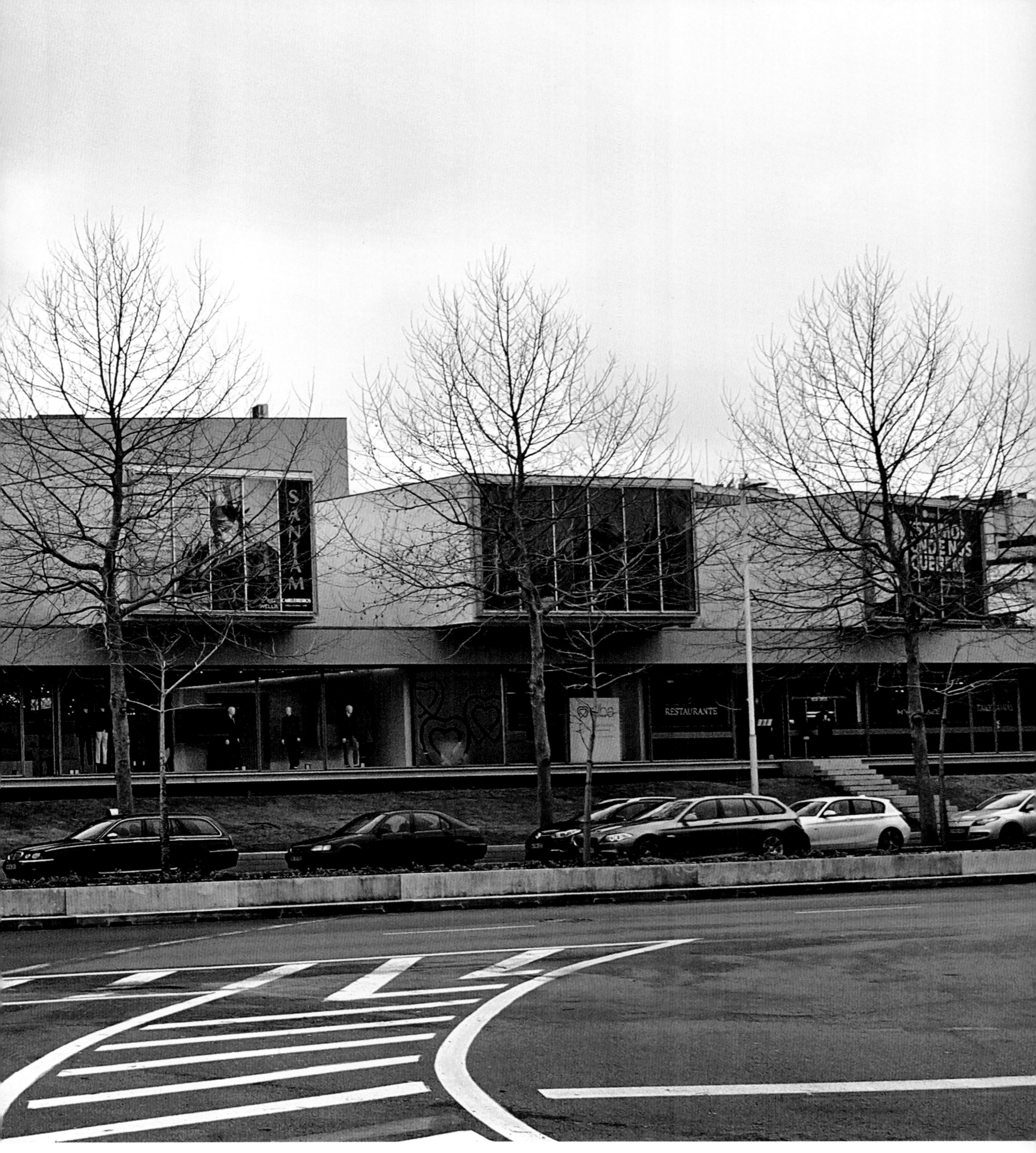

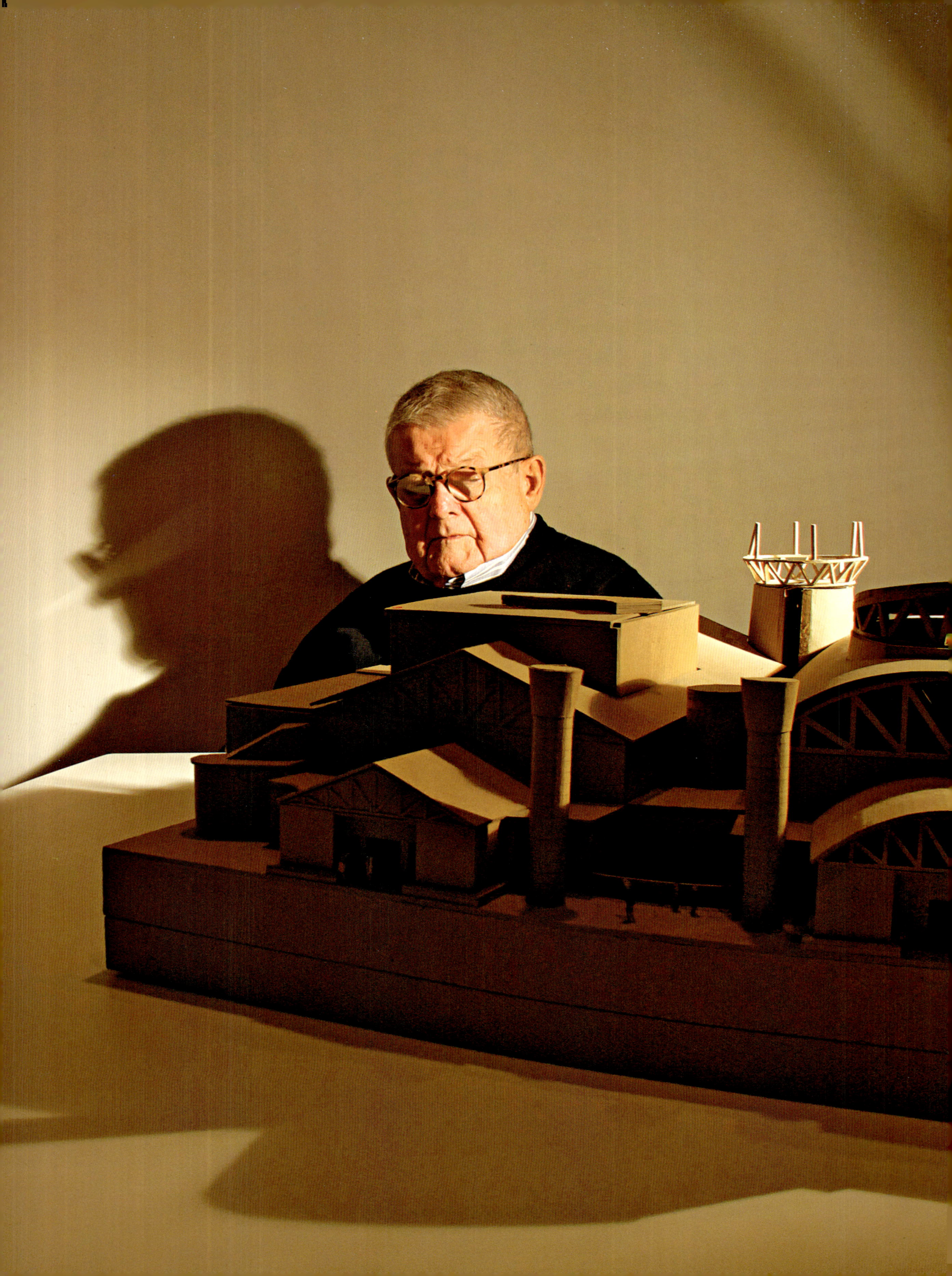

STANLEY TIGERMAN

A founding member of the Chicago Seven, a group of postmodern architects who began protesting the stringent minimalism of Mies van der Rohe in the late 1970s, Stanley Tigerman is a man whose aesthetic lexicon is grounded in emotion. With his firm, Tigerman McCurry, founded in 1982 with Margaret McCurry, he has worked on a number of iconic projects in Illinois, including the 1992 Chicago World's Fair, and the Illinois Regional Library for the Blind and Physically Handicapped in Chicago.

Most iconic of all of these structures is the Illinois Holocaust Museum, a 65,000-square-foot memorial in Skokie. In homage to those who died, the building is laden with symbolism. Divided into two wings, one of which is cast in darkness and the other in light, the sections are joined at a "hinge," where a trail car used to transport German Jews to concentration camps is displayed, symbolizing the rupture in humanity that ocurred during the Shoah. Viewers enter through the dark wing and leave through the light one, symbolizing hope for the future of survivors. Six points of light adorn the museum's exterior, representing the six million Jews who perished.

The building, which eschews the minimal language of traditional modernism, speaks directly to the viewer, rather than acting as a passive receptor for the objects used to fill it. It is not merely a museum for passive learning—it is a place where visitors can mourn.

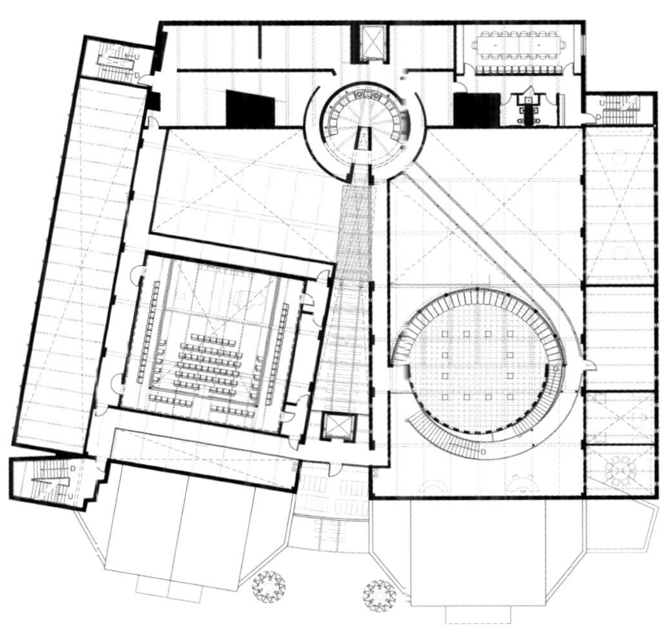

Plan of the Illinois Holocaust Museum.
Opposite: Stanley Tigerman.
Following pages and pages 156-57:
Tigerman McCurry Architects. Illinois
Holocaust Museum, Skokie, Illinois, 2009.

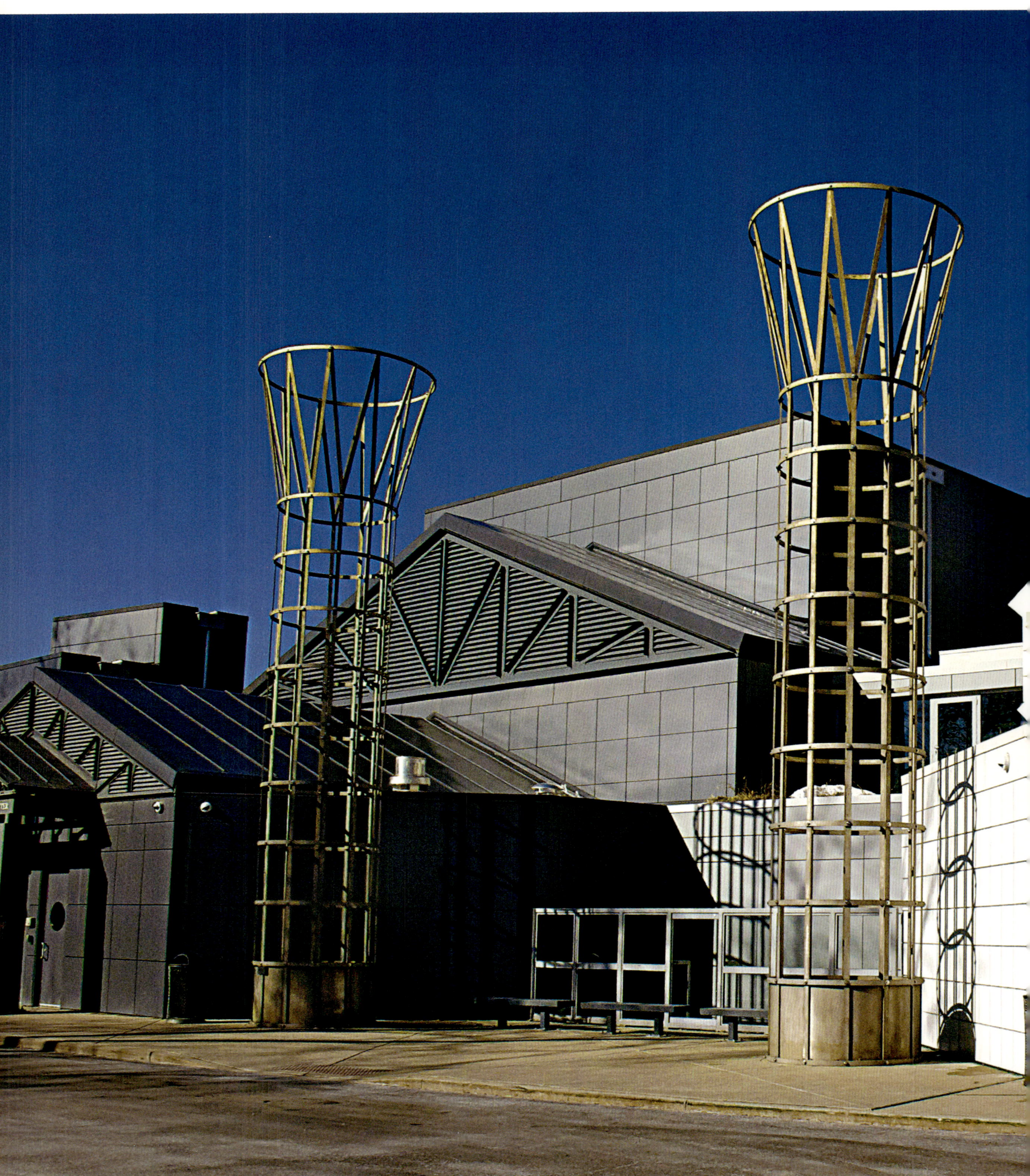

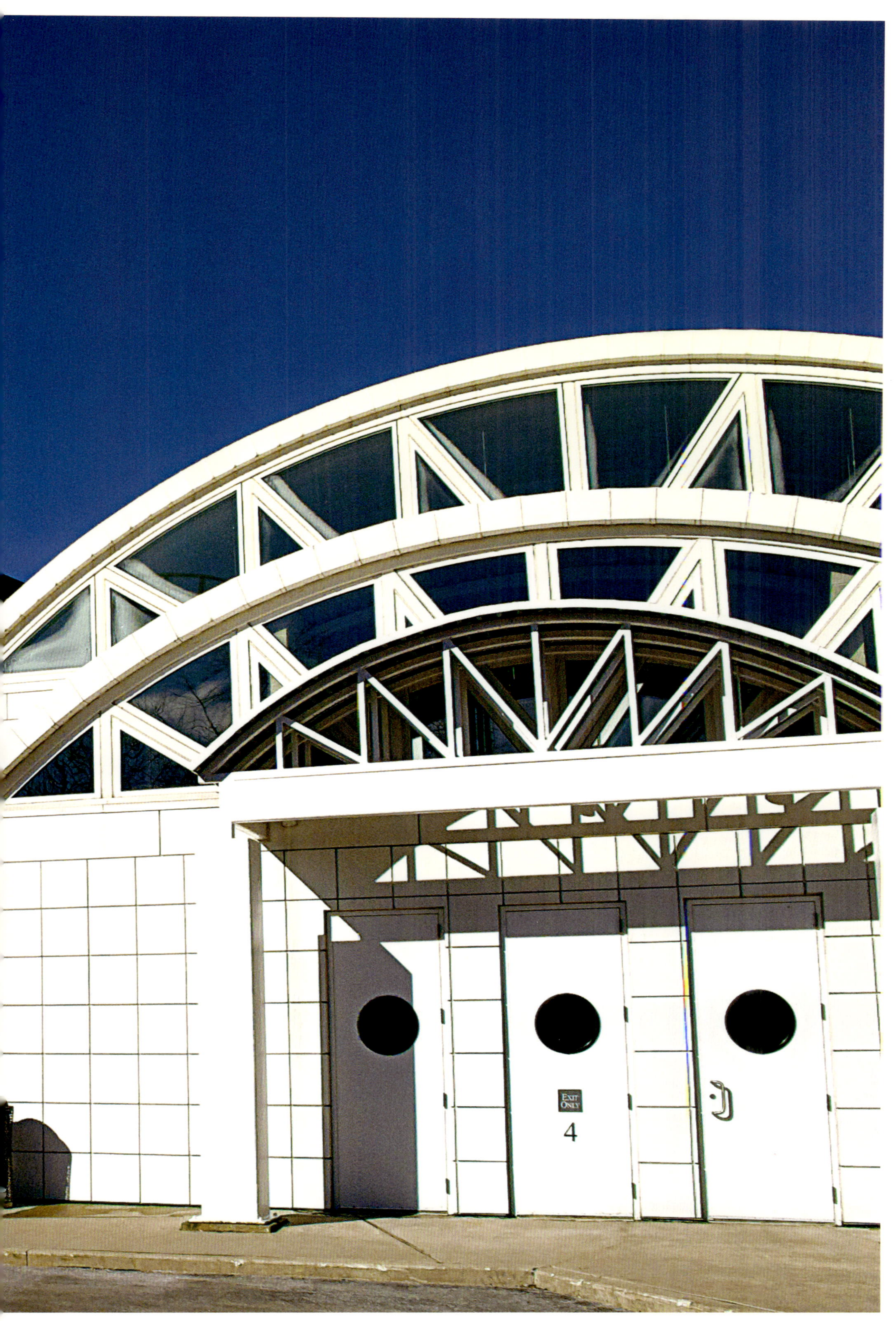
EXIT
ONLY
4

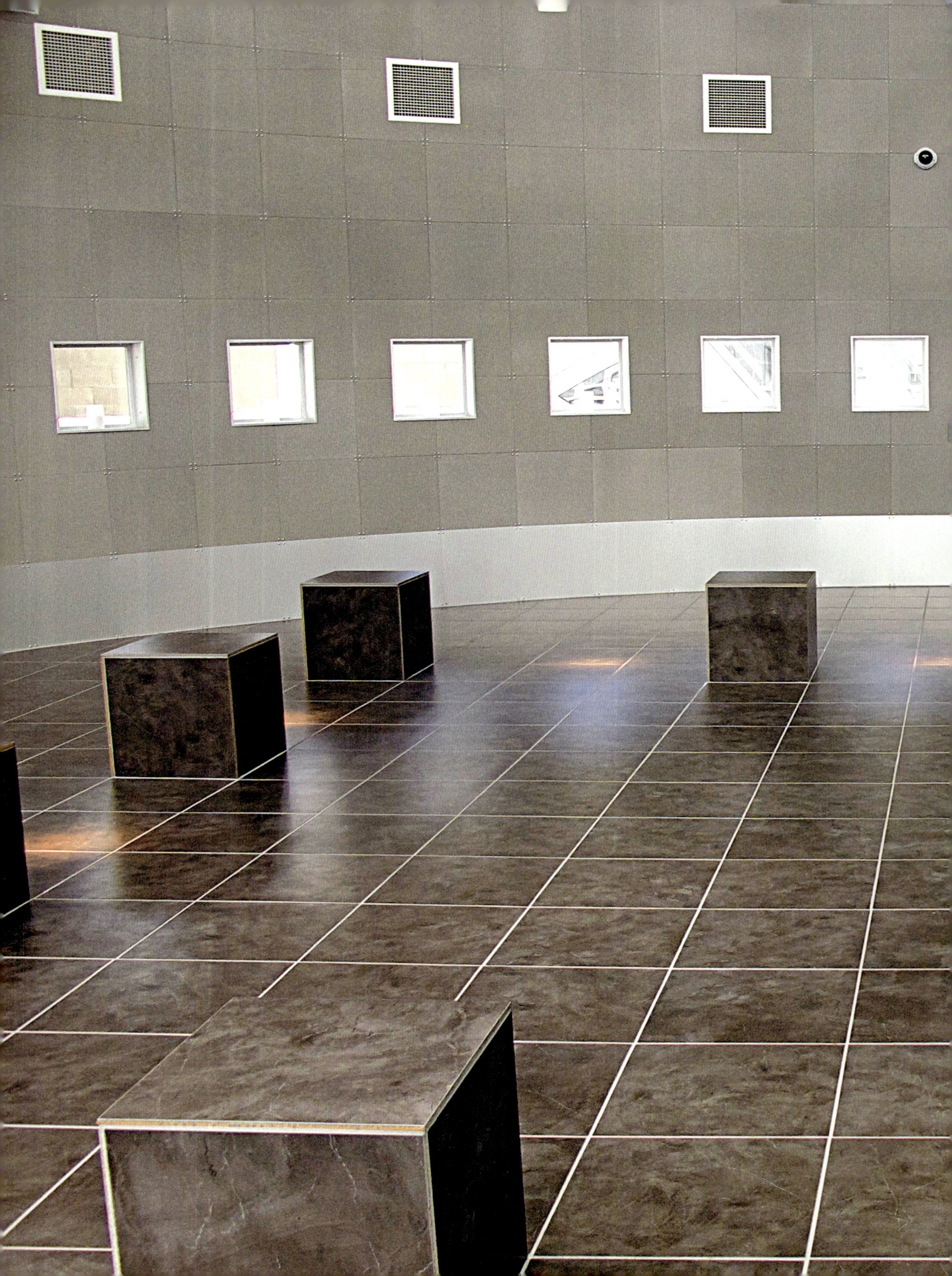

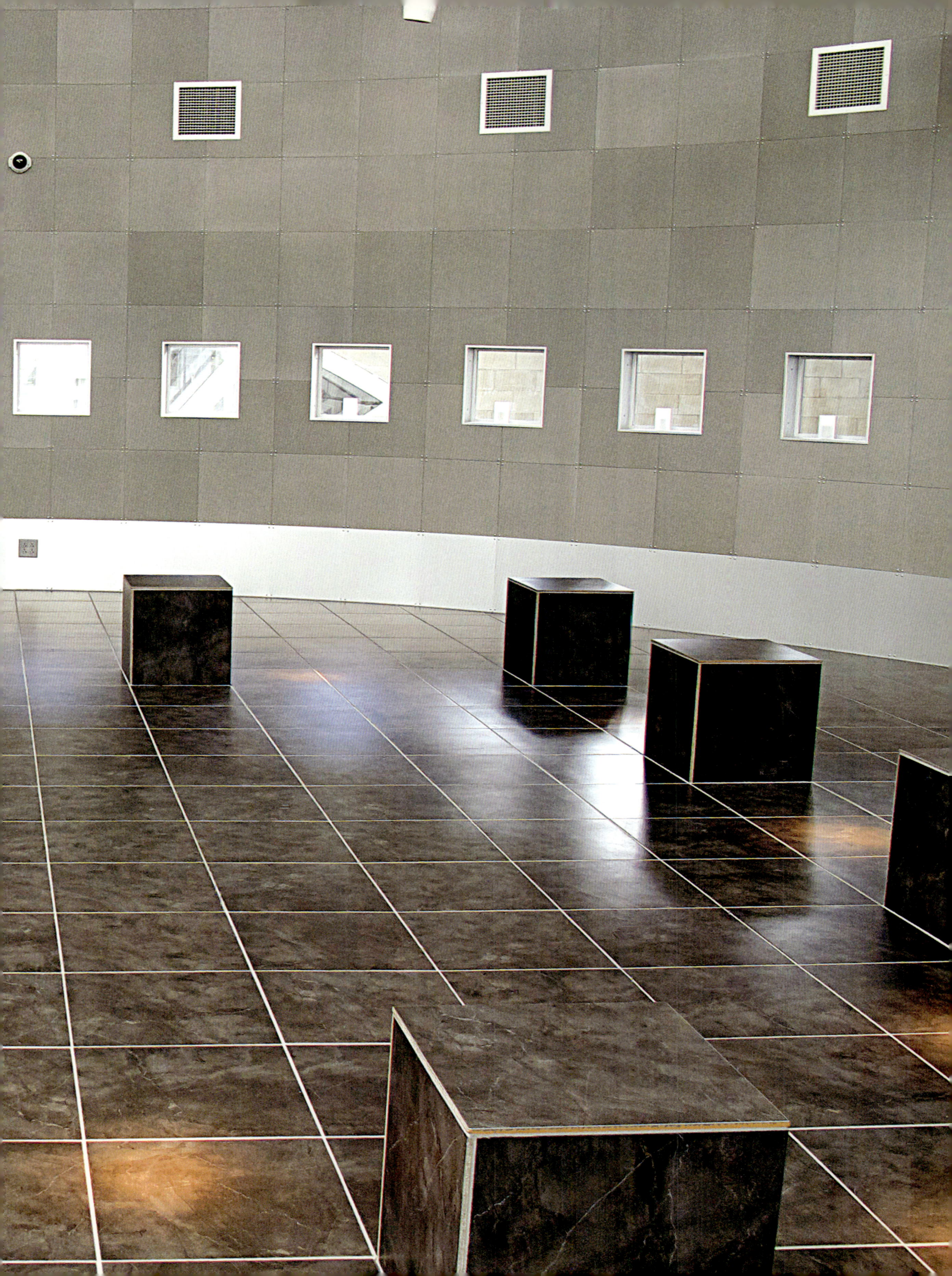

UNSTUDIO
MERCEDES-BENZ MUSEUM

It's no surprise that the Mercedes-Benz Museum in Stuttgart, Germany, designed by Dutch architecture firm UNStudio, functions more like an intersecting pedestrian highway than it does a traditional gallery. Once inside the main atrium, viewers are invited to travel to the top floor, where they then follow one of two pathways—the first leads down a route that shows the brand's car and truck collection, and the second contains historical displays called Legend rooms. At various points, the pathways intersect, allowing viewers to switch course. From the outside, the curves of the structure, stacked at irregular intervals and based on the geometry of a trefoil, hark back to nearby structures such as the Mercedes-Benz test course, the soccer stadium, and the gas and oil tanks lining the river.

Although the structure speaks specifically to the function of the brand it services, it is also a reflection of other works built by UNStudio, which was founded in 1988 by Ben van Berkel and Caroline Bos. Their structures are marked by seemingly simple outer shells that reveal intricately connected internal spaces. These include the Music Theater (2008) in Graz, Austria, an auditorium marked by a spiraling internal structure; and the Het Valkhof Museum (1999) in Nijmegen, Netherlands, in which a staircase again links all of the internal galleries and offices. Look for an increasing presence for the firm in Asia, where they recently opened an office in part to facilitate the completion of Raffles City, a sixty-story housing structure in Hangzhou, China.

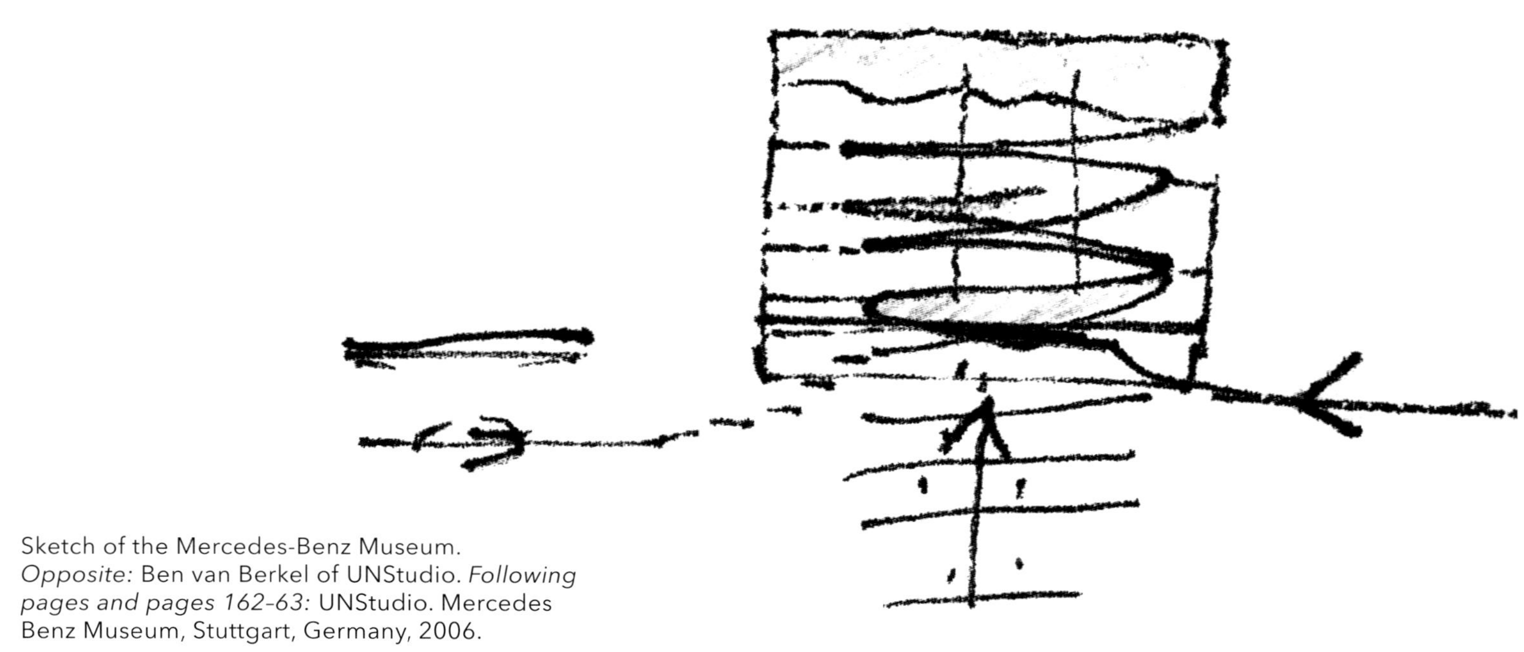

Sketch of the Mercedes-Benz Museum.
Opposite: Ben van Berkel of UNStudio. *Following pages and pages 162–63:* UNStudio. Mercedes Benz Museum, Stuttgart, Germany, 2006.

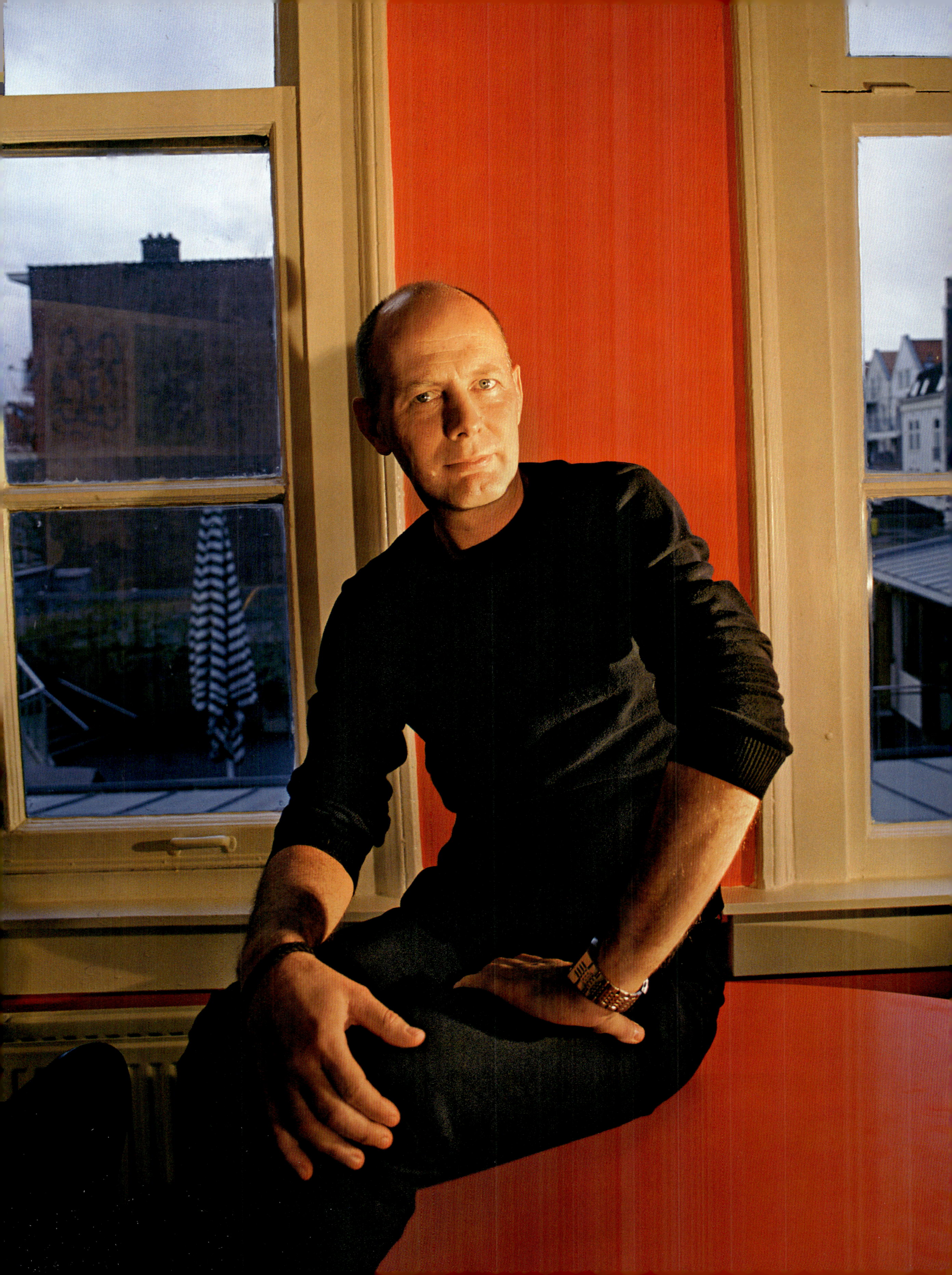

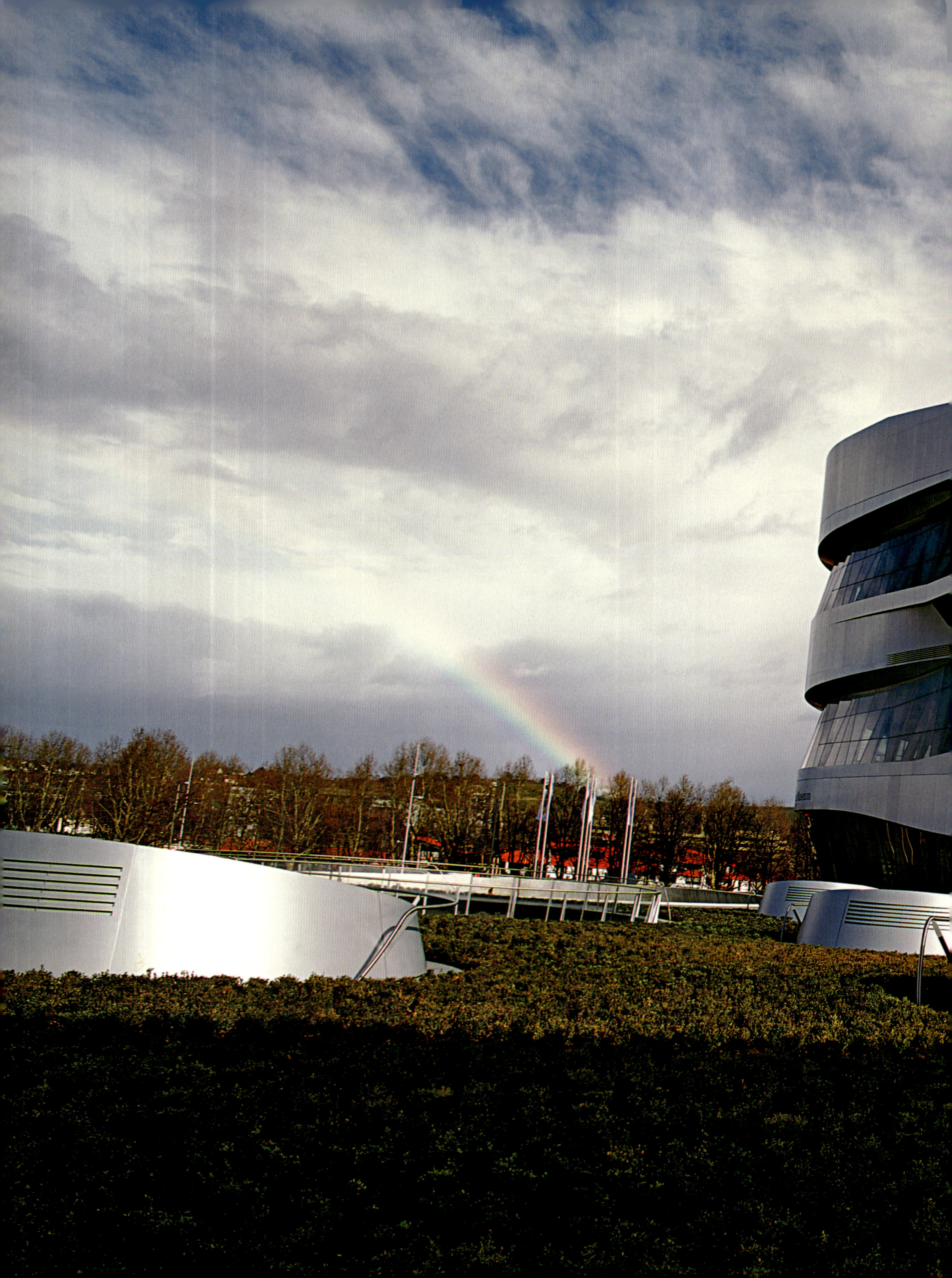

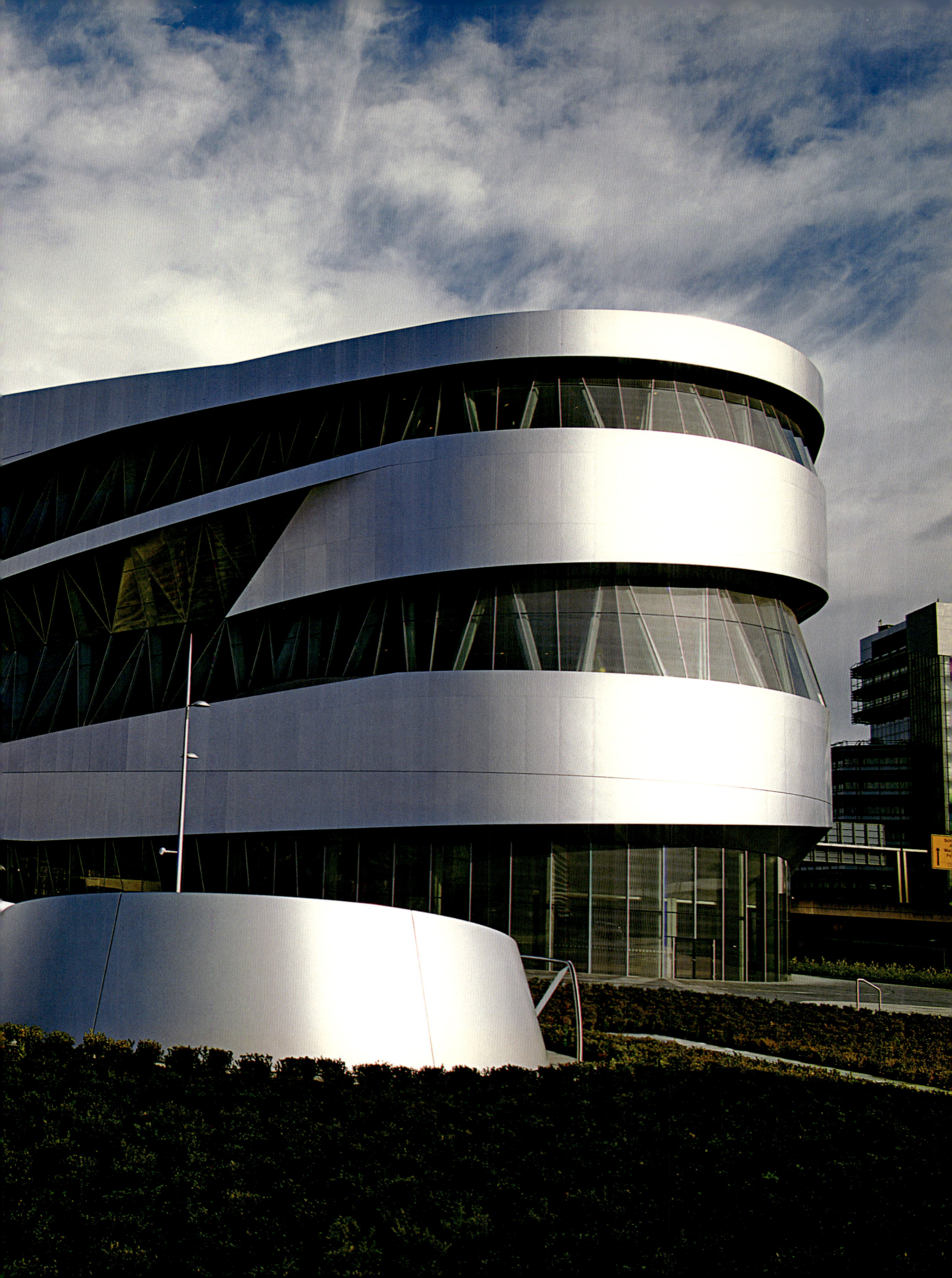

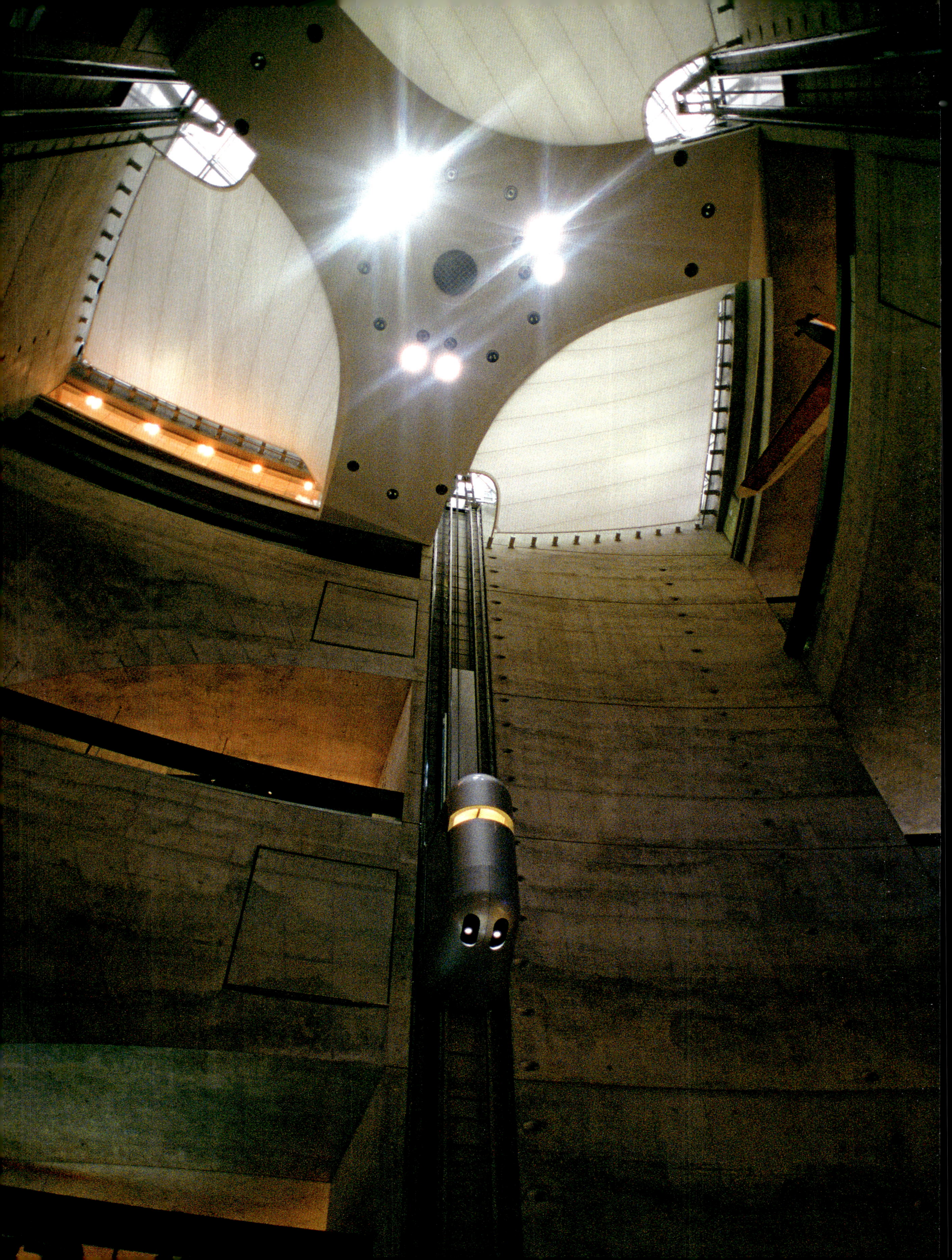

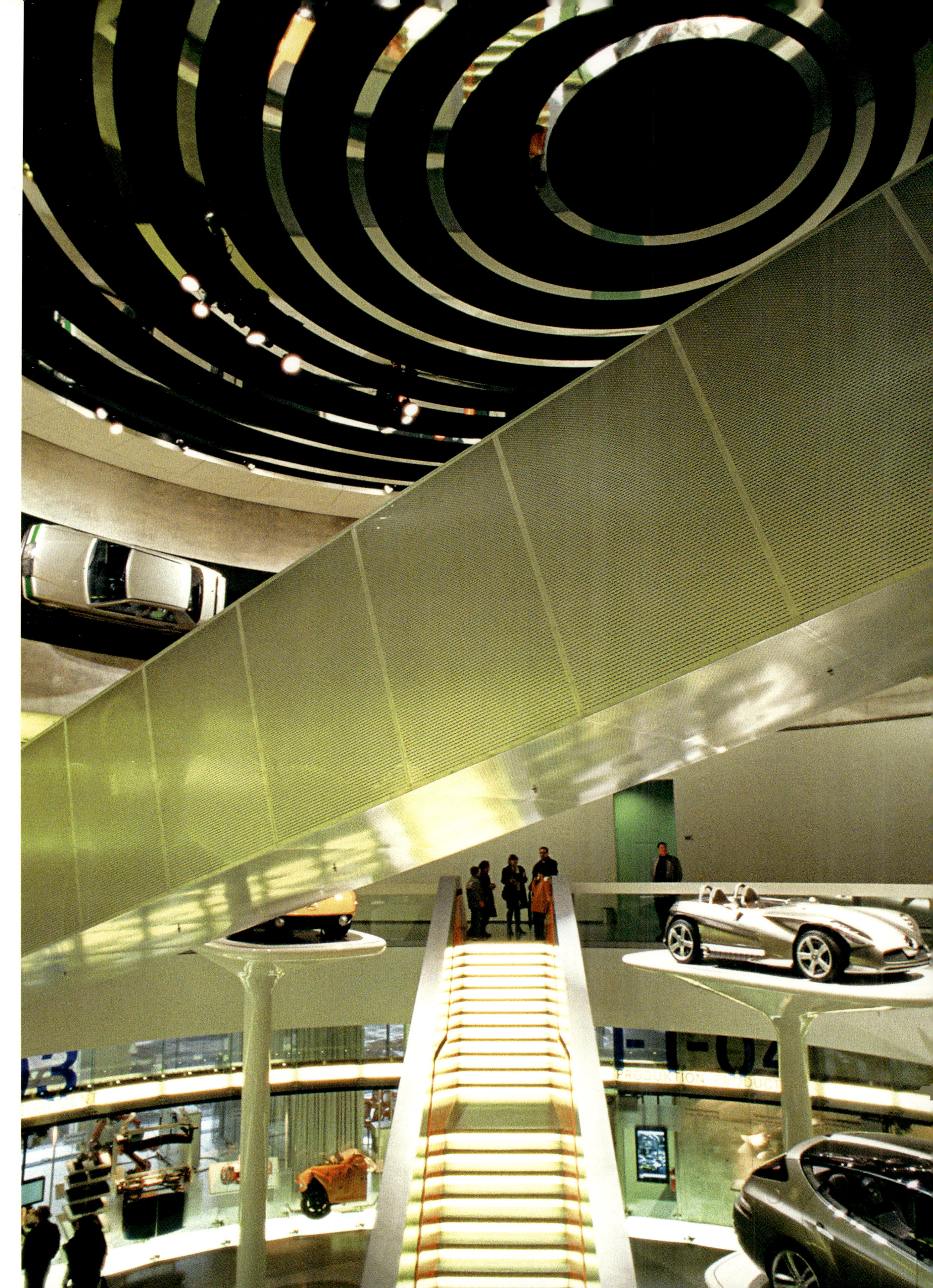

WORK ARCHITECTURE COMPANY

Founded in the 1990s by Alice Waters in Berkeley, California, the Edible Schoolyard Project aims to turn schoolyards marked by urban blight into flourishing gardens that enhance the local community. In 2014, the first Edible Schoolyard opened in New York at P. S. 216 in Gravesend, Brooklyn, an area with one of the lowest percentages of green area in the city.

Work Architecture Company, the New York-based firm that designed the project, was tasked with a number of challenges, including providing space to plant an organic garden on half an acre of parking lot, and creating a structure out of low-cost materials that could function in all four seasons. The resulting complex features three major components—a steel-framed kitchen clad in cementitious shingles tiled together in imitation of the floral pattern on Venturi Scott Brown's Best Products facade in Oxford Valley, Pennsylvania; a greenhouse created from polycarbonate and aluminum; and a "Systems Wall" covered in bright blue rubber. The third component is designed specifically to give students a glimpse into the sustainable systems that support the buildings and garden, including a rainwater collecting system used to irrigate the greenhouse.

The project is both efficient and whimsical. The centers of the flowers on the facade are portholes that allow natural light into the kitchen where P. S. 216's 625 students prepare meals harvested from their own schoolyard. The design accommodates the function— it is both a facsimile of a flourishing garden and a colorful space that encourages students to linger.

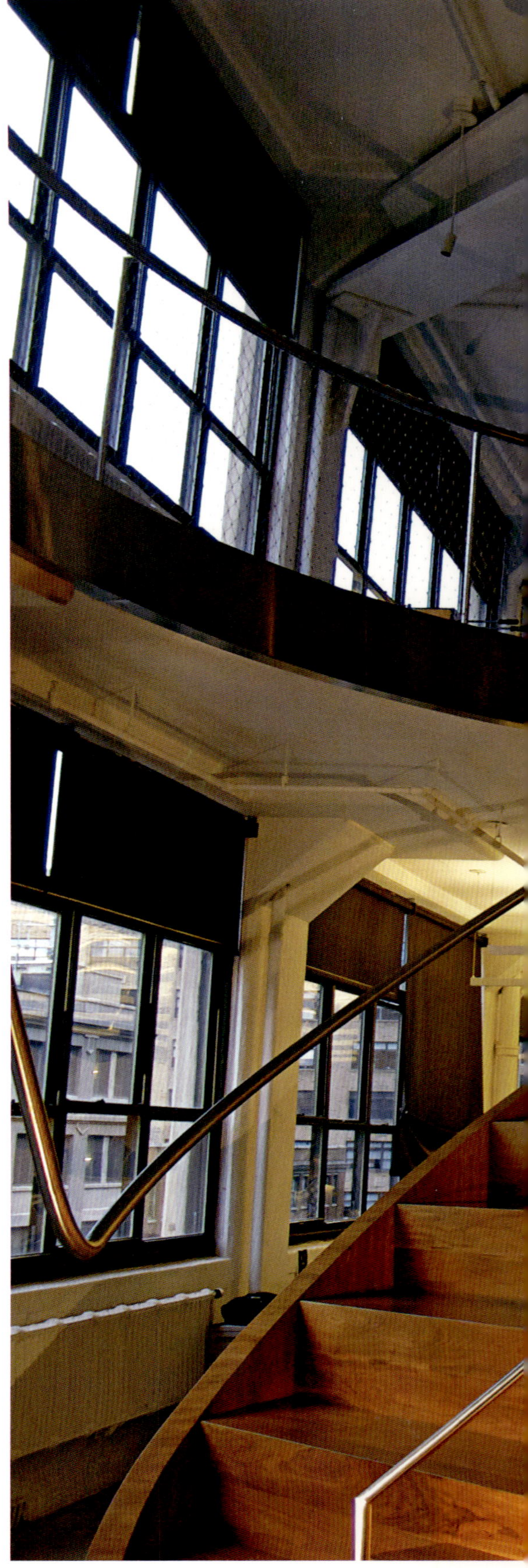

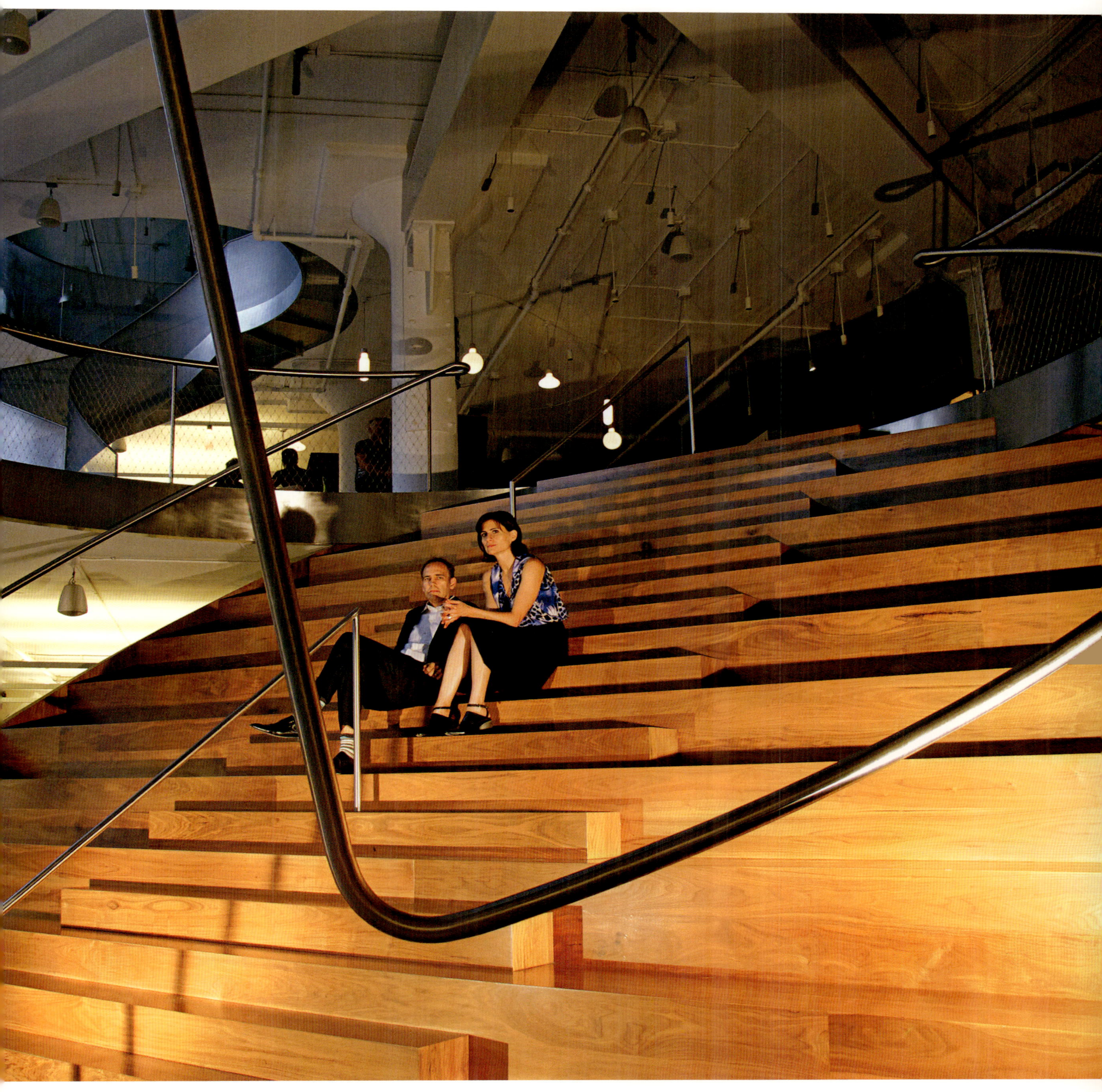

Dan Wood and Amale Andraos of Work Architecture Company.

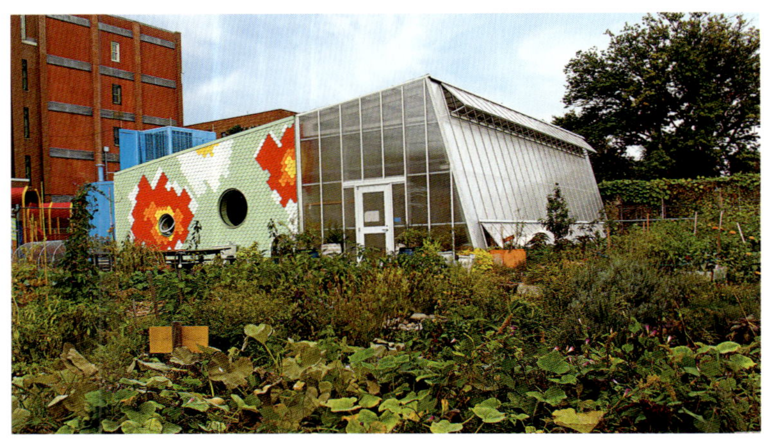

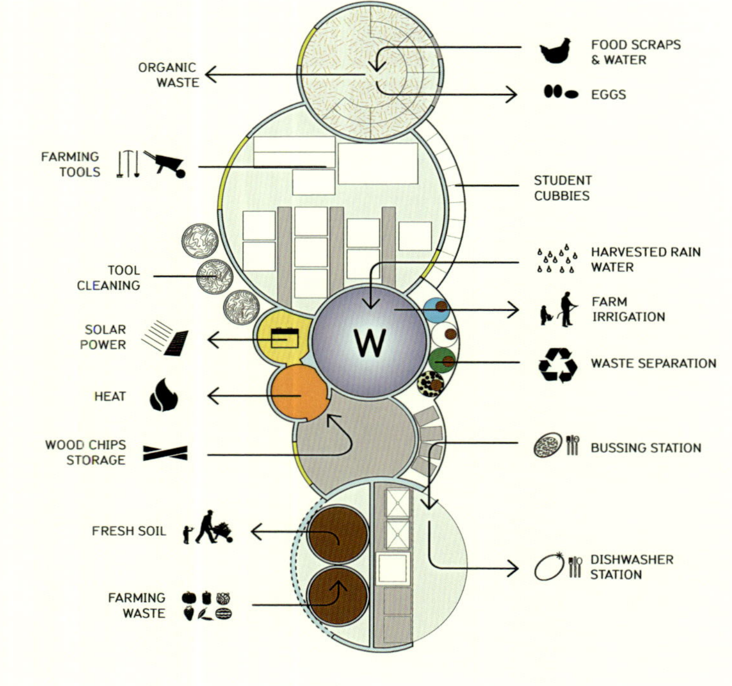

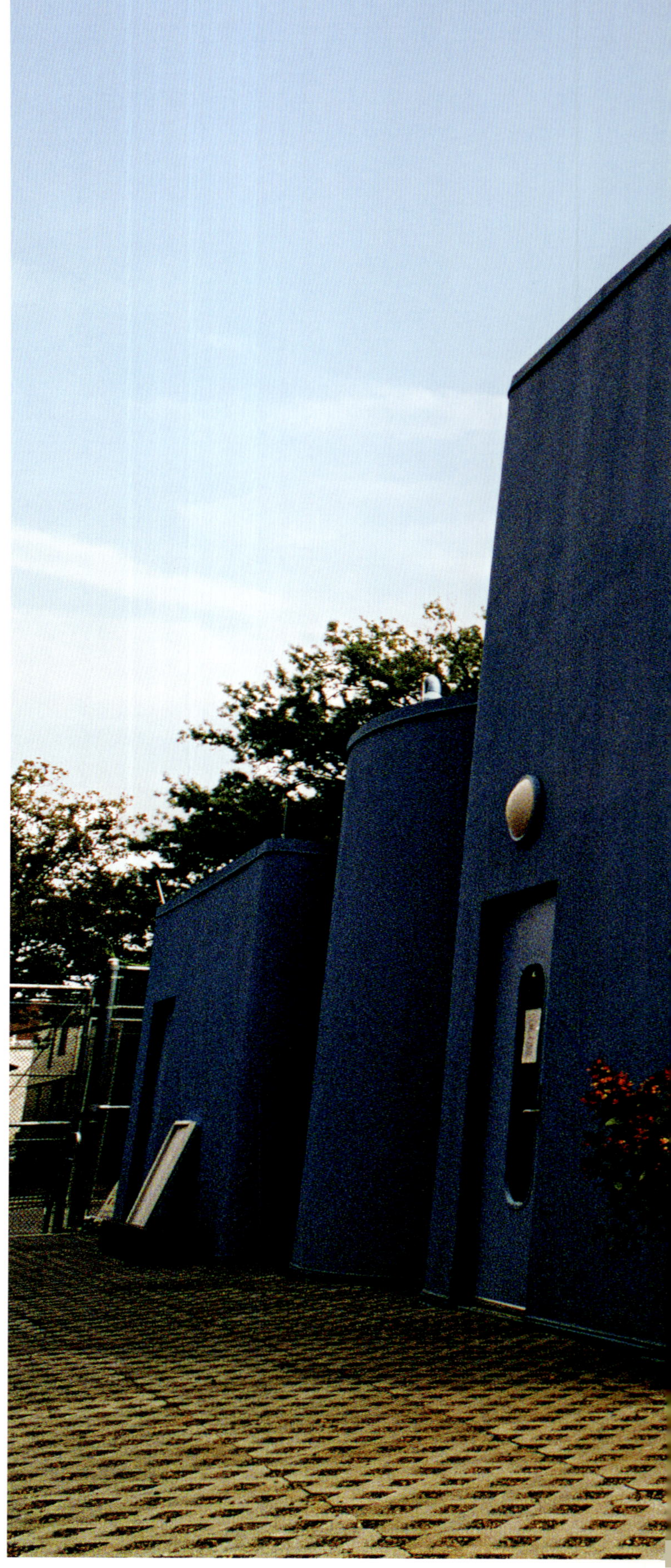

Above, top and opposite: Work Architecture Company. Edible Schoolyard at P. S. 216, Brooklyn, New York, 2014.
Above, bottom: Plan of P. S. 216's Edible Schoolyard.

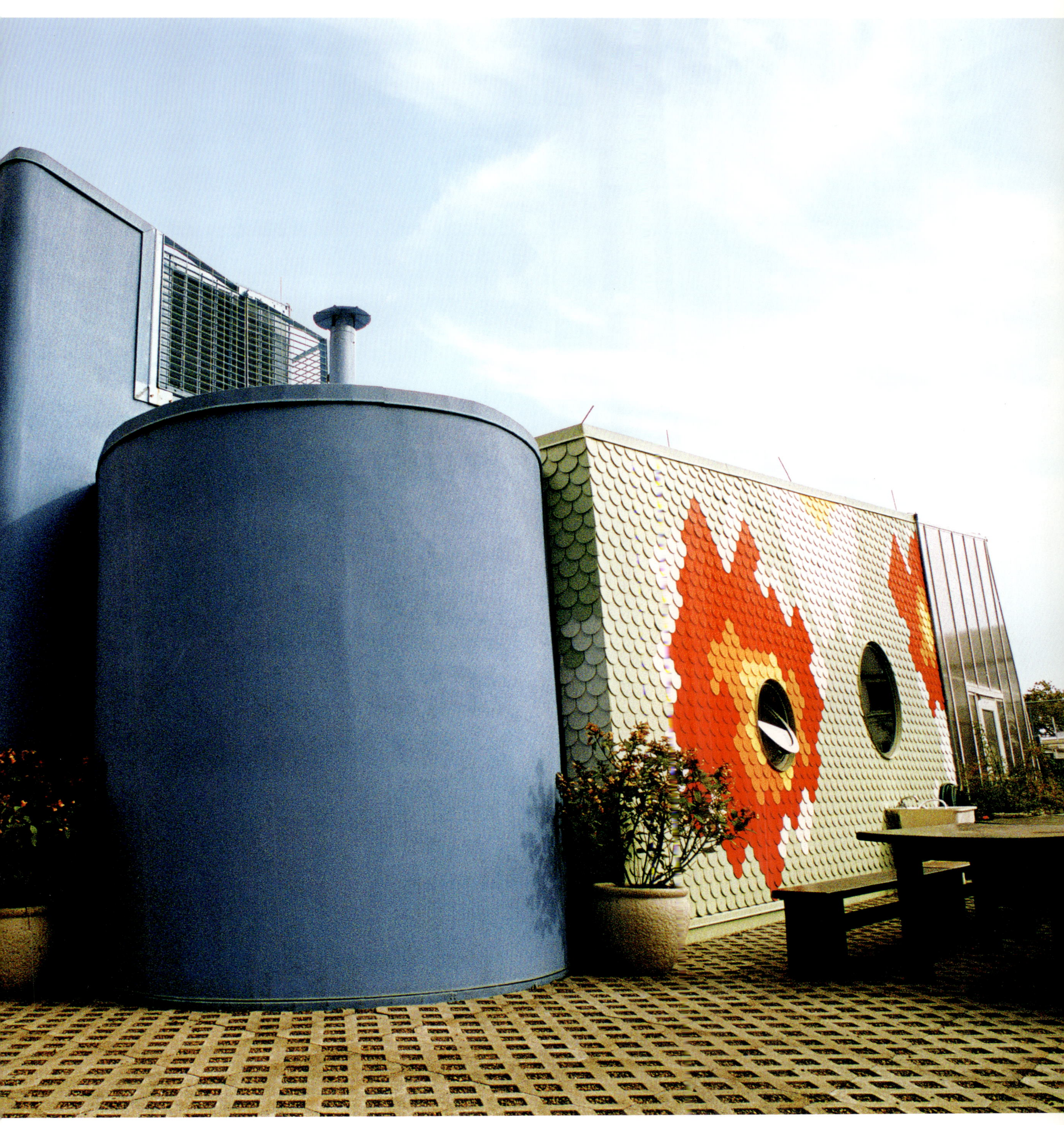

ACKNOWLEDGMENTS

I would like to thank foremost my wife, Barbara. She is my life, my sensibilities, and everything that is important to me. She is unequivocally my rock.
I am grateful to Martine and Prosper Assouline and the entire staff at Assouline for their dedication and efforts toward making this second volume of my photographs. I am totally in awe of the architects and architecture that I was able to photograph for this new volume. Each person and each project has contributed immensely to my world, the world we live in, and our understanding of the unique creative process in the realm of architecture.

CREDITS

All images © Richard Schulman except the following:
Page 15: © Adjaye Associates; page 22: © Bohlin Cywinski Jackson; page 24: Bohlin Cywinski Jackson; page 26: © Bjarke Ingels Group; pages 28-29: © Bjarke Ingels Group; page 32: © Tatiana Bilbao S. C.; page 39: © David Chipperfield Architects; page 40: © Ingrid von Kruse, courtesy David Chipperfield Architects; page 44: © Neil M. Denari Architects; page 46: © Studio Fuksas; page 54: © Studio Gang Architects; page 57: © Grimshaw Architects; page 58: © Rick Roxbrough, courtesy Grimshaw Architects; page 60 (bottom): © Rick Joy Architects; page 66: © Kengo Kuma and Associates; page 74: © Maki and Associates; page 76: © Michael Maltzan Architecture; page 83: © Marmol Radziner; page 86: © J. Mayer H. Und Partner, Architekten; page 93: © Paulo Mendes da Rocha; page 98: © Rafael Moneo; page 100 (bottom): © 2014 Artists Rights Society (ARS), New York / c/o Pictoright Amsterdam; pages 102-103: © 2014 Artists Rights Society (ARS), New York / c/o Pictoright Amsterdam; page 105: © nArchitects, PLLC; page 108: © 2014 Artists Rights Society (ARS), New York/ADAGP, Paris; pages 110-13: © 2014 Artists Rights Society (ARS), New York/ADAGP, Paris; page 115: © Rockwell Group; pages 120-21: © Fernando Romero Enterprise; page 124: © Safdie Architects; page 128: © Selldorf Architects; page 130: © Selldorf Architects; page 136: © Álvaro Siza; page 139: © SO-IL; page 144: © Skidmore, Owings & Merrill/Roger Duffy; page 146: © Skidmore, Owings & Merrill/Roger Duffy; page 149: © Eduardo Souto de Moura; page 153: © Tigerman McCurry Architects; page 158: © 2014 Artists Rights Society (ARS), New York / c/o Pictoright Amsterdam; pages 160-63: © 2014 Artists Rights Society (ARS), New York / c/o Pictoright Amsterdam; page 166 (bottom): © Work Architecture Company.